CARS OF
THE EARLY
THIRTIES

*Illustrated below is Fleetwood's inter-
pretation of the two-passenger Convertible Coupe for the V-12 chassis.
Cadillac V-12 prices range from
$3795, f. o. b. Detroit. G. M. A. C.
terms available on all body styles.*

To ride in the Cadillac V-12 is to know at once why it is ranked so highly among the fine cars of the world — for the appeal of its 12-cylinder performance is well-nigh irresistible. Even those who are accustomed to the foremost automobiles are finding in the V-12 a new conception of motoring luxury. In fact, a V-12 demonstration, almost without exception, makes conventional conceptions of performance and luxury seem commonplace.

CADILLAC V8

CARS OF
THE EARLY
THIRTIES

Tad Burness

CHILTON BOOK COMPANY

Philadelphia · New York · London

ISBN   0-8019-5545-9
Library of Congress Catalog Card Number 74-111379
Designed by Harry Eaby
Manufactured in the United States of America by
Vail-Ballou Press, Inc.

FOREWORD

This book is primarily a continuing, detailed account of the many automobiles produced in the United States during a specific era, in this case, the years 1930 through 1934.

Despite the "Great Depression," when business slowed to what seemed a virtual halt, with millions thrown out of work and with the scarcity of ready money, the automobile continued to advance in design and production.

Let me take you on an informative and, I hope, entertaining motor trip through these years of automotive history, noting as we go some of the most interesting developments of 1930–34, year by year.

However troubled these years were, the early Thirties also were exciting times in which to live. Many interesting things were going on, particularly in the automotive world. Whether or not you remember these days, I hope you will enjoy this book.

ACKNOWLEDGMENTS

I'm most grateful to the following factory officials and antique and classic car enthusiasts; they were kind enough to provide special information helpful in compiling this book:

Bill Adams	Jeff Gibson	Everette Payette
Warren J. Baier	David Lindsay Heggie	Stacy Penning
Robert Brown	Lawrence C. Holian	Raymond Petersen
Emmett P. Burke	Mitchell Ingram	Isadore Rabinovitz
Louis K. Burns	Eric Ismay	Earl Reynolds
Austin Burt	Esto Ludwig	Delbert Rinehart
Swen H. Carlson	H. A. McKnight	David Seedeman
John A. Conde	A. E. McLean	N. L. Sorensen
Dorothy Dase	Robert R. Maskell	Randy Staab
Gary Dobbs	Carl Mendoza	Walt Thayer
Fred W. Dow	Walter E. Messick	Gerald Toth
Wallea B. Draper	Carl Newcomb	Alan Trudeau
Glenn C. Durham	Henry Norton	Norbert R. Valind
John Felletter	L. D. Oaks	E. D. Vosburgh
R. C. Freitag	John F. Osborn	Gates Willard
Joe Gazecki	Warren H. Ott	

CONTENTS

ILLUSTRATIONS

A NOTE ABOUT
THE ILLUSTRATIONS

The pictures in this book are photographs of advertisements that appeared in national magazines forty years ago. As a consequence of their age, some of the original printed advertisements are yellowing at the edges, others bear indelible marks and still others have small tears in them; and as a consequence of the times in which they were printed, some, because of the thinness of the paper used, are somewhat less than opaque. The result is that despite the best uses of photography the pictures are not as good as salon prints. The reader is asked to be indulgent in this matter. There is, however, a plus in the reader's favor, for in photographing advertisements of the times instead of the cars themselves (an impossibility anyway, in that the cars no longer exist for the most part, nor are available) the opportunity is given to read what the manufacturers had to say about their cars—something that can be had in no other way. Such imperfections as appear in the pictures will, thus, be overlooked willingly by all but the most critical, whose interest, perhaps, is more concerned with photography than with the cars in question. The illustrations appeared in such magazines as *Saturday Evening Post, Country Gentleman, Redbook, Sunset, National Geographic* and *Country Life*.

INTRODUCTION

With the crash of October, 1929, the long, dismal Depression was well under way as a few, new "midget" cars were introduced. The appearance of ultra-small economy cars was timely, but buyers did not go for them in great numbers. The only tiny car that sold well was the American Austin, the "Bantam" introduced for 1930.

A total of 2,787,456 new cars and 575,364 new trucks and busses were sold during 1930, a great decline from the more than *5 million* new motor vehicles sold in 1929.

Models for 1930 were, on the whole, not drastically changed from the 1929s, though straight-eight engines were becoming increasingly popular. Auto bodies were still quite high and boxy; accidents caused by top heavy bodies were quite commonplace. So were accidents at unprotected railroad grade crossings.

Wood-spoked "artillery" wheels, with demountable rims, were the most common type. Wire wheels were usually optional. Chevrolet, for several years, had championed the cause of the steel disc wheel, along with Packard, Dodge, Nash and a few others.

Most 1930 cars had four-wheel mechanical brakes, although hydraulics had been available for a few years on some marques. And a new device, freewheeling, was pioneered in midyear by Studebaker.

During 1931, the 50-millionth American motor vehicle was produced. And, years ahead of its time, a *retractable hardtop convertible* was designed and patented by a Salt Lake City resident, B. B. Ellerbeck. It was many years, however, before such a model was commercially produced (by Ford, in 1957).

The N.A.C.C. (National Automobile Chamber of Commerce) * passed a resolution which set the announcement time of new car models for November and December. This was done to stimulate winter sales (spring was usually the most prosperous period) thereby helping to alleviate the usual summertime rush and winter lull in factory production. Another plan, a rather ill-advised one which had been proposed by the N.A.C.C. during the previous year, was also adopted. This was the "bounty" plan, with rewards offered to dealers by manufacturers for the "hide" of every old car. From 1931 to 1933, hundreds of thousands of outdated trade-ins were destroyed by dealers so they would not be resold.

Freewheeling was offered on many new cars for 1931, as well as improved synchro-mesh or constant-mesh transmissions. The improved transmissions were a boon to motorists, eliminating much of the gear stripping and clashing common in earlier days. Grilles began to appear on many radiators. Wire wheels were common, and hubcaps became larger. Simple, one-piece bumpers replaced the double or triple-leaf types seen on many earlier models. And more manufacturers were including bumpers as standard equipment.

1,948,164 new cars and 432,262 new trucks and busses were sold in 1931.

Because of the times, 1932 was the year of lowest production since 1918 when wartime shortages had been the cause. Only 1,103,557 new cars were sold, in addition to 228,303 trucks and busses. With millions more out of work that year, it was little wonder.

Body designs were improved in 1932, with new, enlarged windshields, usually minus the old-style outside visor. On many of the new cars, swing-away sun visors were attached inside to the upholstery panel just above the windshield.

Many cars, especially the large ones, offered new shock absorbers, adjustable from the dash and known popularly as "ride control." Several of the quality marques built models with 12 cylinder engines. The V-16 models of Cadillac (introduced in 1930) and Marmon (introduced in 1931) were also available. Front doors on some 1932 cars swung open at the front, enabling the

* Name changed to Automobile Manufacturers Association, Inc.,/AMA/in 1934.

designers to apply graceful curves to the front edges of the doors. But, the hazards of such doors were obvious, should they accidentally come unlatched at high speed.

Automatic chokes were offered by both Oldsmobile and Packard, with other manufacturers incorporating this feature the following year. Vacuum-operated, semi-automatic clutches were found on many models, including Buick, La Salle, Cadillac, Chrysler, De Soto, Dodge and Plymouth. And Pierce-Arrow introduced hydraulic valve-lifters years ahead of most others.

In 1932, Ford successfully introduced a V-8 engine in the low-price field. This was the first small V-8 which was really any good, and, within two years, the 4-cylinder Fords were discontinued.

"Startix," the anti-stall device which introduced ignition key starter control, was featured on many 1932 cars.

Automotive improvements in 1933 included further streamlining of bodies and grilles, new semi-skirted fenders, power brakes on quality cars, and "no-draft ventilation" featuring side windows with built-in wind-wings. A similar feature was soon adopted by competitors.

Several 1933 cars came with a special starter control actuated by heavy pressure on the accelerator pedal.

Hope that the Depression would soon end boosted 1933 sales, and 1,560,599 new cars and 329,218 new commercial vehicles were sold.

Sales increased, again, in 1934, with 2,160,685 new cars and 576,205 new trucks and busses sold. Freeways, as we know them today, did not exist, but, in a few eastern cities, novel "cloverleaf" split-level intersections were designed and built. They resembled those of today, except that the bridges were more ornate and were crowned by fancy lamp-posts and signals.

Streamlining was the latest note in automotive styling. Chrysler, De Soto, La Salle, Hupmobile, Cadillac, Pierce-Arrow and Studebaker offered models which were aerodynamically designed with sloping windshields and grilles, "fast backs" and bulbous fenders which blended well with hood- and body-lines. Some manufacturers went so far as to offer optional (and detachable) full skirts for rear fenders which completely hid the top halves of the wheels.

The most popular mechanical feature of many 1934 cars was "Knee-Action," or independent front-wheel suspension. The elimination of the old-fashioned solid front axle made for a much smoother ride. Also, some 1934 cars had new steel artillery wheels which resembled the solid-disc type, except for a circle of small openings near the rim.

Hydraulic brakes grew in popularity during the 1930s. By 1939, all full-size American cars had them.

Overdrive was introduced on Chrysler and De Soto "Airflows." This useful device provided a fourth speed for fast cruising, eliminating a considerable amount of engine wear. Three-speed manual transmissions were still the common thing in '34, though Reo dared to introduce a model with an automatic transmission which was years ahead of its time.

And now, a description of each of the many different makes of automobiles available during the early 1930s in this country. The years of 1930 through 1934 are covered in detail.

AUBURN

Auburn, Indiana, was the home base of the Auburn Automobile Company, manufacturer of quality cars since 1900. With the exception of Studebaker, Auburn was the last of many old-time Indiana auto manufacturers to discontinue passenger car production. Auburn dropped out of the picture in 1936.

Auburn, by 1930, was affiliated with two other Indiana automobiles; the new Cord L-29, and the mighty Duesenberg J. Most Auburn dealers handled all three cars.

Perhaps the best-loved of all Auburns, are those built *after* 1930. They are acknowledged by most as true classics, especially the large, elegant speedsters and other convertible models (many of them equipped with superchargers.) Since Auburn was connected with Cord and Duesenberg in the early '30s, the relationship was obvious in Auburn's styling and engineering.

The 1930 Auburn, however, was a different story. In body design it bore a strong resemblance to earlier Auburns dating back to 1925, when Auburn had been completely restyled and had first added a straight-eight model to supplement the 4- and 6-cylinder series. The 1925 Auburn "8-88," with its massive, new McFarlan body, unusual, bowed windshield-and-visor assembly and lower belt line which curved forward over the hood, was more than up-to-date, when introduced. But Auburn styling changed only in minor respects during the late twenties, so that, in appearance, the 1930 Auburn was one of the most old-fashioned of all new cars.

Lowest-priced sedan in the Auburn line for 1930 was the model "6-85," at $995, f.o.b. Delivered in San Francisco to Johnson-Blalack, Inc. (Auburn-Cord-Duesenberg distributors), this car was priced at $1395. The "6-85" had a 6-cylinder, 70-horsepower Lycoming "WR" engine (L-head) and a 120-inch wheelbase. The gear ratio of 4.90 to 1 was quite low; the car would climb well in high gear but was lacking in top speed. A more popular gear ratio on 1930 cars was 4.5 to 1. The 4-speed Chrysler "70" of early 1930 had a top gear ratio of only 3.58, while the lowest-geared of all 1930 cars was the Essex, with a 5.40 high-gear ratio (comparable to *second* gear in many other cars!).

Auburn also offered two straight-eight models in 1930: the 100-horse-power "8-95" had a Lycoming "GR" engine and 125-inch wheelbase. The big "125" Auburn was the top of the line, with a 125-horsepower Lycoming "MDA" engine (bore and stroke of 3¼ x 4½") and a 129-inch wheelbase.

Like the majority of other 1930 engines, Auburn's Lycoming power plants were of the "L-head" variety, with valves at the side of the cylinders. In 1930, Buick and Chevrolet were the only *popular* cars with overhead valves, though Nash and a few others had offered such models before.

Wall Street had taken its disastrous financial nose-dive on October 29, 1929. Many 1930 cars, therefore, were introduced in an atmosphere of fear and uncertainty. Auburn's 1930 cars did not enjoy booming sales, not only because of the times but also because they looked hulkingly old-fashioned. Since styling had become increasingly important, any car without it was in trouble. In its own defense, Auburn paid for a full page of text in the April 19th, 1930 issue of *Saturday Evening Post*. The ad showed no picture of the car but contained a lengthy quotation (from *Cram's Automotive Reports*) about the stability and integrity of the Auburn Automobile Company.

1930 f.o.b. prices of various Auburn models were:

6–85	Sport Sedan	$ 995
6–85	Sedan	1095
6–85	Cabriolet	1095
8–95	Sport Sedan	1195
8–95	Sedan	1295
8–95	Cabriolet	1295
8–95	Phaeton Sedan	1395
125	Sport Sedan	1495
125	Sedan	1595
125	Cabriolet	1595
125	Phaeton Sedan	1695

The world's Smartest low priced car—
119-inch wheelbase Six, low as

$695

*Car illustrated above is the 126-inch
Wheelbase, Straight Eight, 115 Horse
Power, 5-passenger Custom Sedan $1125

Not only does the new Auburn introduce a new high standard of quick acceleration, combined with quiet, smooth, flexible power—not only does it "hold the road" in a manner that makes it easier to drive and safer to ride in—not only does it run in an even, straight line with a minimized tendency to side-sway or roll— But climaxing all these performance-advantages are the many ways in which the new Auburn takes the "work" out of driving. Auburn for 1934 makes automobile driving remarkably easy; more restful; more comfortable; requires less exertion and leaves you refreshed even after long drives. We invite you to ride in and drive the new Auburn models. If the car does not sell itself you will not be asked to buy.

6 CYLINDER MODELS $695 TO $945; 8 CYLINDER MODELS $945 TO $1225; SALON 12 MODELS $1395 TO $1545
All prices at the factory, subject to change without notice. Equipment other than standard, extra
AUBURN AUTOMOBILE COMPANY, AUBURN, INDIANA, Division of Cord Corporation

AUBURN

Unlike its 1930 predecessor, the 1931 Auburn was a beautiful machine. It clearly displayed the influence of its more exclusive sister-cars, the Cord and Duesenberg. The '31 Auburn had a lower, sleeker body, completely redesigned. Hood and radiator grille, also, were new and different. Though the Auburn delivered its power at the rear wheels, it featured a split grille which protruded sharply near the bumpers, suggesting that it had front-wheel drive (like the L-29 Cord.) A new, one-piece bumper dipped in the center (similar to those on the Ford V-8s of the mid-'30s.) Headlamp lenses were bisected by a thin vertical band of brightwork, to harmonize with the split grille. Front fenders were also bisected by a harmonizing moulding at the tip.

Despite the obvious fact that the '31 Auburn had excellent new styling, an Auburn ad in the June, 1931 *House & Garden* magazine read: "We are often asked why Auburn, the originator of designs, never advertises the exterior beauty of its cars. Because, we believe that basically, an automobile is a machine for transportation; also that it is a very important investment. Structural strength, efficiency and endurance, and not outer appearance, are the fundamentals that determine value. The surface may attract, but it is the inner quality that holds the allegiance of Auburn's owners." And most Auburn owners *were* loyal, recalling these cars, as a rule, with a feeling akin to affection. The Auburn was neither the most economical nor dependable of cars, but it was obviously *well built*.

On Auburn's 1931 models, the hood louvres, windshield and front edges of the fore doors slanted slightly, in harmony with one another. There was no external sun visor on the '31 Auburn, though the design of the metal area above the windshield suggested that there *could have been* such a visor, had the designers decided, at the last minute, to include one. All closed models had fabric-covered top quarters, giving closed cars a convertible appearance. The '31 model had the characteristic Auburn belt lines which crossed over the top of the hood and joined at the radiator. With the new styling, this feature was even more attractive than before.

All '31 Auburns featured a silent constant-mesh transmission, and custom models included the popular new device, freewheeling. Freewheeling had been pioneered in 1930 by Studebaker, and was simply a gimmick which made it possible for a car to coast along in neutral whenever pressure was released from the accelerator pedal, even when the transmission was in gear. An additional centrifugal clutch (in a separate unit behind the transmission) did the trick, when the freewheeling control was set in the operative position. Freewheeling proved to be very popular during 1931 and 1932, and most cars offered it for a time, either as an option or as standard equipment. (The

Ford car was a noteworthy holdout. Some Lincoln cars were equipped with freewheeling, but the device was not offered on the Ford, even though Chevrolet and Plymouth featured it as a competitive "extra" at no additional cost.) Freewheeling was designed to save wear and tear on the engine, relieving the driver from the necessity of obtaining the same effect by frequently shifting the gears to neutral and coasting.

Coupes were back in the Auburn line for '31. Strange as it may seem, a few auto builders had occasionally dropped 2- and 3-passenger coupes from their line for a few seasons, until obvious public demand warranted their return.

Wire wheels with racing-type "knock-off" hubcaps were optional, though the standard equipment, wood artillery wheels, did not fit in as well with the graceful design of the car. Tire size was 6.00 x 17 inches (small in diameter for 1931, when the 19-inch wheel was still the most popular size), and 18-inchers were beginning to be popular.

There was no longer an Auburn six in 1931. The "8-98" was the only model available, though the custom models were known as "8-98-A." The engine was a new, straight-eight Lycoming "GU" of 98 horsepower, and not a continuation of any of the three 1930 engines. Gear ratio was 4.45 to 1, and standard wheelbase was 126 inches (136 inches on 7-passenger sedan, priced at $1195.) Other 1931 Auburn models:

8–98 2-Door Brougham	$ 945	$1145
8–98 4-Door Full Sedan	995	1195
8–98 Business Man's Coupe	995	1195
8–98 Convertible Cabriolet	1045	1245
8–98 Convertible Phaeton-Sedan	1145	1345

(Prices at right are for Custom 8–98–A Models.)

The '31 Auburns, in addition to their many other features, had sturdy X-type frames and automatic chassis lubrication. Midland "steeldraulic" brakes were of the mechanical variety, but were actuated by cables in flexible, metal sheathing. And Auburn boasted the widest rear seat of any production car, as well as the widest door on any car (brougham and coupe.)

Auburn styling remained virtually unchanged for 1932, as did the 8-cylinder engine. However, a powerful new "12-160" series was introduced, featuring an interesting 45-degree, V-12 engine of 160 horsepower, known as the

Lycoming "BB". Another dramatic development was "Dual-Ratio," a two-speed Columbia rear axle which provided a power ratio of 4.5 to 1, or a cruising ratio of 3 to 1. The latter ratio was remarkably high for its time, and enabled the engine to loaf along with little effort at speeds far above the limits posted in most states in 1932. The control for the Dual Ratio was a simple lever located in the center of the dash panel just below the speedometer.

Ride control also was provided, with shock absorbers that could be adjusted by another lever on the dash. And "Startix" was featured, a device that automatically restarted the engine if ever it should stall with the ignition on.

The 12-cylinder Auburn had twin carburetors, one for each block of six. The 12-160 Auburns also had hydraulic brakes, though "steeldraulics" were continued on the 8s. Wheelbase was 127 inches on the 8s, and 132 inches on the new 12-160. As a styling and safety improvement, dual outside horns were featured on some models.

During 1932, a speedster model was once again offered, for the first time in the Auburn line since 1929. The speedsters are the most desirable Auburns, so far as present-day collectors are concerned, though *any* 1932 Auburn would be of interest. With the exception of the revived speedster, all other body-types were continued from 1931, and, on the 8s, at the same prices. The f.o.b. price of the new 12s ranged from $1345 to $1895.

Auburn made a few, noticeable changes for 1933. Two-piece V-windshields were introduced (similar to Chrysler's) and the grille now featured small, horizontal bars, as well as six fine, vertical bars and one large divider down the center. Below the grille was an extended metal pan which replaced the lower grille extension of the '31–'32 models. The shape of the bumper and front fenders was simplified, to no good effect. Though the '33 Auburn was attractive, it was an example of how a beautiful design could be spoiled with a little tampering for the mere sake of modernizing.

The chassis frame of the 1933 Auburn featured a new A-member at the front end to bolster the sturdy X-member. A new "Salon" series was added to the standard and custom 8s and 12s. Though the 12s continued to be rated at 160 horsepower, the 8 was boosted to 100. Wheelbases were now 127 or 133 inches. With more models, the price range was wider; $745 to $1845. The Auburn was a lot of automobile for the money!

Additional 1933 improvements on the "Salon" models were vacuum boosters for the hydraulic brakes on the 12s, air-cushioned rubber engine mounts, and all-metal side top quarters to replace the formerly fabric-covered panels.

Big changes came on the 1934 models. Auburn cars were completely restyled. At the time, the '34s may have appeared more streamlined than their predecessors, but, looking back from today, the models from the *earlier* '30s were far better looking. The '34 had a heavy look which made it appear somewhat awkward.

Though the brougham model admittedly contained some wood in its superstructure, the '34 Auburns featured "all-steel" bodies of "advanced but not 'freakish' streamlined design." This may have been a subtle dig at the new Chrysler and De Soto "Airflows" which were certainly the most modern-looking of all popular cars. The only other streamliners were the '34 La Salles, a few custom Cadillacs, "Aerodynamic" Hupmobiles, and the limited-production dream car, the Pierce "Silver Arrow."

Horizontal, streamlined vent mouldings were used on the hood of the '34 Auburn, and the grille was slightly modified from '33, with a continuation of the grille pattern on the lower pan (as in 1932). Fenders were skirted, in keeping with the latest trend.

However, Auburn's most important development for 1934 was not its new styling, but the new 6-cylinder model. The car was driven by an 85-horsepower Lycoming "WF" engine, had a 119-inch wheelbase and hydraulic brakes. It was the first 6-cylinder Auburn available since 1930, and prices started at only $695.

The standard 8-cylinder model (with Lycoming "GF" engine) had 100 horsepower, with a cast-iron cylinder head and a compression ratio of 5.3. The custom eight had a 6.2 compression ratio, using an aluminum head on a Lycoming "GG" engine. Both eights had a piston displacement of 279.9 cubic inches, but the higher-compression "GG" developed 115 horsepower. The eights had a 126-inch wheelbase and were priced from $945 up, as in earlier years.

The 12-cylinder Auburn (model 12-165) was still available in 1934, but sales were disappointing, even though prices began at $1395. As in '33, wheelbase was 133.

Dual-Ratio was still available (for *all* Auburn models, even the sixes) and was Auburn's most unique feature. At this time, Auburn was directly affiliated with the Columbia Axle Company, makers of the Dual-Ratio unit.

AUSTIN
(American Bantam)

The American Austin Car Company, Inc., located at 7300 Woodward Avenue, Detroit, produced in 1930 a car that delivered fuel economy of 40 miles per gallon, the new American Austin. First cousin of the famous British Austin Seven, the American version was, indeed, a midget; it had a 75-inch wheelbase, and a total weight of approximately half a ton! The little car used an engine and mechanical parts similar to those of the smallest British Austins, but the body was especially designed for America. The first model of 1930 was a two-passenger coupe, with a straight, vertical back like that of a two-door sedan. A package-delivery model was also added to the line, and, for 1931, a roadster was introduced.

Known by its makers as "the Bantam car" (a bantam rooster was adopted as its insignia), the American Austin was advertised in a circular entitled the "COCK-CROW," which boasted such Austin feats as, "55.07 miles in one hour on one (imperial) gallon of gasoline," and, "200 miles at 83.53 miles per hour." The latter feat was obviously accomplished by a larger model of the British Austin, and anyone expecting performance of more than 50 from the miniscule American version was in for a disappointment.

Though the American Austin was launched just in time for the great Depression, many drivers rejected the economy car as a "toy," and as "too small to be safe."

The Austin was continued with few changes until 1934. The company failed in '34, but soon reorganized as the American Bantam Company. Changes were made in the car which enabled American Bantam to avoid paying patent royalties to the original Austin Company of England. With new headquarters in Butler, Pennsylvania, the Bantam Company produced a wider variety of models later in the '30s; even a station wagon was added, in '38.

The most popular body-type for the American Austin was the two-passenger coupe, with its sedan-like shape and the seat set well back in the body to provide sufficient legroom for driver and one additional passenger. During the early '30s, the tiny, 4-cylinder engine developed less than 15 brake horsepower, and the *total* piston displacement was a piddling 45.6 inches (less than the displacement of just one cylinder in many modern American engines.)

Needless to say, 45 miles an hour was a brisk speed for such a little car. And, with its excessively low-geared 5.25 to 1 differential, 50 miles an hour for any great length of time could cause serious engine damage!

In 1930, the American Austin was advertised at $445, f.o.b., but the price dropped as low as $275 during the Depression, then rose again later. Because of their size, American Austins were the convenient butt of many jokes. By some strange magic, circus clowns often emerged in surprising numbers from these midget machines, and the bantam cars were frequently used in stage comedy acts.

Though these cars were discontinued shortly before World War II, quite a number of American Austin and Bantam cars have been saved from oblivion, probably because they were "too little and too cute" to scrap. Reportedly, fewer than 7000 were built. Yet, a safe estimate probably would be that more than 2000 remain today in conditions varying from perfect to miserable.

BUICK

Motor Land magazine for August, 1929, announced the July arrival of the new 1930 Buick. It was completely restyled, leaving the 1929 model a one-year style known as the "Silver Anniversary Buick" (also, as the "Pregnant Buick," because of its bulging side panels.)

The 1930 model was Buick's last 6-cylinder car. The new body design was so well-received that it was continued, unchanged, on the following year's new 8s. *Motor Land* had this to say:

"Offered in fourteen new models, the 1930 Buick made its bow to the motoring public last month (July, 1929.) Announcements from the factory featured increase of power, longer wheelbase, lower and longer bodies, and many mechanical improvements and refinements.

"The Buick line, as in former years, is divided into three series. The wheelbase and horsepower of all models of the three sixes have been increased. The wheelbase of the six models of the '40' series has been increased from 116 to 118 inches, and the engine has been stepped up to 80½ horsepower (at 2800 RPMs.)

"Wheelbases on the two models in the series '50' line are increased from 121 inches to 124 inches, and on the six models of the '60' series from 129 inches to 132 inches. Models in the 50 and 60 series have an engine which will de-

Body by Fisher

Assurance of Complete Motoring Satisfaction

CARRY in your mind's eye this portrait of the stunning new Buick beauty. But also call up in memory all you have heard of the supreme satisfaction which comes to the Buick owner. He is the envied among motorists. His car is known everywhere for rugged dependability, for blithely doing the things which other owners hesitate to ask of their cars.

Then know that in all Buick history there has been no Buick to equal these new ones. Incredible as it may seem, it is a fact that they elevate dependability to a far higher level. Through the most alert and modern of engineering, they are greatly advanced in safety, and comfort, and convenience. The owner smoothly rides with the gliding ride as only Buick gives it. In fact, in every phase of his motoring he enjoys the utmost of satisfaction.

This *new* kind of motoring in Buick is attuned to modern desires, modern needs and modern conditions. It is the kind you want in your new car. It is to be had in full and generous measure only in the new Buick Eight.

BUICK for 1934

velop 99 horsepower. All models have a speed in the seventies, it is stated."

Among the many mechanical refinements for 1930 were thermostatically-operated shutters in the redesigned radiator shell, and a steering wheel road-shock-eliminating-device that was coupled with a fully adjustable worm- and roller-type steering assembly for improved handling. New Lovejoy Duo-draulic shock absorbers were used, with new longer rear leaf springs to check annoying bounding and rebounding motion on rough roads.

Other improvements included a redesigned transmission and clutch, improved rubber engine mountings and a wider chassis frame. Buick's four-wheel mechanical brakes were of the new "Controlled Servo Enclosed-Type," internally expanding, and actuated by sealed cables. They were claimed to be more efficient than hydraulic brakes because, though they might require more foot pressure, they, at least, contained no fluid which might leak out unexpectedly. Sudden failures experienced with some early hydraulic brake systems led many drivers in the early '30s to stick with mechanical brakes.

A notable styling feature, designed for safety as well, was the slightly tilted, "non-glare" windshield, one of the major features on all General Motors 1930 cars. It was duly appreciated by night-driving motorists, for the reflection from headlights of following cars could create an annoying glare on an absolutely vertical windshield, thus dazzling the driver. The new windshield sloped at a slight seven-degree angle.

The instrument panel of the 1930 Buick was unspectacular, but tastefully conservative in design. The entire dash was finished in glossy black, with the set of circular gauges framed within a thin rectangular band of chrome. All-black dashboards (with few exceptions) were the new rage for '30, at General Motors.

Gear ratio was a comparatively low 4.55 to 1 in the small "40" series, and 4.27 to 1 in larger models. Obviously, the "50" and "60" series with their larger engine and more favorable gearing were to hold together better at high speeds, as they lasted through the years to follow.

More than *two million Buicks* had been sold by the time the 1930 models arrived, and Buick's advertising spoke justifiably of the continuing loyalty of the many owners who preferred Buick to any other medium-priced automobile. The 1930 prices ranged (f.o.b.) from $1225 for the least expensive "40" model, to $1995 for the best of the "60s." By May, 1930, the top of the price range was extended to $2070.

Buick kept the same successful exterior styling for 1931, but all-new engines were under the hoods. Though Buick's traditional valve-in-head engine design was retained, the 1931 Buick engines were all straight-eights. The new straight-eight was such a great car that Buick stood by straight-eights exclusively until the new Buick V-8 was introduced for 1953.

In addition to the new engines, another 1931 Buick refinement was the silent-shift syncro-mesh transmission which proved to be remarkably smooth. Low and second gears produced a throaty whine, not unlike the sound of a modern truck transmission.

There were now four series of Buicks: "50," "60," "80" and "90" models. The "50" series had 77 horsepower at 3200 RPM and was capable of 75 miles per hour. The 90-horsepower "60" series and 104-horsepower "80" and "90" series were able to reach an honest 80-mile top speed.

The oil temperature regulator was a welcome addition for '31, and it kept the engine oil reasonably cool, even at prolonged high speeds. A new air intake silencer eliminated much of the hissing noises heard from earlier types of carburetor intakes.

Though Buick's Fisher body for 1931 resembled the '30, outwardly, it contained improved insulation for greater comfort and quietness. Closed-car upholstery came in mohair, whipcord or broadcloth, with leather in the various convertible models. The dash panel of the '31 was redesigned, with new squarish gauges set in a wood-brown panel with silver-finished borders, and two, modernized map lights above. Between the windshield and the recessed area of the dash, there was, also, an attractive, wood-colored panel, not unlike those in the 1929 and 1930 Chryslers.

The Buick "50" had a 114-inch wheelbase and a 4.55 gear ratio. The price range was only $1025 to $1095, f.o.b.; less for an eight than for the previous year's lowest-priced Buick six. The "60" models sold for $1285 to $1355, had a 118-inch wheelbase and 4.45 gear ratio. Highest-geared was the new "80" series, with 4.27 ratio, a 124-inch wheelbase and price range of $1535 to $1565. The 132-inch wheelbase "90" series had a 4.36 gear ratio and sold for $1610 to $2035.

As before, Buick was early in announcing its new models, for the '31s appeared on July 26, 1930. The straight-eight was very well received, and by May, 1931, Buick claimed that it was selling more cars than the thirteen other builders of 8-cylinder cars combined! Buick announced, in 1931, that it would not make its usual summer model change, but would continue the popular model until close to the year's end.

Until the 1960s, there were thousands of 1931 Buicks still in regular service as transportation or work cars. They were exceptionally reliable and durable, and outlasted many later Buick models and other cars. The '31 was durable because it was a heavy car built for speed and power, yet it was remarka-

Body by Fisher

Possession · · · **MAKES THE HEART BEAT FASTER** · ·

BUICK this year is widening the tremendous favor it holds with people who live in the modern manner. Its beauty, its luxury, its quiet sophistication, are in their language, as its sturdy dependability and mighty performance are in the universal language of motoring.

Buick engineering creates a different and finer kind of motoring—the Buick kind. It adapts Knee-Action wheels to Buick's own requirements for the gliding ride. But it doesn't stop there. It goes all the way to the gliding ride as only Buick gives it. It builds in a new balance of weight and springing, and a new ride stabilizer; it equips with new air-cushion tires.

Then it provides center-point steering for your greater surety of control; vacuum-power brakes for your greater safety; automatic starting and other operations for your greater convenience and ease, and your car's increased efficiency.

In less than an hour you can learn why Buick is cresting the flood of popularity—and discover that just the thought of possessing it for your own makes your heart beat faster.

· BUICK ·

WHEN · BETTER · AUTOMOBILES · ARE · BUILT — BUICK · WILL · BUILD · THEM

Body by Fisher

LISTEN—*in any smart summer gathering*

 In the lively conversation of any social gathering today, you hear Buick's name repeatedly. Buick style, beauty, and comfort are spoken of in warm approval. Everyone is enthusiastic about the Knee-Action gliding ride as only Buick gives it.

Women freely express their great liking for Buick's automatic conveniences. For they no longer fuss with choke, throttle and spark to start the engine. They just press down on the accelerator pedal.

You are almost sure to catch some owner of an earlier model loyally remarking that he can't imagine a car more dependable than his. He may be right. At any rate, the new cars carry every proven feature that makes Buick so wholly dependable.

An hour's driving of any new Buick will reveal all that is truly fine in modern cars. Every model in each of the four groups—from 117 to 136 inch wheelbase—yields the super-smooth, powerful performance of Buick's Valve-in-Head straight eight engine. Take a Buick demonstration and acquaint yourself with the year's most noteworthy advancements.

Series 40—$795 to $925. Series 50—$1110 to $1250. Series 60—$1375 to $1675. Series 90—$1875 to $2175. List prices at Flint, Mich., subject to change without notice. Special equipment extra.

◆ BUICK ◆

WHEN · BETTER · AUTOMOBILES · ARE · BUILT—BUICK · WILL · BUILD · THEM bly uncomplicated, with few of the fancy gimmicks found on many of the big cars.

There seemed to be one fault common to many of the '31 Buicks, and that was the double-jet carburetor. When worn, it would draw in too much air, causing noise and cutting down the natural smoothness of the engine. It was a minor flaw in a car that was nearly perfect in all other respects. The only other common problem in this model was that the hydrostatic (thermometer-type) gas gauge had a tendency to lose its indicating fluid as it aged. The various models of the '31 Buicks averaged from 12 to 18 miles per gallon. And for the convenience of the owner, a portable oil-can was attached to a bracket on the firewall, the same shade of green as the engine.

As on many 1932 cars, the old-fashioned outside sun visor was eliminated on the '32 Buicks, and the metal area above the windshield was slightly curved. New, door-type hood vents were featured, and the horns (dual) were now mounted outside the car, below the headlights.

A notable new feature for '32 was "Wizard Control," the combination of an automatic clutch and free wheeling. It was now possible, in most instances, to shift gears without bothering to use the clutch pedal which, of course, was still provided. Free wheeling was a new feature in the Buick line, as well as the new "silent-second" transmission. Gone was the truck-like whine of low and second gear as heard on the '31 Buicks.

Inside the 1932 Buicks, the dash had been completely redesigned once again, with all instruments grouped at the left. The 90 MPH speedometer was of the new "sweep-hand"-type that had just come into vogue. On the right side of the dash was something new; a glove compartment. Formerly, the pockets in the doors had been used for storing small articles.

The vacuum-operated windshield wiper was designed to operate properly at *all* speeds.

With the Depression at its worst, Buick prices were at their lowest since the days of the 4-cylinder models in 1925. F.O.B. prices on the "50" series ranged from only $935 to $1155. The "50" had 78 (later 82) horsepower (with a 230.4 cubic-inch straight-eight engine.) It had a 114-inch wheelbase, and a low-geared 4.60 to 1 rear axle ratio.

The "60" had a larger engine of 272.6 cubic inches that developed 90 horsepower. The wheelbase was 118-inches and gear ratio 4.55 to 1. The 4-door sedan in the "60" series sold for $1310 at the factory in Flint.

The "80" and "90" series shared Buick's largest (344.8 cu. in.) 104-horsepower engine, though once again the "80" series was higher-geared (4.27 to 1 as opposed to 4.36 in the "90.") Wheelbase of the "80" was 126 inches, with the "90s" being eight inches longer. For $1570, f.o.b., you could buy an "80" series sedan in 1932. The comparable "90" model was priced at $1805.

All 1932 Buicks had 18-inch wheels.

An optional feature found on most '32 Buicks was the "Ride Regulator," a switch on the steering column which enabled the driver to regulate the shock absorbers to suit road conditions.

Buick, in 1932, advertised top speeds of over 80 mph, and while this was easily true of the larger models, the small "50" models were working hard at 75. Still, all the Buicks of this era were extremely hardy, and they were advertised to last from 150,000 to 200,000 miles or more, as many did.

The 1932 Buick was making more than half of all sales of the fourteen 8-cylinder cars in its price range. There were twenty-six Buick models in all, and they were advertised nationally by radio.

In 1933, with Depression austerity the general rule, Buick continued to advertise its remarkable durability. For instance, a 1914 Buick in Los Angeles had already traveled over 500,000 miles. Another case was cited of a 1926 Buick in Minneapolis which had been driven for 370,000 miles and was still going strong. Still another story was told of a *1908* Buick which had currently logged 240,000 miles! By 1933, over 2,700,000 Buicks had been built, and over one and a quarter million of them were still in use. More than 47% of all previous Buicks had survived to that time!

For the second year in a row, Buick's styling changed. The 1933 models had a new "Wind-Stream" body, with semi-skirted fenders, added vent doors on either side of the hood, and a brand-new, V-shaped grille which sloped considerably. Seventeen-inch wheels were standard.

General Motors' most notable improvement for 1933 was "No-Draft Ventilation," featured on Buick and all other General Motors cars. This was, simply, a swinging "butterfly" section in each front door window (as well as in the rear quarter side windows), which made it possible to open a portion of a window without creating a draft. This feature, in similar forms, was soon found on nearly all makes of cars, but General Motors' Fisher Body Company was the first to use it widely.

Glove compartments were here to stay, and the '33 Buick had one which could be locked.

Buicks and other General Motors cars were known for their superior upholstery in the '30s, and the 1933 Buick closed cars came with a choice of broadcloth, whipcord or mohair. Window curtains were still offered but they were concealed when not in use. Safety glass was standard in windshields and vent windows.

"Automatic" shock absorbers replaced the unique, manually-adjusted-type of the previous year. A new X-type chassis frame was adopted.

Twenty body-types were available, in the same four series, as before. However, wheelbases had been lengthened, and horsepower increased. The 86-horsepower "50" series had a 119-inch wheelbase. The "60" had a 127-inch wheelbase and 97 horsepower. The "80" and "90" Buicks had 113 horsepower and, respectively, 130 and 138-inch wheelbases. Besides being longer, the 1933 Buick was a heavier car. Models ranged in weight from 3866 to 4901 pounds. Prices were still low, but prices of the "50" series were slightly higher for 1933. The sedan sold for $1045, f.o.b.

Buick, for 1934, adopted styling it would retain, unchanged, for 1935. The "Wind-Stream" bodies were similar in many ways to those of '33, but the door-type hood vents had been replaced by horizontal ventilating slots. Trumpet-type outside horns (of the sort used in 1932) replaced the curved ones of '33. Separate parking lamps were eliminated, as an extra-dim beam was added to the headlights.

The most important 1934 feature was the "Knee Action" independently suspended front wheels, with coil springs. This improvement gave new smoothness to the famous Buick ride, but was likely to be a liability in later years on cars so equipped. Some of the "Knee Action" cars tended to shimmy and wander badly when they grew old, though independent front-wheel suspension was a good (later improved) principle.

Other Buick features for '34 were the "Ride Stabilizer" (a rear sway bar which prevented body roll) and vacuum-power mechanical brakes which required only half as much pedal pressure as previously (because of the new Bendix "BK" booster). An automatic choke was a novel feature, and both manifold heat and spark controls were automatic.

"Center point" steering control was also new, as were the 16-inch "Air Cushion" tires.

A new "40" series was added to the Buick line, in midseason. It was the predecessor to Buick's later special models. The new "40" had 93 horsepower, would reach 85 miles per hour, averaged 15 miles per gallon and sold for only $795, and up, at Flint. The "80" series was dropped, but later returned as the famous "Roadmaster."

Body by Fisher

ℐt would greet you with a Smile ◆ ◆ ◆

If your motoring has become a sort of hum-drum transportation, there is that in the Buick which will bring back the zest of driving your first car.

Just to see the Buick is to realize how vivacious and new it is in its smart beauty. To drive it and ride in it but once is to recognize that it brings to modern motoring something new and all its own.

For there is a difference that goes beyond the gliding ride as only Buick gives it, beyond the matchless ease of superb performance and the convenience of automatic features. There seems to be the vigor and exuberance of youth in all that Buick does; and it is not difficult to imagine that, if it were human, it would always greet you with a smile.

You can take that kind of car to your heart—which perhaps explains the undying loyalty of Buick owners, and the even more wide-spread favor which Buick is winning today among motorists of all classes.

· BUICK ·

WHEN · BETTER · AUTOMOBILES · ARE · BUILT—BUICK · WILL · BUILD · THEM

Can you do THIS in YOUR automobile?

Can you shift *all* gears, first, second, third or reverse, swiftly and easily without even touching the clutch pedal—a major advantage of Wizard Control?

You CAN *in a Buick*

Can you obtain Standard or High pression (without cost) in a Valve-i Straight Eight even the fine p Buick which won sales leadership in i

You CAN *in a*

Can you have either Free Wheeling or Conventional Drive at will— changing from one to the other *instantaneously* to meet varying driving conditions?

You CAN *in a Buick*

Can you sweep o road at 80-plus wi feeling of absolute and security impa the Torque Tube and an extra-r finely balanced

You CAN *in a*

Can you enjoy a *truly silent* second speed as well as acceleration up to forty miles an hour or more before shifting noiselessly into high?

You CAN *in a Buick*

Can you *choose* yc by means of a Ri ulator, to assure comfort according conditions, num passengers and car

You CAN *in a*

Can you place personal articles or packages in an attractive built-in convenience compartment in the instrument panel—handy, spacious, fitted with lock?

You CAN in a Buick

Can you count upon 200,000 miles and more of fine, dependable performance, knowing that your motor car has a 28-year record of just such performance-ability?

You CAN in a Buick

Can you adjust the full front seat swiftly and easily—moving it forward or backward to desired driving position—even while the car is in motion?

You CAN in a Buick

Can you motor with perfect peace of mind, derived from the knowledge that a nationwide service organization with more than 3,000 authorized stations reinforces your car's reliability?

You CAN in a Buick

Can you secure positive, vacuum-controlled windshield wiper action at all engine speeds—and gain instant protection from sun glare at any angle via an Adjustable Interior Visor?

You CAN in a Buick

Can you obtain these advantages, with a choice of twenty-six luxurious Fisher body types, assuring exactly the model you want, at prices ranging from $935 to $2055, f. o. b. Flint, Michigan?

You CAN in a Buick

You CAN if you own
THE NEW BUICK EIGHT

Body by Fisher

Assurance of Complete Motoring Satisfaction

CARRY in your mind's eye this portrait of the stunning new Buick beauty. But also call up in memory all you have heard of the supreme satisfaction which comes to the Buick owner. He is the envied among motorists. His car is known everywhere for rugged dependability, for blithely doing the things which other owners hesitate to ask of their cars.

Then know that in all Buick history there has been no Buick to equal these new ones. Incredible as it may seem, it is a fact that they elevate

dependability to a far higher level. Through the most alert and modern of engineering, they are greatly advanced in safety, and comfort, and convenience. The owner smoothly rides with the gliding ride as only Buick gives it. In fact, in every phase of his motoring he enjoys the utmost of satisfaction.

This *new* kind of motoring in Buick is attuned to modern desires, modern needs and modern conditions. It is to be had in full and generous measure only in the new Buick Eight.

BUICK for 1934

CADILLAC

In September, 1929, the General Motors Corporation's Cadillac Motor Car Company of Detroit made its twenty-eighth annual presentation of new models, as it announced the 1930 "353" series.

There were a few noteworthy styling changes from '29, such as the slant of the non-glare windshield, with its new "cadet-type" metal visor above. Headlights were enlarged to 13 inches in diameter, and there were now dual globular tail and stop lights at the rear.

Open Cadillacs had vertical louvres on the sides of the cowl, to match those along the hood. Radiator shutters were standard equipment, as was "Security-Plate" shatter-proof glass (in windshield and in all windows).

Inside the 1930 Cadillac, the dashboard was redesigned with a lower edge that dipped gracefully in the center. All six instruments were circular and set in a row, while the center two (speedometer and clock) were larger than the others. A band of chrome ran along the lower edge of the dash and additional chrome trim encompassed the row of instruments in caliper fashion. As in 1929, the basic color of dash and instruments, on most models, was black.

Though the change was hardly noticeable, the rear seat in the sedan was four inches wider than before. Also, seven-passenger sedan bodies were lengthened by three inches. These were minor improvements, to be sure, but

Cadillac felt it worthwhile to mention them to prospective buyers. A touch of true luxury was found in the folding top of the convertible coupe, for the top was fitted with an additional interior lining. Thus, the top bows and other "unsightly" mechanical parts were hidden from view, and the interior of the cab resembled that of a coupe with the top up.

Fisher bodies were standard, though de luxe Cadillacs had Fleetwood bodies. Here is a list of the various types, from Cadillac's 1930 catalog:

7 FISHER BODIES:

2-Passenger Coupe with Rumble Seat
2-Passenger Convertible Coupe with
    Rumble Seat
5-Passenger Coupe
5-Passenger Sedan
5-Passenger Town Sedan
7-Passenger Sedan
7-Passenger Imperial Sedan (limousine)

14 FLEETWOOD SPECIAL CUSTOM BODIES:

"Fleetdowns"	2-Passenger Roadster	"Fleetmere"	5-Passenger Imperial Cabriolet
"Fleetway"	4-Passenger All-Weather Phaeton	"Fleetdale"	7-Passenger Sedan
"Fleetwind"	4-Passenger Sedanette Cabriolet	"Fleetdale"	7-Passenger Imperial
"Fleetwind"	4-Passenger Sedanette	"Fleetwick"	Town Cabriolet with Opera Seats
"Fleetdene"	5-Passenger Sedan	"Fleetmont"	Town Cabriolet with Quarter Window
"Fleetmere"	5-Passenger Sedan Cabriolet	"Fleetcrest"	Town Cabriolet with Full Rear Quarter
"Fleetdene"	5-Passenger Imperial	"Fleetbourne"	Limousine Brougham

Standard wheelbase was 140 inches, and tire size was 7.00 x 19. 12-spoke wood artillery wheels with demountable rims were standard, though disc, wire, or demountable wood wheels were obtainable at extra cost. The four-wheel mechanical brakes had massive $16\frac{1}{2}$-inch drums, and the 1930 Cadillac V-8 sedans had a lower gear ratio than any other Cadillac of that era—5.08 to 1! However, there were optional ratios of 4.75 or 4.39 which were better suited to high-cruising speeds.

Cadillac had been building V-8 engines since late in 1914, and among the mechanical changes in Cadillac's latest 1930 V-8 engine was a horsepower boost to 95, as well as redesigned combustion chambers, 4-ring pistons, larger valves. A new double-reduction starter was introduced, to insure faster turn-

This ONE *alone*

The gentleman who owns this car can drive from one end of the earth to the other—and not *once* will he see another car precisely like his own. The car pictured is No. 27 of the 1934 production of the Cadillac V-16—the world's most distinguished automobile. Only 400 of these magnificent cars will be produced within the year, and early reservations are sincerely advised.

CADILLAC

V-Sixteen

over of engine without drawing additional current. The fuel tank held 25 gallons.

Despite the improvements on the V-8 Cadillacs, the company's greatest news for 1930, which was disclosed to the public on January 28, was the all-new V-16 model. With the exception of Duesenberg, the new 16-cylinder Cadillac was America's most powerful production car that year. It developed 185 horsepower at 3400 RPM. The new model was this country's first full-production 16-cylinder car. The V-16 engine was actually two separate straight-eights that shared a common crankshaft. Each half of the gigantic engine had its own carburetor, water pump and accessories. The car could actually run on half an engine.

Yet, performance of the V-16 was not what one would expect. Top speed was about 85. The three-ton car would not accelerate rapidly, and gas mileage ranged from 4 to 10 miles per gallon. The engine held ten quarts of oil!

The V-16 models had new door-type hood vents and a screen-type stone guard in front of the radiator. Price range of the Cadillac V-8 was $3195 to $7500, but the V-16 prices started at nearly $6000, f.o.b. Detroit! Prospective buyers at the motor shows held during 1930 were given a beautiful ivory-colored 10″ x 14″ catalog that illustrated eleven custom "Fleetwood" models of the Cadillac V-16. The catalog came in its own protective envelope and included (within the back cover) a packet of designer's scale-drawings of the various models. The catalog proclaimed that, "in such details as color, finish of panels, upholstery fabrics and trim, it is possible for each owner to have the treatment he prefers." The catalog also suggested that a buyer could use the designer's drawings to pencil in the custom modifications that were desired. In fact, modified versions of these drawings could be presented at any Cadillac-La Salle dealer for a careful estimate of what such a custom-creation might cost.

Prices of the new Cadillac V-8 models for 1931 were reduced, with a range of $2695 to $3795, and the styling was upgraded to give the V-8 Cadillac the look of the previous year's V-16. Vent doors in hood, stone guard, and other such details were added.

But that wasn't all. For 1931, another multi-cylinder engine was offered, the V-12. Cadillac featured three distinctively different engines! Models of the new, 135-horsepower V-12 were priced from $3795 and, for such a large car (140 to 143-inch wheelbase), it filled a fair amount of sales.

The 16-cylinder models were priced from $5350 to $15,000 in 1931! Movie star William Boyd, later known to millions of children as "Hopalong Cassidy," owned a beautiful V-16 convertible sedan in 1931 when he was

LEADERSHIP RESTS ON ACHIEVEMENT

Cadillac WAS FIRST WITH SYNCRO-MESH TRANSMISSION

It was a significant day, indeed, when the Cadillac Motor Car Company announced that it had perfected a non-clashing transmission — one that would enable the driver to shift without reducing his speed, and without noise or grinding of gears! . . . This great advancement, called then and now the Syncro-Mesh Transmission, has resulted in a complete transformation of the act of gear-shifting — and made motoring infinitely safer and more enjoyable. . . . The same spirit of pioneering which enabled Cadillac to produce the Syncro-Mesh Transmission is kept endlessly alive in the Cadillac laboratories, and is evident everywhere in the new Cadillacs and La Salles. In fact, among many other advancements, these new cars reveal an improvement in the transmission itself, for the Cadillac-La Salle Syncro-Mesh is now silent in operation in *all* forward speeds — low, second and high. . . . This constant pioneering has caused many persons to hold to Cadillac and La Salle during year after year without so much as considering the purchase of other cars — for they know that every practical advancement will be given them in these two distinguished creations. . . . Your Cadillac-La Salle dealer will gladly acquaint you with today's Cadillacs and La Salles — now, as always, foremost examples of the finest automotive craftsmanship. La Salle list prices start at $2245, Cadillac at $2695, f. o. b. Detroit.

The Syncro-Mesh Transmission, one of the great developments in the history of the automobile, was introduced by Cadillac in August, 1928. It was, and is, a marked example of Cadillac's leadership in the fundamental advancement of the motor car

MAGELLAN, FIRST TO CIRCUMNAVIGATE THE GLOBE

THE CADILLAC V-12 ALL-WEATHER PHAETON

playing romantic leads in the early talkies. And Douglas Fairbanks had a town car. Jean Harlow also bought a Cadillac (cabriolet) in '31, and Ramon Navarro took delivery of a new roadster at the factory and drove it home to Hollywood.

By 1931, many motorists had forgotten that, in the early 1900s, Cadillac had built small 1- and 4-cylinder "gas buggies" at fairly low prices (well under $1000.) With the new multi-cylinder models (which were planned as early as 1927), Cadillac enhanced its reputation as a luxury car.

For 1932, Cadillac bodies were restyled, with sun visors moved inside and bodies more rounded. Radiators were also restyled, with the removal of the stone guard. Freewheeling and an automatic clutch were added, also a new transmission with silent helical gears in all forward speeds.

By redesigning the intake manifold, Cadillac engineers raised the horsepower of the V-8 engine from 95 to 115. All models were equipped with combined air cleaners and silencers, and "straight-through" mufflers for reduced back pressure. Diaphram-type fuel pumps replaced the old-style vacuum tanks. New carburetors were used on the V-12 and V-16.

The V-8s and V-12s had 17-inch wheels; 18-inchers were used on the V-16s. A most unusual model was the V-16 "Town Coupe," which was actually a two-door sedan with a long hood, short body and a separate trunk. This body was also used for a time on the other series of Cadillacs.

For 1933, Cadillac offered many new styling features; V-shaped radiator, new horizontal vent doors in hood, "No-Draft" ventilation, and, most noticeably, deeply skirted fenders which were considerably streamlined in appearance.

An advertisement in the April, 1933 *Fortune* magazine declared that a limit of 400 V-16 automobiles would be built by Cadillac that year. However, there was certainly a wide variety of V-8 Cadillacs available, as indicated:

Body Type	Weight	Price f.o.b.
134" wheelbase models		
Roadster	4695	$2795
Coupe	4855	2695
Convertible Coupe	4825	2845
140" wheelbase models		
Sport Phaeton	4975	——
Phaeton	4865	$2895
All-Weather Phaeton (side windows)	5110	3395

Body Type	Weight	Price f.o.b.
5-Passenger Coupe	4850	2895
Sedan	5000	2895
Town Sedan	5060	2995
7-Passenger Sedan	5105	3045
7-Passenger Imperial	5140	3195
With Fleetwood bodies		
Touring Car	4925	——
Sedan	5000	$3295
7-Passenger Sedan	5101	3445
7-Passenger Limousine	5140	3645
Town Cab. (5-pass.)	5010	3995
Town Cab. (7-pass.)	5200	4145
Limousine Brougham	5225	4145
Town Coupe	4890	——

As in 1932, the 353 cubic-inch V-8 engine developed 115 horsepower. The bore and stroke measured $3\frac{3}{8}$" x $4\frac{15}{16}$," and six-point rubber engine mountings were used. Safety glass was used throughout the 1933 Cadillac.

Even though cars during the early '30s were offering new improvements each year, prices were often reduced each season as the Depression curbed prosperity. For 1933, Cadillac again reduced prices, with the V-8 range beginning at $2695, f.o.b.

In a colorful series of magazine advertisements, The Cadillac Motor Car Company pictured famous discoverers, Marco Polo, Magellan and others, along with illustrations of the latest Cadillac models. These advertisements listed many of Cadillac's "discoveries," such as the electric self-starter, interchangeable parts, enclosed bodies, the 90-degree V-8 engine, the 16-cylinder engine, syncro-mesh transmission, thermostatic carburetor, and others.

Each of the 400 V-16 Cadillacs for 1933 was to be custom-built to individual order, and each car was to be inscribed with the owner's name. Fleetwood bodies were used on the V-16s, and one such car, a beautiful $8000 convertible sedan, was ordered by singer and screen star Al Jolson. Despite the price of Jolson's car, the planned f.o.b. price range of the 1933 V-16 was only $4500 to $6000, which is considerably less than the present value of such a car in good condition.

Cadillac had new, streamlined bodies on its most expensive 1934 models. And the "streamliners" were most attractive, not unlike the designs Cadillac would be offering on all its models by 1936.

For 1934, Cadillac joined other General Motors cars in offering "Knee-Action" front suspension. Compression ratio was raised and was now 6 to 1. Engine speed was increased to 3400 RPM on the V-8, giving it 130 horsepower. An unusual feature on Cadillacs (as well as on the subsidiary La Salle cars) was the cold air intake, a large flexible tube that connected the carburetor air intake with a hole in the top tank of the radiator.

All '34 Cadillacs had 17-inch wheels, with graceful pontoon fenders. The new bumpers, too, were smartly styled in the form of two horizontal blades, one above the other and slightly "veed." All models had Bendix vacuum-mechanical brakes, though the lower-priced La Salle featured hydraulic brakes in 1934. (Other '34 cars that already offered hydraulic brakes were Auburn, Chrysler, De Soto, Dodge, Duesenberg, Franklin, Graham, Oldsmobile, Plymouth, Reo and Stutz. The last major producer to offer hydraulic brakes was Ford in 1939.)

There were thirty-three different body models in Cadillac's V-8 series, and nineteen V-12 variations. The V-16s again featured Fleetwood custom-built bodies tailored to the buyers' demands, and, as before, production was limited to 400 a year. Respective horsepower ratings for the twelves and sixteens were 150 and 185, and these multi-cylinder models, not noted for economy in gasoline consumption, now carried 30-gallon tanks. The 30-gallon gas tank was the largest used on any American car at the time, the next largest being on the 29-gallon tank on Marmon's ill-fated V-16. On the other hand, the smallest automobile fuel tank (5 gallons) was found on the little Austin.

Prices of the 1934 Cadillacs began at $2395., f.o.b. Detroit. The 1935 models which followed were not much different in outward appearance except that they had a more conventional and less imaginative bumper.

The V-12 model was discontinued during 1937. The V-16 was continued all the way to the end of the 1940 season. The L-head, V-8 engine was replaced by an overhead-valve, Kettering-designed version when the 1949 Cadillacs appeared.

LEADERSHIP RESTS ON ACHIEVEMENT

Cadillac WAS *first* TO USE THE 90 DEGREE V-TYPE ENGINE . . . .

Nowhere has Cadillac's leadership been more consistently maintained than in the design and construction of its engines. . . . Nineteen years ago, Cadillac committed itself to the V-type engine principle by introducing the first 90-degree V-type power plant ever used in an automobile. During all the years since, Cadillac has held to this principle without a single interruption— and has become, by virtue of this experience, the acknowledged authority on the V-type engine. . . . This fact becomes of the utmost significance when it is recalled that engines with more than eight cylinders are impractical with any other design. Thus, in the multi-cylinder field, Cadillac obviously stands alone in its ability to design and construct power plants. . . . You sense this leadership the moment you drive a modern Cadillac or La Salle. For in no other cars are the engines so smooth, so quiet, or so generally satisfactory in their performance. La Salle list prices begin at $2245, Cadillac at $2695, f. o. b. Detroit. Liberal G. M. A. C. terms may be arranged on any model.

MARCO POLO
OF VENICE
FAMOUS TRAVELER
AND EXPLORER

CADILLAC V-12 CONVERTIBLE COUPE . . . A GENERAL MOTORS VALUE

Leadership rests on Achievement

.. AND LEADERS ARE *MADE BY DEEDS*

ANTOINE de
la MOTHE CADILLAC,
FOUNDER OF DETROIT

When the writer of history dips his pen and starts his record of life, he looks about him for accomplishments and deeds. The hopes and aims and aspirations of those who walk across his pages are interesting, of course; but only in *things done* does he find the substance of which his record must be made. . . . And as in the history of human affairs, so is it in the chronicle of business. When the buyer of anything that's built looks into the record of him who built it, he goes beyond the claims and creeds, and hunts for facts and works. . . . And this is the reason why Cadillac has won first place in the fine-car field. Out of the welter of claims and hopes, the record of Cadillac stands clear. For, true to the spirit of Cadillac himself, intrepid discoverer and leader of men, the motor car company that bears his name has constantly been a pioneer. The electric self-starter, the 90-degree V-8 engine, the 16-cylinder engine, the Syncro-Mesh transmission, interchangeable parts, the thermostatic carburetor, enclosed bodies—these are but a few of the Cadillac "firsts" which have contributed so much to the development of the automobile. . . . It is out of this long record of achievement that the new Cadillacs and La Salles of today have had their being—the finest cars, in every way, that Cadillac has ever built.

CADILLAC MOTOR CAR COMPANY • • Division of General Motors

Cadillac

CADILLAC V-12 5-PASSENGER SEDAN

It is impossible to arrive at an adequate conception of the Cadillac V-16 until you have

experienced a demonstration — for there is no mode of transportation, whether on land

or sea or in the air, more completely luxurious than travel in this distinguished car.

Custom Coachwork by Fleetwood   *Priced from $5,350 to $15,000 f. o. b. Detroit*

C A D I L L A C   V - 1 6

CADILLAC MOTOR CAR COMPANY   DIVISION OF GENERAL MOTORS

Illustrated below is the Cadillac V-16 five-passenger All-Weather Phaeton, created by Fleetwood especially for the V-16 chassis. Prices of the V-16 range from $5350, f.o.b. Detroit.

To sit at the wheel of the Cadillac V-16 is really an exceptional experience—for there is no precedent at all for *what* this car does, nor for the *manner* in which it does it. The V-16 was planned, of course, as an entirely new embodiment of motoring luxury; and not a single tradition or limitation was permitted to influence its design. As a result, it is a highly individualized creation—a car so irresistibly inviting in appearance, so superbly behaved in action that it must inevitably revolutionize your highest opinion of motoring. Your Cadillac-La Salle dealer will gladly arrange to demonstrate the truth of these statements.

CADILLAC V8 12 16

Cadillac V-8 prices range from $2695, f. o. b. Detroit — with G.M.A.C. terms available on all body types. The model illustrated below is the V-8 5-passenger sedan, with coachwork by Fisher.

Until 1927, Cadillac's entire reputation as a master builder was based upon the Cadillac V-8. This fact has never been forgotten; and though the Cadillac line now includes three other distinguished cars—the La Salle, the V-12 and the V-16 —the V-8 is built, to this day, as if it were the sole protector of Cadillac's good name. In fact, no eight-cylinder Cadillac ever produced could compare with the present V-8. Yet, due to a vastly enlarged manufacturing program, this finest of V-8 Cadillacs is priced as low as $2695, f. o. b. Detroit.

CADILLAC V8 12 16

Long, low and graceful—and possessed of the exceptional performance assured by Cadillac's V-type engine design— the V-8 all-weather Phaeton is one of the smartest creations to have borne the Cadillac name. Cadillac V-8 prices range from $2695, f. o. b. Detroit. G. M. A. C. terms available on all body styles.

It has often been said that deep in the hearts of a majority of motorists is the ambition, some day, to own and drive a Cadillac. Mindful of this, the Cadillac Motor Car Company has striven constantly, year after year, to bring its products within reach of an ever-increasing number of people. Today, this purpose has been fulfilled in exceptional measure—for the distinguished Cadillac V-8, expressive of everything that has come to be associated with the name Cadillac, is offered at prices ranging from only $2695.

CADILLAC V8 12 16

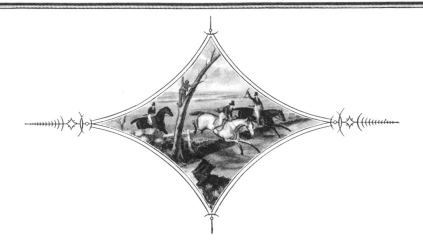

SIXTEEN CYLINDERS

The Cadillac sixteen-cylinder engine goes far beyond the contemporary conception of brilliant performance. It multiplies power and subdivides it into a continuous flow...constantly at full-volume efficiency...flexible... instantly responsive. This, plus complete individuality in styling, is—in brief—the story of the "V-16"

CADILLAC MOTOR CAR COMPANY   DIVISION OF GENERAL MOTORS

CHEVROLET

Because Chevrolet had made a major styling change, and had switched from a 4- to a 6-cylinder engine in 1929, changes in the 1930 line were relatively few. However, all '30 Chevrolets had the new black instrument panel, with circular dials, including an electric gas gauge.

Wheel diameter was reduced from 20 inches to 19 inches, but steel disc wheels were still standard equipment, with wire wheels optional.

The 1930 Chevrolets had an increase of 4 horsepower, giving the new engine a rating of 50 brake horsepower at 2600 RPM. Physical improvements included an enlarged "hot-spot" manifold, and lightweight pistons with bronze bushings. There were also unseen, but important, improvements in the clutch, transmission and rear axle. Wheelbase of 107 inches was the same as in 1929.

Though 1930 styling of Chevrolet was little changed from 1929, the windshield on each '30 model (closed cars) was tilted slightly to prevent glare.

With the Depression under way, prices were reduced; roadsters and phaetons sold for only $495, f.o.b. Flint.

The "Imperial" sedan, which in 1929 had been a landau model with fully folding rear quarters, was changed in 1930 to the "Club Sedan." The new model had a solid top, without landau irons, and sold for $625 ($50 less than the standard 7-window sedan.) However, by the summer of 1930 the club sedan had again sprouted landau irons and was priced at $665. At this time a special sedan was added to the line at $725, featuring *six wire wheels* as standard equipment. During the course of 1930, wire wheels appeared on more and more of the new Chevrolets.

Although Fisher bodies were used on many pre-1929 Chryslers and other makes in the 1920s, by 1930 the Fisher body was a General Motors exclusive. General Motors had long since owned Fisher, and Fleetwood was also a property. To quote a Chevrolet advertisement, *Country Gentleman,* August, 1930: "The Chevrolet Six offers you a *Fisher Body.* It is the only car in the lowest price field that does. And, as you probably know, the Fisher emblem (a royal coach) is accepted everywhere as the one sure guide to *extra value* in modern automobile coachwork.

"*Body by Fisher* stands for comfort and completeness . . . . for fine-car style. Even more important to those who give cars long, hard usage— — — *Body by Fisher* means composite wood-and-steel body construction, the strongest, most durable type known . . . . the same type as used exclusively in the highest priced cars. The framework is of selected hardwood, fortified at all points of stress by staunch braces. Over this strong wood framework are mounted steel panels, so that the wood reinforces the steel and the steel reinforces the wood."

The one fault with wood-framed composite bodies, however, was that dampness could eventually seep into the wood frame and rot it, seriously weakening such bodywork. And today, "wood-rot" can be a severe problem in some composite-bodied old cars that collectors are restoring.

During the summer of 1930, Chevrolet announced that it had produced more than *two million automobiles* in just the few months since January, 1929! There could be no doubt that the Chevrolet Six had been fully accepted.

For 1931, Chevrolet introduced several changes. The wheelbase was lengthened to 109 inches, and more vertical, hood louvres were added, now framed by an embossed panel. The slant of the windshield was more noticeable, and the external visor was shortened. The rear window was wider than before. Sport models featured an attractive screen, or stone guard, over the radiator, Cadillac-fashion. Wire wheels were standard equipment on *all* models.

Prices in 1931 ranged from $475 to $650. A new model for 1931 was the very stylish "Landau Phaeton," at $650. It was a convertible 2-door sedan, with folding windshield and a top that fitted neatly in line with the body when down. Also new was the 5-passenger coupe at $595. Other models and prices:

Roadster	$475	Standard 5-window Coupe	545
Sport Roadster (with rumble seat)	495	Sport Coupe (with rumble seat)	575
Phaeton (touring car)	510	Convertible Cabriolet	615
Standard Coupe	535	Standard Sedan	635
Coach (2-door sedan)	545	Special Sedan (6 wire wheels)	650

During 1931, Chevrolet reduced the price of its standard truck chassis to only $355!

Because the 1931 Chevrolet was an attractive and reliable car, many survived. Only a few years ago, they were easy to find in the back rows of used car lots, for about $65, apiece. That kind of bargain is hard to come by today. Most cars that old are worth at least a few hundred.

The only real fault with the early Chevrolet Sixes was that their rear axles were somewhat undersized and tended to break under considerable stress.

Despite bad times, the 1932 Chevrolet was well publicized in newspaper and magazine advertising and on the radio. One hundred and seventeen improvements were found in the new, '32 Chevrolet. There were numerous styling changes, but *Motor* magazine and other automotive critics considered the most important development to be in the engine. Horsepower was increased to 60, at 3000 RPM, because of a new downdraft carburetor, improved manifold, and changes in the valve timing. As a result, the torque was greatly improved; hill-climbing was easier, and acceleration was obviously better. Top speed was now advertised "65 to 70 miles per hour."

The engine was the same size as before, but there were many other, unseen improvements. For example, the main bearings were now pressure-lubricated.

A new, syncro-mesh transmission brought easier gear-changing at all speeds, and freewheeling also was included. Plymouth had adopted the feature in June, 1931, and Chevrolet decided to offer it, too, despite the added production expense.

Bodies were greatly improved, with the external visor eliminated. The windshield was high, for greater visibility, and the area directly above was gracefully curved, as on the other General Motors cars for 1932. The radiator featured a fine, built-in grille, and headlamps were connected by an attractive, double tie-bar. On each side of the hood were four vertical ventilating doors instead of the old-style louvres. These vent doors were chrome-plated on de luxe models.

Six new
sport models

styled in the modern manner

The vogue for using the Chevrolet Six as a personal car is particularly noticeable in those sections where standards of living are above the average. At the country club—the fashionable resort—or in the quiet atmosphere of fine homes—Chevrolet is unusually well represented . . . Six very logical reasons for this are presented at the right: Chevrolet's new sport models, styled in the modern manner. . . . A certain casual air of quality has been captured in the lines of these cars—a nice balance of smartness and simplicity, which good taste always approves. The low streamline treatment has been carried out cleanly and effectively. The rich color-tones are enlivened with the sparkle of chrome plate, with the flash of de luxe wire wheels. Interiors, too, not only make allowance for the comfort and convenience of driver and all passengers, but reveal many novel and interesting smart-effects. . . . Like all 14 other Chevrolet body-types, these sport models are available in a wide choice of color harmonies, to suit the individual fancy. Each, being a Six, gives the multi-cylinder performance to which two- and three-car owners are accustomed. Each is a car that fits very naturally into the environment of those who live well.

Chevrolet prices range from $475 to $650, f. o. b. Flint, Michigan. Special equipment extra. Product of General Motors. Chevrolet Motor Company, Detroit, Michigan

NEW
CHEVROLET
SIX

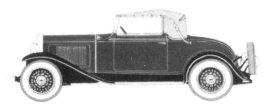

NEW CHEVROLET CONVERTIBLE CABRIOLET $615

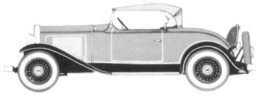

NEW CHEVROLET SPORT ROADSTER $495

NEW CHEVROLET SPORT COUPE $575

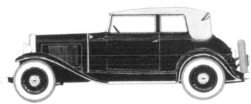

NEW CHEVROLET CONVERTIBLE LANDAU PHAETON $650

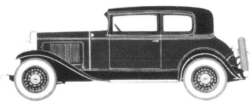

NEW CHEVROLET FIVE-PASSENGER COUPE $595

NEW CHEVROLET SPECIAL SEDAN $650

In all, there were twenty versions of the 1932 Chevrolet, with prices starting at $445. Because of their peculiar second-gear whine, these cars could be distinguished in sound from those of all other years.

The new "Master" and "Eagle" Chevrolets for 1933 included a new device known as the "Starterator." The engine could now be started merely by pressing hard on the accelerator treadle. It was a feature found on a few other cars during the course of the thirties.

Horsepower was 60 in the 107-inch wheelbase "Standard" models, and 65 in the Master and Eagle series which had 110-inch wheelbases. A new "Aer-Stream" body was used on the '33 models, with curvier corners, "No-Draft Ventilation," and a distinctive, arched rear window. A new, sloping, V-shaped grille was introduced, and three slanting vent doors were located on each side of the hood, near the cowl (except on Standard models, which had sloping hood louvres, instead.)

New semi-skirted fenders were added. All models had wire wheels as standard equipment (the rule since 1931) and standard models had 17-inch wheels, with the better Chevrolets featuring 18-inch wheels, as in 1932.

A "silent second" transmission was introduced, eliminating the high-pitched whine of the '32 gearboxes. And an interesting new gadget on the distributor was known as the "octane selector." It consisted of a pointer, a degree scale, and knurled screw and lock nut. The owner or mechanic could now make easy adjustments in advancing the spark in order to best adapt the car to various octanes of gasoline (different in certain localities.) In the early '30s, "regular" gasoline had an octane rating of only 65, while Ethyl had a usual rating of 78. Times have changed since then!

The Standard coupe of 1933 was priced at only $445. Chevrolet had edged ahead of Ford in sales since 1931, and the competition was especially fierce in the low-price arena.

Just before the 1933 Chevrolets appeared, each of the 10,000 Chevrolet dealers participated in a nationally-broadcast "sales school" which opened on December 12, 1932, to familiarize salesmen with the details of the '33 model before its December 17 introduction.

Chevrolet's big news for 1934 was "Knee-Action" independent front wheel suspension. It was offered in the 80-horsepower "Master Six" series, with prices starting at $540 for the roadster, a body-type which, along with the phaeton, was dropped by Chevrolet after 1935. The Master Six (model DA) had a 112-inch wheelbase and 5.50 x 17" tires.

The Standard Six (model DC) had a 107-inch wheelbase, a 60-horsepower engine and a 181 cubic-inch piston displacement. Masters had the "Blue Flame" engine with 206.8 cubic inches and 80 horsepower. The Standard had 5.25 x 17″ tires, and the roadster price was only $465., f.o.b.; a real value for the money!

All models had three horizontal ventilating louvres on each side of the hood, diminishing in length from the top down.

The 1934 Chevrolet Standard was to be continued, virtually unchanged, for 1935. However, the 1935 Master De Luxe models had a completely new body with all-steel "turret top," V-windshield, metal-spoke wheels and many other improvements.

With Chevrolet's great success in the late 1920s and the 1930s, it is hard to imagine that General Motors considered Chevrolet's future "hopeless" in 1921. In '34, Chevrolet celebrated its twenty-third anniversary and built its ten millionth car.

CHRYSLER

The first Chrysler was the 1924 model which, by 1926, had become the "70" series. The Chrysler, a high-compression light six in the medium-price field, had been an instant success. In mid-1925, a Chrysler "Four" had been added to the line, replacing the Maxwell car, and during '26 a smaller Chrysler six, the "60" had joined the Chrysler line, as had the big Imperial. Chrysler model numbers indicated the guaranteed top speed. By 1929, the three Chryslers, all sixes, were the "Imperial 80," the sporty "75" and the utilitarian "65"; each had been drastically restyled, and featured Chrysler's attractive new, narrow-profile radiator design.

Chrysler featured five distinctively different models in the 1930 line, each with its own engine, instrument panel, radiator design and other details. In descending order of price and size, the five 1930 models were the "Imperial," the "77," "70," "66," and the "CJ" Six (which was introduced after the 1930 season was under way.)

The final year in which Chrysler offered all sixes and no straight-eight engines was 1930. The 1930 Imperial was, with the exception of its transmission, a continuation of its 1929 predecessor. The exterior was virtually unchanged. The Imperial was mounted on a massive 136-inch wheelbase. Glamorous custom bodies were created by Locke, the most popular being the rak-

Airflow CHRYSLER

Come on Along . . . !"

MOTORING IS FUN AGAIN!

★　　★　　★　　★　　★　　★　　★　　★　　★

THE NEW AIRFLOW Chryslers give you thrilling new driving sensations that result from interesting scientific facts.

You get a glorious sense of freedom at high speeds because the authentic streamline design eliminates vacuum and wind drag. For the same reason, acceleration from 40 to 60 is as spirited as it is from 15 to 30.

You enjoy a Floating Ride over even the worst of roads because the new distribution of weight slows down the periodicity of the springs . . sharp jolts are lengthened into easy glides.

You feel a magical sensation of effortless ease when the *automatic overdrive changes

gear ratios for you as you pass 40 miles an hour . . . cutting engine speed one third . . . reducing fuel consumption as much as 20% at 40 miles an hour, 25% at 60.

You can actually feel the safety you get from the Airflow Chrysler's unit body and frame. Forty times as rigid as an ordinary frame, this strong bridgework of steel not only contributes vastly to steadiness on the road but also prevents road shocks and jiggling vibrations from assaulting your nerves.

In everything it is and does, the Airflow Chrysler provides a whole new travel experience. You can easily prove it for yourself!

Four Distinguished 1934 Models

CHRYSLER AIRFLOW EIGHT . . . 122 horsepower and 123-inch wheelbase. Six-passenger Sedan, Brougham and Town Sedan, five-passenger Coupe. All body types, $1345.

CHRYSLER AIRFLOW IMPERIAL . . . 130 horsepower . . . 128-inch wheelbase. Six-passenger Sedan and Town Sedan, five passenger Coupe. All body types, $1625.

AIRFLOW CUSTOM IMPERIAL . . . 150 horsepower . . . 146-inch wheelbase. Individualized body types, prices on request.

1934 CHRYSLER SIX . . . With independently sprung front wheels . . . for a smooth, cushioned ride . . . 93 horsepower. 7 body types on 117-inch and 121-inch wheelbase. Priced from $775 up. Four-door Sedan, $845. *Automatic overdrive standard on Imperial and Custom Imperial. Available at slight additional cost on Airflow Eight. Duplate safety plate glass in all windows of all models at only $10 additional. List prices at factory Detroit, subject to change without notice.

Write for the interesting free Floating Ride booklet. Chrysler Sales Corporation, 12193 East Jefferson Avenue, Detroit, Mich.

ish sport roadster. Boxing champ Jack Dempsey drove one of these. The Imperial roadster of '29–'30 had a long rear deck which sloped gradually down toward the rear. This deck contained a comfortable rumble seat which was easily entered, not only by the usual trap door, but also by an additional side door at the right. Though a side door for the rumble seat was found on some earlier models (such as Auburn), the feature was most uncommon. It afforded new dignity to passengers who would otherwise have had to scramble in and out of the rumble seat in the ordinary way.

The engine under the Imperial's long, notched hood developed 100 horsepower, and the displacement was 309.6 cubic inches. This was the last of the big 6-cylinder Imperials, and prices began at $2895. Chrysler's all-new "Multi-Range" 4-speed transmission was standard equipment.

"Multi-Range" was also featured on "77" and "70" Chryslers. These two models had the de luxe "narrow-profile" radiator with vertical shutters, as did the Imperial. Early "77s" and "70s" (beginning July, '29) had distinctive "pennon" (dart-shaped) hood louvre groups. Though very attractive, the "pennon" louvres did not allow enough air circulation through the hood, and in January, 1930, they were changed to conventional, vertical louvres. The parking lights were moved down from their unusual position on the windshield posts to a more conventional location, attached to the cowl band. When these changes were made, horsepower was also boosted to 93 on the "77" and "70" Special, with Standard "70" rated at 75.

Instrument panels on the "77" and "70" models were tastefully designed in the latest, modernistic fashion, with each black-faced gauge mounted separately on a flaring, silver-finished panel. The dashboard was finished around the panel in black and had a straight-across lower edge. For the first time, provisions were made for optional radio installation.

Though the "77" was a beautiful car, some owners considered it unlucky (despite its double-seven model number!). The "77" used more gasoline than its "75" predecessor, and its new transmission was not always reliable. The Stock Market crash of October 29, 1929, occurred not long after the "77" had made its debut. One of these cars, in fact, figured prominently in a sad tale from San Francisco. It seemed that a prominent West Coast stock broker had overplayed the market and had also purchased a new "77" roadster just before the fateful fiasco. When he discovered that he'd lost a fortune, the broker went berserk and hurled himself through his office window. He plunged to death, crushing in the top of his new sport roadster parked directly below.

The "66" was the next-to-lowest-priced of Chrysler's 1930 models. Mechanically, it was more or less a continuation of the "65" model, being a small, De Soto-sized six with a seven-main-bearing engine of 66 horsepower. Early "66" Chryslers had a vacuum-tank fuel supply; models, after December, 1929, had a mechanical fuel pump and two additional horsepower.

Though it had the narrow-profile radiator shell, with most of the radiator's depth concealed beneath the hood, the "66" did not have the radiator shutters found on the larger models. Also, the "66" had vertical hood louvres from the very start of its model run. Wheelbase was 112¾ inches, and the price range was $985 to $1065. For a few months, the "66" was the lowest-priced Chrysler model. Then the "CJ" was introduced.

Heralded as the "lowest-priced six ever to bear the Chrysler name," the model "CJ" (better known as the 1930 Chrysler "Six") was launched early in the year, starting at only $795 for the business coupe. The "CJ" had the narrow-profile radiator shell, without shutters, and the front cover of the upper pan was embossed and painted black to match the radiator core directly below it. It was an unusual design, imitated in recent years by certain heavy trucks. As on the De Soto Six, the hood louvres on the "CJ" were placed in three vertical groups on each side. A few louvres were merely dummy openings stamped along the hood to match the real ones.

The "CJ" was the first of a succession of alphabetical designations for Chrysler; after 1935, the letter "C," followed by a number, designated the model.

The 1930 "CJ" had a new engine of 62 horsepower and 195.6 cubic inches displacement. This engine differed from earlier Chrysler engines in that it used timing gears instead of a chain, the exhaust manifold was tubular and was carried down at the front of the engine in order to keep heat and fumes as far as possible from the passengers and the distributor shaft was inclined, through the block. Spark control was fully automatic (vacuum-controlled). Because it was designed for economy, the "CJ" engine did not have seven main bearings as on bigger Chrysler sixes. It was, nonetheless, an extremely reliable and durable unit.

The "CJ" had a new "Steelweld" body with a steel frame, containing few parts of wood. With the exception of Dodge (which had long used Budd all-steel bodies), the "CJ" was Chrysler's first "all-steel" car. Other Chrysler-built models appearing after the spring of 1930 followed suit with similar body construction. The "CJ" was low-geared (4.7 to 1) and would peak out at less than 65 miles per hour.

The Chryslers for 1931 were first introduced during the autumn of 1930. They were completely restyled. The new models had an attractive, classic grille, V-shaped. The hood was much longer in proportion to the body, with

THE FINEST EXPRESSION OF CHRYSLER ENGINEERIN

A new dynamic beauty that refreshes the eye . . . a flashing brilliance in performance that makes every ride an adventure . . . tremendous power under effortless control . . . superb good taste and luxury in every minute detail . . . such are the new Chrysler Imperial Eights. Designed and built without restr tion or stint, they nevertheless represent values that appeal wise and discriminating buyers. They are a satisfying inve ment . . . as well as a fascinating and thrilling possessi

TWO NEW
CHRYSLER IMPERIALS

1933 CHRYSLER SIX; 83 HORSEPOWER; 117-INCH WHEELBASE; SIX BODY TYPES, TO $1055. 1933 ROYAL EIGHT; 90 HORSEPOWER; 120-INCH WHEELBASE; FIVE BC TYPES, $945 TO $1195. 1933 IMPERIAL EIGHT; 108 HORSEPOWER; 126-INCH WHE BASE; FIVE BODY TYPES, $1355 TO $1595. 1933 CUSTOM IMPERIAL; 135 HORSEPOW 146-INCH WHEELBASE; SIX BODY TYPES, $2895 TO $3595. ALL PRICES F. O. B. FACTO

"The finest cars ever to bear my name" *W. P. Chrysler*

1933 CHRYSLER IMPERIAL CONVERTIBLE COUPE,

CHRYSLER
IMPERIAL EIGHT

Front view and rear view of the Chrysler Imperial Eight Close-Coupled Sedan . . . faultlessly beautiful, viewed from any angle . . . 145-inch wheelbase . . . 125-horsepower . . . Multi-Range 4-speed transmission with Dual High gears . . . a motor car for the connoisseur of motor cars.

5-Passenger Sedan $2745; Close-Coupled Sedan $2845; 7-Passenger Sedan $2945; Sedan-Limousine $3145.
Custom Body Styles: Coupe $3150; Roadster $3220; Convertible Coupe $3320; Phaeton $3575. F.O.B. Factory.

a long panel of vertical louvres on each side. Instrument panels were new and different, with circular gauges. The 1931 Chryslers also were the first to offer straight-eight engines, as well as sixes.

Prices ranged from $885 for the Chrysler "Six" coupe, to $3575 for the beautiful custom phaeton on "Imperial Eight" chassis. The "Imperial Eight," by the way, was a superb car, inevitably destined to become a sought-after classic. It had a wheelbase of 145 inches (on some models) and its long straight-eight engine developed 125 horsepower with ease. Also featured was the Multi-Range four-speed transmission, first offered on three of the five '30 Chrysler models.

The 1931 "Imperial" had graceful, sweeping fenders, a remarkably long hood, and a new V-windshield (both sections of which could be swung open separately.) Most beautiful of all was the custom roadster, originally priced at $3220. It had a low, slanting stationary two-piece windshield that made the car look years ahead of its time.

Late in 1930, when the new Chrysler Eights were first introduced, a dramatic test of the Chrysler's steel body strength was staged at Coney Island, N. Y. In front of a crowd of fascinated onlookers, a 10,000-pound elephant was led from a raised platform onto a wooden pallet placed on the roof of a new Chrysler sedan. The elephant failed to crush or even damage the body of the car as it stood on the roof, and all doors could be opened and closed with ease! Many cars of that time would have been mashed like beer cans under such weight!

In addition to the "Imperial Eight" and 90-horsepower Chrysler "Eight" (later the 95-h.p. "De Luxe Eight" at $1495 and up), there was a 1931 "70" model (93 horsepower, priced at $1245 to $1295), as well as the 116-inch wheelbase Chrysler "Six" with 70 horsepower.

The 1932 Chryslers were similar to the '31s in appearance, but the new models featured many mechanical improvements. The most unusual was Chrysler's patented "Floating Power," a vastly improved method of mounting the engine on resilient rubber cushions, with a flexible leaf spring for the rear mounting. The engine was, indeed, so flexible in its housing that it could, literally, thrash around beneath the hood when rapidly accelerated. However, the "Floating Power" engine mounts eliminated nearly all vibration and provided remarkable smoothness in every driving situation. "Floating Power" was introduced on the 4-cylinder Plymouth "PA" model, in June, 1931, giving the little engine "the smoothness of an eight with the economy of a four." So it was inevitable that Chrysler would include the feature on all their other cars the following season.

Freewheeling and an automatic clutch were also a part of the '32 Chryslers. The clutch pedal was there but, when the freewheeling unit was in action, use of the pedal was unnecessary in forward speeds.

"Oilite" bushings were used between the leaves of Chrysler springs, to prevent dryness, squeaking, and ultimate wear. Oilite was a porous, bronze material containing 40 percent oil, and Chrysler put it to various useful applications during the thirties.

Chrysler prices began at $885, f.o.b., for the 82-horsepower six.

One minor problem that was given considerable thought from automotive engineers was fan noise. Chrysler tried an "X-type" fan in 1932, a marked improvement.

The most luxurious Chrysler of 1932 was the "Custom Imperial," which had an extra-long hood that extended over the cowl, all the way back to the base of the windshield. Manufacturer Walter P. Chrysler had been inspired by a custom-built Lincoln in 1931, and hurriedly decided that his engineers should install such hoods on the forthcoming Custom Imperials. Chrysler also chose to include vertical ventilating doors on this model, one of which was later restored by the late singer and automobile collector, James Melton.

External sun visors were not used on any 1932 Chryslers, and all closed models (as well as some open varieties) had the new two-piece windshield originally featured on the 1931 "De Luxe" and "Imperial Eights."

During the first ten months of 1932, only 24,620 Chryslers were sold. Twice as many had been sold during the same period of the previous year, but, in 1932, Chrysler's low-priced Plymouth was the "bread and butter" of the company. Plymouth was the only American make that gained in sales during the dark year of 1932.

An unattractive Chrysler innovation for 1933 was the redesigned hood, with all models featuring the vertical ventilating doors. The doors did not harmonize with the slope of the grille and windshield posts, and gave the hood an awkward side appearance.

Front fenders were not skirted, but were carried further toward the bumpers in an early attempt at streamlining. The new Chryslers did not have cowl lamps; three-beam headlights were adopted.

A silent, helical-gear transmission served all models but the "Custom Imperial"; the latter had a four-speed transmission with silent third gear. Freewheeling was included, as before, but, in 1933, a pendulum valve was added to the automatic clutch to eliminate sudden "jack-rabbit" starts.

A new starter switch was actuated by the accelerator pedal. Unseen but important improvements were made in the engine, such as redesigned pistons and improved valve seats. Chrysler's high-compression cylinder head (the "Red Head") was still available, having been introduced in the late '20s to give even greater power and speed to the engines. The standard cylinder head was known as the "Silver Dome." Four Chrysler engines were available in '33 and three different eights were featured, the smallest eight being a new 90-horsepower model. The price leader was the 83-horsepower six, at only $795 for either business coupe or brougham. By August, the minimum price was down to $745; "lowest in history" for a Chrysler Six.

At the upper end of the scale, Chrysler's finest "Custom Imperial Eight" models, with 135 horsepower and a 146-inch wheelbase, were available in six body types, priced from $2835 to $3595. Walter P. Chrysler claimed that they were the best ever to bear his name. And they were the last of the long, narrow, classic Imperials dear to so many auto buffs.

During 1933, a man named Childe Harold Wills (better known as C. H. Wills), at sixty, became the chief metallurgist for the Chrysler Corporation. A dozen years previously, Wills had founded C. H. Wills and Company in Marysville, Michigan, and had manufactured the advanced Wills Ste. Claire automobile from 1921 to 1927. He was well-suited to the position of metallurgist in the 'thirties, for his own V-8 automobiles had been built mainly of a special molybdenum steel. Finding greater security with Chrysler than he had known in his own venture, C. H. Wills remained in his position for the rest of his life (until 1940, which also marked the passing of Walter P. Chrysler).

Chrysler dropped a "bombshell" on the automotive world of 1934, when the new Chrysler "Airflow" models were revealed. All Chryslers except the 6-cylinder series were "Airflows," with a startlingly different, unitized body of radically streamlined design. Picture if you can, a car shaped somewhat like a giant Volkswagen "bug" of today launched in an era of high, boxy automobiles. You can imagine the impact of the first "Airflow"! It stood apart from all the squarish designs of the competition; there were a few other manufacturers with modernized, limited-production models, but none of the others was as completely streamlined nor well-engineered as the Chrysler "Airflow." It was truly three years ahead of its time in appearance and, in its unique construction, it offered many ideas not seen in other cars for years to come.

The "Airflow" was a super-car. With overdrive, it could cruise effortlessly along a rough road at eighty miles an hour, almost silently, and with such smoothness that the rear-seat passengers could sit and read books as comfortably as though in a library!

The idea of designing an "Airflow" body was first conceived in mid-1927, by Carl Breer, a top Chrysler engineer. He felt that an automobile body did not have to be square just because all others had been. Why not design a body using airplane principles, with smooth, curved surfaces which would slip easily through air currents at high speeds?

On the recommendations of the famed pioneer aviator, Orville Wright, an experimental wind tunnel was set up, and scale models were used in various tests until the most satisfactory design was chosen. However, more than six years passed before the first "Airflow" was ready to be shown.

Though the "Airflow" was an engineering triumph, it was not a sales success. It was too different in appearance from ordinary cars, and many an admirer of the new model was afraid he would be continually stared at if he were seen driving one. Only 11,292 "Airflow" Chryslers were built in 1934. The number sold diminished in following years, as 7751, 6275 and 4600 were sold in 1935, 1936 and 1937, respectively.

Some believed that this type of streamlining was better suited to the latest trains. The "Airflow" bore a marked resemblance to Union Pacific's new yellow-and-brown "M-10000" train, which also made its debut in '34. Interestingly enough, the car and train were often pictured together in various books and magazine articles.

In 1934, many thought the Airflow's snub nose and waterfall-like grille were particularly ugly. So, 1935 and later-date "Airflows" were given grilles more in line with the conventionally-designed "Airstream" models which were selling better. The "Airflow" was not offered after 1937.

No convertible "Airflows" were built; the ultra-streamlined Chryslers were available only with sedan bodies, in either four-door or two-door "fastback" models. The *smallest,* two-door sedans were described by their manufacturer as "coupes," though they were actually sedanettes. A 6-cylinder De Soto "Airflow" also was produced from 1934 to 1936.

CHRYSLER

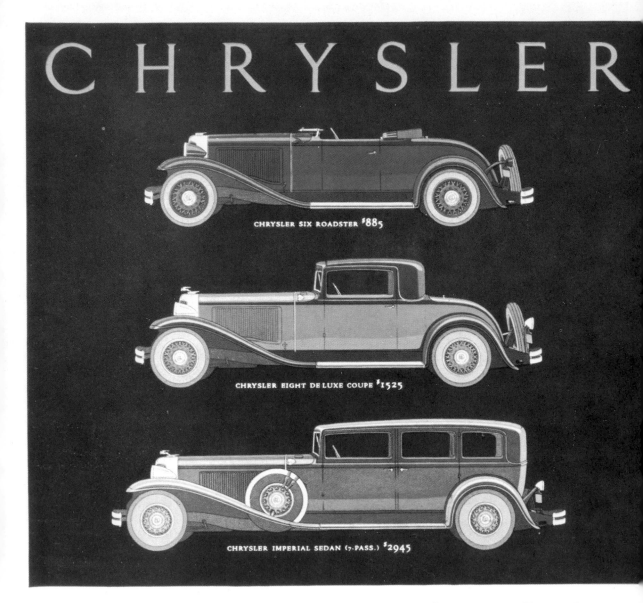

CHRYSLER SIX ROADSTER $885

CHRYSLER EIGHT DE LUXE COUPE $1525

CHRYSLER IMPERIAL SEDAN (7-PASS.) $2945

Only Chrysler Engineering Gets Chrysler Results

CHRYSLERS at every price are *Chryslers*—and therefore joyously different from other cars. More alive, more responsive, smoother in action.

All Chrysler cars are definitely related to each other by the same general design, by the same general basis of quality, by the same general excellence of engineering, by the same general spirit of performance.

Today there is a Chrysler for practically every purse—each outstanding in value.

The Chrysler Six. A fine, big Six of sterling ability. 116-inch wheelbase. Quiet 78-horsepower engine. Quick, quiet gear shift. Staunch, rigid double-drop frame. Low center of gravity. Safety bodies of steel rigidly welded into one piece. Internal self-equalizing hydraulic brakes. And with Chrysler's *perfected* free wheeling optional at slight extra cost.

Or the new Chrysler Eight De Luxe—*de luxe* in everything, inside and outside. Divided windshield. Unusually roomy bodies. Unusually deep, soft cushions. An easy-riding 124-inch wheelbase. Unusually long springs. A smooth 95-horsepower straight eight engine that gives you eighty miles an hour if you want it—with the safety of low-swung balance of weight and the positive, easy control of internal hydraulic brakes . . .

CHRYSLER SIX . . . . . . $885 to $935

CHRYSLER EIGHT DE LUXE $1525 to $1585
(Five wire wheels standard; six wire wheels $35 extra)

CHRYSLER IMPERIAL EIGHT $2745 to $3145
(CUSTOM MODELS $3150 to $3575)

All prices f. o. b. factory; special equipment extra

Or the magnificent Chrysler Imperial Eight Chrysler's very finest—a motor car for connoisseu of motor cars. An ultra-fine car of 145-inch whe base and 125-horsepower — winner of 12 offici A. A. A. Contest Board stock car speed recorc

Both the De Luxe Eight and the Imper Eight have the exclusive Chrysler Dual Hi, gear transmission. TWO high gears, and y can shift from either to the other *instantly*— any car speed—without clashing. One high ge is for flashing action in traffic. Another st higher gear gives faster car speeds at *slower* e gine speeds.

Drive a Chrysler — *any* Chrysler — and enj the difference. Enjoy the brilliant zest of Ch sler pick-up, the smoothness of Chrysler spee Learn why Chrysler value is better value.

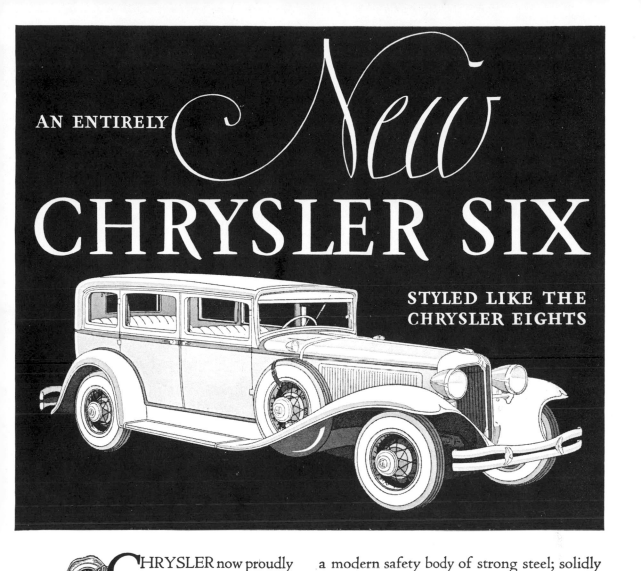

AN ENTIRELY *New*

CHRYSLER SIX

STYLED LIKE THE
CHRYSLER EIGHTS

CHRYSLER now proudly presents a new Chrysler Six styled in the manner of the Chrysler Straight Eights—a very remarkable new Six at a very remarkable low price. It has a heavy double-drop frame with the great advantage of an extremely low center of gravity. The low-swung unity of chassis and body results in unusual smartness, perfect balance, greater steadiness and real safety at all speeds. It has a long easy-riding wheelbase of 116 inches . . . It has a big 70-horsepower engine . . . It has a modern safety body of strong steel; solidly welded, with no joints to cause squeaks . . . It has self-equalizing weatherproof internal hydraulic brakes . . . It has hydraulic shock absorbers . . . It has adjustable front seat . . . It has five wire wheels at no extra cost . . . It has everything it needs to be the outstanding value among sixes. The performance of the new Chrysler Six is really something to experience. Something to get excited about. Something that says better than words can say . . . "*This* is a *great* motor car."

AT A LOW PRICE

$895

SEDAN—F. O. B. FACTORY

That *something* which makes a Chrysler a *Chrysler!*

THERE is a certain thrilling something about Chrysler performance that one never senses or enjoys in any other car. It is "something" and yet somehow *everything.* It is the spirit and sure stride of Chrysler speed. It is the gliding sensation of Chrysler smoothness. It is the electric aliveness of Chrysler pick-up. The answer, of course, is Chrysler engineering. With new, roomier bodies of dreadnought construction; with new, bigger, more powerful engines—with Down-Draft carburetion in the "77" and "70", together with the Multi-Range 4-speed transmission and gear shift — these latest Chryslers further out-distance all attempts to equal Chrysler performance. And besides, there is more style in Chrysler beauty, just as there is more *go* in Chrysler power and more *stop* in Chrysler brakes—weatherproof hydraulics, the safest brakes known. Get a personal experience at the wheel—and you will realize with full conviction why a Chrysler inspires a pride all its own.

There is a Chrysler for every purse and every need from
$795 to $3575

The "77"
9 body styles, $1625 to $1825

The "70"
7 body styles, $1295 to $1545

The "66"
6 body styles, $995 to $1095

New Chrysler Six
5 body styles, $795 to $845

The Imperial
8 body styles, $2995 to $3575

All prices f. o. b. factory

© 1930 by Chrysler Corporation

CHRYSLER "77" ROYAL COUPE $1725 *f. o. b. factory (special equipment extra)*

CHRYSLER
CHRYSLER   MOTORS   PRODUCT

3 NEW CHRYSLERS

TO SURPASS and thereby to render obsolete the transportation standards established by more than a quarter-century of motor car building—that is the revolutionary achievement of Chrysler engineers in these newest products of their science. ≈ ≈ There is no more basis of comparison between these latest Chryslers and cars of the past than between today's great tri-motored passenger planes and the first Wright Brothers gliders that took the air at Kittyhawk. ≈ ≈ These latest Chrysler creations are motor cars, just as the earliest and the latest air vehicles are both flying machines. ≈ ≈ There the comparison stops between Chrysler and earlier automobiles. For Chrysler again transcends all standards and ideals of power, of riding ease, of roomy luxury, of smooth operation, of quality and of value. As for beauty, Chrysler now brings to the automobile an entirely new art. Five years ago, Chrysler genius set the pace — equally revolutionary in 1924 — which the whole industry has striven since to equal. ≈ ≈ Today, Chrysler antiquates even its own accomplishment —and sets a new standard which the future cannot fail to acclaim the most astounding revolution in all motordom's history. ≈ ≈ All Chrysler dealers cordially invite you to an early inspection.

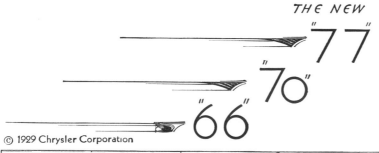

THE NEW "77" "70" "66"

© 1929 Chrysler Corporation

THE NEW "70" ROYAL SEDÁN

CHRYSLER

CHRYSLER MOTORS PRODUCT

HERE'S SOMETHING NEW

A CHRYSLER DEVELOPMENT
THAT REVOLUTIONIZES PERFORMANCE

TRY IT

SOMETHING startling has happened. Three sensational new Chryslers are abroad in the land.

In the thick of city traffic—on the streets and boulevards—along the highways and byways — in the mountains — on the plains—their unprecedented performance is changing every notion of what a motor car can be expected to do.

The new Chrysler "77" and "70" introduce such epochal new developments as:

**MULTI-RANGE GEAR SHIFT
DOWN-DRAFT CARBURETION
SYNCHRONIZED POWER
PARAFLEX SPRINGS
ARCHITONIC BODIES**

Come to the salesroom. Examine these new Chryslers at your leisure. Then take one out; drive it; and you'll experience the supreme sensation.

$1595 NEW CHRYSLER "77" PRICES — 9 Body Styles, priced from $1595 to $1795. F. O. B. Factory (Special Equipment Extra).

$1245 NEW CHRYSLER "70" PRICES — 6 Body Styles, priced from $1245 to $1395. F. O. B. Factory (Special Equipment Extra).

$985 NEW CHRYSLER "66" PRICES — 6 Body Styles, priced from $985 to $1065. F. O. B. Factory (Special Equipment Extra).

CHRYSLER

CHRYSLER MOTORS PRODUCTS

WITH MULTI-RANGE GEAR SHIFT — NEW "77"

WITH MULTI-RANGE GEAR SHIFT — NEW "70"

A CHRYSLER SIX UNDER $1000 — NEW "66"

CONTINENTAL

Nearly everyone has heard of the luxurious Lincoln "Continental," but back in 1933 and 1934 there was a new car known as the "Continental" which was strictly an economy model; it had no connection with Lincoln, nor with the Ford Motor Company.

The Continental car of 1933 and 1934 was produced by the Continental Automobile Company, a subsidiary of Continental Motors Corporation. It was promoted by interests which had backed the well-made but ill-fated De Vaux car of 1931 and 1932. The Continental fared no better.

A series of three was introduced. The best was the "Ace," a 6-cylinder car. In the middle was the "Flyer," a lighter six. Smallest was the 4-cylinder "Beacon" model, with f. o. b. prices starting just above $400!

The little "Beacon" had a 101½-inch wheelbase and weighed from 1950 to 2160 lbs., depending on body type. The 4-cylinder engine developed 40 horsepower at 2800 RPM, and could deliver 33 miles per gallon. Maximum speed was reported to be from 60 to 65 m.p.h., and the tire size was 5.25 x 17.

Continental suspension was unique in that the rear springs were cantilevered pairs, clamped to the frame at the third crossmember, and pinned at the rear to the axle, above and below. The front spring was mounted transversely, as on a Ford. This set-up was used on the "Beacon" and "Flyer" models.

The intermediate "Flyer" models had 65 horsepower, 6-cylinder engines and a 107-inch wheelbase. All 1933 Continentals had "steeldraulic" brakes, as did many of the other cars that year. Bodies were all-steel, and at a quick glance, the general design was reminiscent of the '32 Ford (except on the "Ace" series.)

Though the two smaller models had vertical hood louvres, the 114-inch wheelbase "Ace" had four vertical ventilating doors on each side of the hood. The Ace coupes and sedans also had rakish V-windshields and winged radiator mascots. Standard models had wire wheels and 5.50 x 17 tires, while de luxe models carried six wood wheels and modern 6.50 x 16 tires. The 6-cylinder Continental "Red Seal" engine of the "Ace" was rated at 85 horsepower. Both 1933 and 1934 Continental cars used "Winged Power" engine mountings of flexible live rubber.

In the 1934 series there was less of a choice of models. Concentration was on the 4-cylinder car, which was renamed the "Red Seal" model. Over-all design was similar to the '33 models, though the 1934 car had three long, horizontal hood louvres which gave it a side resemblance to the 1934 Chevrolet. Continental sales during 1933 had amounted to fewer than 3000 units, and the car was in twenty-fourth place, trailed only by Lincoln, Pierce-Arrow, and Franklin.

The Continental Automobile Company had dreamed up a strange sales plan, which they hoped would save the day for their car. In addition to having a few dealers, the company was to sell cars *by mail,* with delivery and servicing to be handled by independent, authorized repair garages. In addition, department stores such as Gimbel's of New York, and others, were also designated Continental "dealers." Though sales were minimal, many years later (in the early '50s) Kaiser Motors tried this idea again. Kaiser built an "Allstate" version of its compact "Henry J" car, and the "Allstate" was sold through Sears Roebuck stores. Also, "King Midget" cars have been sold by mail-order for many years by Midget Motors Corporation of Athens, Ohio.

Volume sales of automobiles by mail order have never been feasible though, and, after 1934, Continental returned to building engines, only.

CORD

E. L. Cord didn't find time to finish high school back in the early 'teens; he was too busy making big money in the Los Angeles used car business. Before the age of twenty, he had made, and lost, remarkable sums in reselling used Model T Fords. After a couple of other business ventures, Cord (at the age of twenty-four) took his last twenty dollars, went east and started work in Chicago for a Moon dealership. This was in 1919, when the Moon "Victory" model was new and popular.

Cord earned a small fortune as a Moon salesman during the early '20s; as much as $30,000 a year, at a time when many skilled workers were pleased to earn $2000! But, eventually, the popularity of the "Victory" Moon (which resembled a little Rolls-Royce) began to fade. Cord became interested in the Auburn Automobile Company, which in 1924 was "on the rocks."

A shrewd promoter and salesman, Cord was given carte blanche by Auburn's receivers to reorganize the company. He did, and the 1925 Auburn (with all-new styling and a choice of six- or straight-eight engines) was a great success.

After continued triumphs with Auburn (which he built into a large Indiana manufacturing complex), young Cord, in 1929, decided to produce a new, front-wheel-drive car that would bear his name.

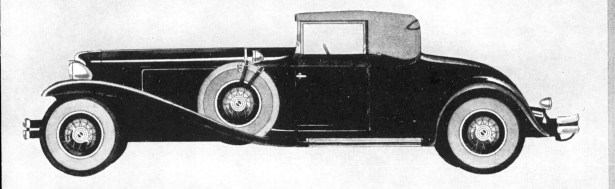

FINE CAR LEADERSHIP

The leadership of the Cord front-drive in the fine car field daily becomes more pronounced. This is traceable to the accumulative experience of Cord owners who enjoy advantages not obtainable in any other automobile. Included among these exclusive advantages are effortless handling, a different roadability, a sense of security, and an absence of fatigue for driver and passengers that obsolete any car less efficient and commodious. And now, an improved Cord car is available at prices comparable with ordinary standard cars—a sensational value in the fine car field.

CORD
FRONT DRIVE

By October, 1929, the new Cord (Model "L-29") was creating a sensation in every Auburn showroom where it was displayed. It was certainly *not* a car for the average man, however; the price (f.o.b.) was $3095 for either the sedan or brougham. Convertible models (cabriolet or phaeton sedan) were priced at $3295. Powered by a 298.6 cubic-inch Lycoming FDA straight-eight engine (125 h.p.,) the "L-29" Cord bore somewhat of a resemblance to the fabulous "J" series Duesenberg (another new product of the Auburn empire.)

The "L-29" dashboard was most unusual, with a modern glove compartment in the center but with very behind-the-times twin instrument panels and control sets at either end. The right-hand panel (difficult for the driver to see), contained the gas gauge, oil level gauge and ammeter. The dials and controls resembled those of an early radio, though no provisions for a radio were made in the "L-29" dash.

The "L-29" was continued, with few changes, from 1929 to mid-1932; a beautiful car, extremely long and low, with a 137½-inch wheelbase and a massive hood which dominated the classic silhouette. A total of less than 6000 units were built during that time. But the front-drive mechanism developed problems, especially with the universal joints which transmitted power to the wheels. This, and the $3000-plus price, eventually brought about the discontinuance of the L-29.

After a three-year pause in Cord production, and some rough times for Auburn and Duesenberg, E. L. Cord decided to produce an all-new car which would, once again, bear his name. The '36 and '37 Cords (Models "810" and "812") were not commercially successful, but they were admired by many and became prized collectors' items once they were out of production. So great was the demand for the V-8 powered "810s" and "812s," that, in the mid-1960s, an enterprising Oklahoman and long-time Cord admirer, Glenn Pray, offered shortened, but well-built, reproductions for sale. Compromises had to be made, in order to keep the price of the "new" Cord under $8500. Pray's model used a Corvair engine and a fiberglas body. After a number of the "new Cords" were sold, Pray decided to revive the classic Auburn speedster of the mid-'30s.

DE SOTO

Chrysler introduced its first De Soto car in the latter half of 1928. (There had been a De Soto "Six" in 1913, though it had no connection with Chrysler's car except that both had 6-cylinder engines and happened to have 55 horsepower.) The first 1929 De Soto, the "K" series, was continued without noticeable change for twenty-two months, until the spring of 1930. In May, the "K" was replaced by the new "CK" De Soto, also a six, which had a new "Steelweld" body which did not have the wooden framework of the earlier, Hayes-bodied De Sotos. The new "CK" also had a conventional radiator shell that was deeper than the narrow profile '29 models. The "CK" had 60 horsepower. Under the hood, and inside the car, the De Soto "CK" was nearly identical to the Chrysler "CJ" which was being produced concurrently.

De Soto's biggest news for 1930, however, was the new model, "CF" with 72-horsepower straight-eight engine introduced early in the season while the '29-style model "K" was still in production. Getting the jump on the redesigned six, the new, De Soto "Eight" received much attention for a few months. The De Soto "Eight" had a comparatively small (207.7 cubic inches) engine, and at $965 and up, f.o.b., it was advertised as the "lowest-priced eight in the world." The radiator design of the "CF" eight was not unlike that of the "CK" six, but the eight had one long vertical group of louvres on each side of the hood, rather than the three vertical groups of louvres that characterized the six. The eights also had a different body design, with only a small belt line above the door handles.

The De Soto "Eight" had a low (4.9 to 1) gear ratio, and was an outstanding hill climber. At Ligonier, Pennsylvania, De Soto arranged a test with their new eight, pitted against three other 8-cylinder makes all costing over $2000 each (twice as much.) The De Soto made an excellent showing, on grades of 10 percent and more. On level ground, the De Soto "Eight" was hampered by its 4.9 rear axle, and would only reach a top speed of just over seventy.

For 1931, both the De Soto "Six" and "Eight" were changed, with one-piece bumpers and a new narrow-profile radiator shell with built-in grille resembling shutters. At a glance, the 1931 De Sotos, especially the sixes, bore a marked resemblance to the very beautiful and larger Chrysler "75" of 1929. Now that a radiator emblem had been temporarily eliminated, the new De Sotos were identified by a badge on the headlamp tie-bar. Inside the 6-cylinder "SA" model, the instrument board was also somewhat reminiscent of the Chrysler "75," as it, too, contained five gauges in a row, behind a long glass panel.

Horsepower of the 6-cylinder "SA" series was increased to 67, then to 72. On the eight, horsepower was also boosted (to 77) as the displacement of each engine was enlarged. With a new gear ratio of 4.33, the De Soto "Six" was capable of 75 miles an hour. Top speed of the "Eight" also was increased as its gear ratio was changed from 4.9 to 4.6.

In midyear, De Soto discontinued its use of an outside sun visor, and added a new, easy-shift transmission and a $20 optional free-wheeling unit. Despite the improvements, De Soto's minimum price was trimmed to $695.

The 1932 De Soto was dramatically new in design. With its introduction, came several national magazine and newspaper advertisements bearing the endorsements of such celebrities as racing driver Peter De Paolo, artist Neysa McMein, commentator Floyd Gibbons, and Robert ("Believe it or Not") Ripley.

The front end of the '32 De Soto was unlike any other design, though it somewhat resembled the special speedster built three years earlier by Du Pont. The De Soto had a European-looking curved grille of fine horizontal bars, in front, two long trumpet-like horns, and a dashing winged goddess radiator mascot. The body was slightly streamlined, with a windshield that was divided down the center by a chrome strip. All windshields swung open at the front and, on certain open models, they could be folded flat on the cowl.

In 1932, De Soto adopted the well-known "Custom" name to designate luxury models. All the 1932 De Sotos were sixes, for the eight had not sold well and had been dropped during 1931. No further 8-cylinder De Sotos were built until the introduction of the V-8 "Firedome" De Soto for 1952.

All '32 De Sotos had "Floating Power" and freewheeling. For only eight dollars extra, an automatic clutch could be ordered. Prices started at only $675 for the standard roadster, and the new De Soto was billed "America's Smartest Low-Priced Car."

Strange as it may seem, ultra-modern 7.00 x 15 "airwheels" were included on some of the new De Sotos for 1933. Fifteen-inch wheels were virtually unheard-of in the early 1930s, and did not become common for another fifteen years.

The 1933 grille design was similar to that of the previous model, but sloped at a greater angle, and the fenders came down further in front. Twin outside horns were standard equipment on more models, and headlights were divided by a chrome strip down the center, to harmonize with the dividing strip on the windshield. Bodies were somewhat more rounded at the corners, especially just above the windshield, on closed models.

The stroke of the '33 engine was increased to $4\frac{3}{8}$" and the bore was $3\frac{1}{4}$. Horsepower was 79 (or 86, with the 6.2 to 1 high-compression "Red Head" engine).

New mechanical features also included an automatic choke, automatic manifold heat control, silent helical transmission and accelerator pedal starter control.

Interiors were more beautiful than ever, with fine, tufted upholstery, an attractive tan "marbleized" steering wheel, and a handsome dash panel with four small gauges around a large, circular speedometer, all mounted behind an intricately-decorated glass panel. Indeed, De Soto would never match the beauty of its 1933 interiors for years to come. The checkerboard tufting of door upholstery in the Custom sedans was a feature equalled only in the finest automobiles.

De Soto's price range (f.o.b.) for 1933 was only $695 to $975. Seldom before, or since, has a car of so little cost been so finely appointed.

In 1934, despite the beauty of the earlier models, De Soto made the most complete change in its entire history, introducing its all-new "Airflow" model. The car was similar to the Chrysler "Airflow" in design, but considerably smaller. With a 6-cylinder, 100-horsepower engine and the famous Airflow "floating ride" (passengers sat ahead of the rear axle rather than directly above it), advertisements claimed that one could read a newspaper in the car at 80 miles an hour over a rough dirt road. Also, the ads continued, the steel unit frame and body were forty times more rigid than a conventionally built car. The four-door "Airflow" sedan weighed 3570.

Like the early Chrysler "Airflows," the 1934 De Soto "Airflow" had no trunk. But luggage space was provided inside the car, concealed behind the back cushion of the rear seat.

There were eleven unexciting color choices: Black, Star Blue, Fisherman Blue, Explorer Blue, Baden Green, Cedar Bird, Dusty Gray, Eel Gray, Dorset Gray, Palm Beach Gray, and Gunmetal Gray. Understandably, there were a great many gray De Sotos on the road in '34!

The 1934 De Soto's engine was started by a pushbutton on the dash. Tire size was 6.50 x 16. And, unlike the Chrysler which offered a conventional model, no other series except the "Airflow" was offered by De Soto in 1934. This proved to be a sales disaster, and only 13,940 De Soto "Airflows" were built in 1934.

The "Airflow" was continued by De Soto in 1935 and 1936, but conventional "Airstream" models were also offered for those two years. Only 6797 De Soto "Airflows" were produced in 1935, and 5000 in the final year. All De Soto "Airflows" are understandably scarce today.

The De Soto was durable and reliable. As the 1930s progressed, De Sotos were used more and more frequently in taxi service. By the 1940s, the major portion of Yellow Cab Company's nationwide fleet was made up of De Soto sedans and limousines.

Nevertheless, De Soto sales began to decline, and the last De Soto 1961 models, were discontinued in the first week of December, 1960. The De Soto name was retained by the Chrysler Corporation, however, for use on a series of trucks sold overseas.

DE VAUX

The April 25th, 1931 issue of *Saturday Evening Post* contained an intriguing advertisement. In part, it read as follows:

"PRESENTING AN EXCEPTIONAL MOTOR CAR.

An ideal of perfection has been attained . . . and its achievement climaxes the distinguished careers of two men who have performed staunch work in shaping the destinies of the automotive industry.

"Americans now are witnessing the world premiere of a low-priced automobile that boldly upsets tradition . . . that reaches beyond the limits of the conventional . . . that confidently carves its niche in the competitive field on the basis of a surpassing excellence.

"Crowds gather in a twinkling . . . eyes sharpen with healthy curiosity . . . wherever (this car) is displayed throughout the country. An unmistakable aura of achievement surrounds this car. For modern persons it is magnetic. Eagerly their questions come: How fast? . . . easily, 70 to 80 miles an hour. What motor? The (car) is powered by the new Hall Motor, the first of its kind anywhere. It was perfected over a period of five years in the Hall Laboratories by Col. Elbert J. Hall."

What new car was this, that was so boldly launched in 1931, in dark days of the Depression? It was the all-new automobile, the 1931 De Vaux, created jointly by Norman De Vaux (president and executive owner of Durant Motor Company of California,) and by Col. Elbert J. Hall, the founder of Hall-Scott

Motor Company, and a former consulting engineer to General Motors, Ford, and other auto manufacturers.

The new De Vaux was a strikingly attractive car. Its Hayes-built body and harp-shaped radiator grille were designed by M. Comte Alexis de Sakhnoffsky, Grand Prize winner for excellence at the 1930 Monte Carlo Motor Salon. M. de Sakhnoffsky, a designer who was already well-known in Europe despite his youth, was to become an important influence in the world of auto styling, along with such personalities as Raymond Loewy, Pinin Farina, Harley Earl, Virgil Exner, and Gordon Buehrig.

The De Vaux's 6-cylinder Hall engine was of L-head design. It was built in cooperation with Continental Motors, and had an improved 6-port intake manifold, which gave it 70 horsepower on regular fuel. The car would get moving from 5 to 55 m.p.h. in 19 seconds, a good figure for 1931. On a 113-inch wheelbase, the De Vaux was of average but comfortable size. It had "steeldraulic" cable brakes, and an easy-shift transmission with quiet second gear. Tire size was 5.00 x 19.

Prices of the De Vaux "6-75" were amazingly low, in view of all that it offered. Prices began at only $595, f.o.b., and plants were located at Grand Rapids, Michigan and Oakland, California. It was obvious that the car was planned to sell at a loss until its good reputation had been established.

Most buyers were afraid of "off-brand" cars that could easily become orphans. But those who became acquainted with the new De Vaux judged it to be an outstandingly good car. In the first ten months of 1931, some 4315 De Vaux cars were sold. If not impressive, this, at least, put the newcomer in twenty-sixth place, ahead of such famous names as Pierce-Arrow (4056 cars), Franklin (3267), and Lincoln (3178).

For 1932, a redesigned De Vaux was produced, but for a very short time. The 1932 model had more body curves, and the external sun visor was eliminated. However, the second series of De Vauxs fared poorly, and after the initial flurry of orders in mid-1931, the De Vaux was headed for oblivion. It sank into obscurity in months, and was discontinued within a year.

And what became of the De Vaux cars that were built and sold with such high hopes? In a few years, most Americans had forgotten them, or were never aware that they had existed. Yet, the De Vaux was such a well-engineered car that several specimens remained in daily use for years to come.

DODGE

The early 1930 "Standard Six" Dodges were merely continuations of the successful 1929 model, but later the new "DD" was introduced. The Dodge "DD" had a deeper-looking radiator, and a slightly different body. The windshield was now sharply angular at the lower corners, instead of being rounded as on the earlier "Standard" and "Victory" models. Parking lights on the "DD" were mounted far back on the cowl, near the base of the windshield posts.

Dodge's big event of 1930 was the introduction of the "DC," which, like one of the new De Sotos, had a straight-eight engine. Dodge's new eight was larger than the De Soto version, having a 114-inch wheelbase, and a 220.7 cubic inch engine that developed 75 horsepower. The price of the new eight was $1095 and up. All closed Dodge "Eight" models were factory-wired for the installation of a radio. Automobile radios were still an expensive and complicated luxury in 1930, though, and few cars were fitted with them that year.

Like the bodies of the 1928 and 1929 "Victory Sixes," the body of the Dodge "Eight" was of the "Mono-Piece" all-steel type, secured to the chassis without body sills.

"Dodge Dependability" was a slogan frequently used in 1931 advertising, as in other years. The 1931 Dodges had new bodies, with very shallow external visors. The metal area above the visors was somewhat rounded at the cor-

The New DODGE SIX AND EIGHT

with FLOATING POWER
with Automatic Clutch
with Silent Gear Selector
and Free Wheeling

The New Six Sedan

IN THE new Dodge Six and Eight, Dodge presents a new achievement in silent, effortless motion and easy positive control.

The splendid new engineering features of these cars are united with already-proved factors of body and chassis design and craftsmanship which carries on the fine traditions of Dodge Dependability.

Modern beauty, modern action, modern safe[ty], greater size, power and comfort, Dodge Depen[d]ability . . . in all these, the new Dodge cars gi[ve] definite sales advantages to Dodge Dealers. Th[ey] reflect a Dodge institution that is aggressively d[e]voted to the spirit of progress . . . building solid[ly] on principles and policies which have been prov[ed] sound for seventeen years.

ners, giving the cars a sturdy look. Radiators had built-in shutters which gave the new model a more expensive appearance. The '31 Dodge was 4 inches lower than earlier models, owing to the new double-drop frame.

Horsepower of the "Six" was boosted to 67; the "Eight" had 84. Wheelbases were lengthened to 113⅝" for the "Six," 118" for the "Eight." Bedford cord upholstery was available in closed models. Wire wheels were standard.

Later in 1931, optional free-wheeling and a "Positive Easy-Shift" transmission became available.

Especially attractive in the '31 Dodge line was the 8-cylinder coupe for five, at $1135. It was a revival of a Victoria body-type that had fallen out of favor in the late '20s, but which was to be the predecessor of the popular "club coupe" of later years. In fact, several 1931 and 1932 competitors offered Victoria coupes as "new" models. This particular Dodge offered a pleasing and practical design, yet a five-passenger "club coupe" was not offered in Chrysler's lower-priced Plymouth line until the '42 models appeared.

Among the latest Dodge features for 1932 were "Floating Power," an automatic vacuum-operated clutch, silent-second transmission with freewheeling unit mounted directly behind, and a heavy X-brace in the double-drop frame. Bodies were new, with the external visor eliminated. Over the windshield (on closed models) was a smart-looking moulding which resembled a right-hand bracket set sideways. Hoods were longer. The radiator design was similar to that of the 1931 model, and, though shutters were included, the new Dodge was one of the few cars which still had a flat radiator rather than a new V-grille.

The Dodge "Eight" now featured "Oilite" springs, prelubricated in metal covers. Wheelbase on the "DK" Eight was 122⅜", and the gear ratio was comparatively high: 3.9 to 1 on coupes and convertibles. Instrument panels and garnish mouldings were finished in walnut grain. The "Eight" now had a 282.1 cubic inch engine of 90 horsepower, and, with the high gearing, was a speedy model. Prices of the Dodge "Eight" ranged from $1115 to $1185, and the 78-horsepower Dodge "Six" (Model "DL," 114⅜" wheelbase) was priced from $795 to $895. All closed models were wired for radio.

In 1933, an excellent year for Dodge, new bodies were offered, as well as a slanting, slightly V-grille, with vertical bars. New, one-piece bumpers were introduced, and the most expensive models had twin trumpet horns in front. As in 1932, a choice of wood or wire wheels was available, with 16-inchers on the "Six" and 17s on the "Eight."

1933 was the final year for wooden wheels, also for the Dodge "Eight," which had never caught up with the popular sixes in sales. The last Dodge "Eight" was known as the model "DO," with an engine that delivered 100 horsepower. Prices of the "Eight" began at $1115 for the rumble-seat coupe, and, at the top of the line, was the rare convertible sedan, at $1395.

The "DP" was the 6-cylinder '33 model on a 115-inch wheelbase. It had 75 horsepower. Of all older Dodges, the 1933 "Six" was, until recent years, among the most common. In fact, Dodge sales for 1933 increased by 203.7%, with 75,256 cars sold in ten months. No other car could boast such a dramatic rise in sales volume during that time. Most of the new sales were in the 6-cylinder series, which was priced well below the "Eight." With the Dodge "Six" selling from $595 to $695, f.o.b., and prices of the "Eight" starting at $1115, there was a considerable price gap between the two models. There's no doubt that low prices of the "Six" helped to kill off the Dodge "Eight" that much faster.

Two wheelbases were available on the new Dodge "Six" for 1934. There was the 117-inch "DR" model, and the 121-inch "DS" Special. Both models featured a slightly larger engine, from 201.3 to 217.8 cubic inches. The horsepower rating of the "DR," was 82, and in the "DS" an additional five horses were gained with the use of the optional aluminum cylinder head which boosted compression from 5.6 to 6.5. A new voltage regulator was added to the generator to prevent overcharging of the battery on long runs. Other mechanical improvements were adopted, such as independently coil-sprung front wheels. "Floating Cushion" tires were standard equipment.

Bodies were somewhat similar to the '33 models, though on the '34s, swinging "butterfly" windows were included for draft-free ventilation. These swinging windows could be rolled down into the front doors, along with the main window sections. This 1934 Chrysler Corporation feature was popular with the men who drove on long newspaper routes, for with the side windows clear of obstructions, they could throw their newspapers with ease.

Hoods looked much longer on '34 Dodges, with four new horizontal hood louvres on each side (twelve on each side of the Special models.) Sedans had a small space for luggage behind the swinging back-half of the rear seat. The sportiest, by far, of the closed models was the unusual "Brougham" on the long-wheelbase chassis. It was a 4-door, 5-window club sedan which listed at $835 and had a "fast back" nearly as extreme as that of the "Airflow" Chryslers and De Sotos. However, the front section of the "Brougham" was similar to other "DS" models. Also worthy of mention was the $875 4-door convertible sedan in the "DS" series. It had a windshield which folded flat for those balmy days when driver and passengers could enjoy the feel of the breeze in their faces. Jaunty side-mounts and twin horns in front were also a part of this model's classic look. Most unusual of all, a special Dodge station wagon, on the truck chassis, was available. It had a special wooden body by Cantrell.

A New Eight Coupe, $1095

A New Six Sedan, $845

New *Beauty* now graces

DODGE DEPENDABILITY

Dodge Brothers present a new Dodge Six and a new Dodge Eight — the most beautiful, comfortable and able cars in Dodge history. ∞ It continues to be Dodge Brothers conviction that the most important thing about a motor car is that it be a *good* motor car — so designed and so built of sound materials that it may last long and operate dependably. ∞ The new Dodge Six and Eight demonstrate that it is possible to incorporate in cars of Dodge quality at Dodge Brothers traditional price-levels a measure of beauty, size and performance far beyond anything that moderate price has previously commanded. ∞ The value represented in such cars will be instantly apparent to every motor car buyer.

New Dodge Six $815 to $845, New Dodge Eight $1095 to $1135; Standard Six $735 to $835, Standard Eight $995 to $1095. Prices f.o.b. factory

"I bought my first Dodge nearly twenty years ago

...and this new '8' is the finest car Dodge ever built!"

SHE: This is the best looking car I've ever seen, Dad.

HE: Isn't it a beauty? I've driven Dodge cars for nearly 20 years—and this beats them all!

NO MATTER what kind of car you've been driving . . . no matter what price you're used to paying, the new Dodge "8" will be a revelation to you.

122-inch wheelbase . . . 100-horsepower—it's big, powerful, fast! And it is ultra-modern in appearance, in comfort, in driving ease.

Floating Power engine mountings give you unbelievable smoothness . . . freedom from vibration. A new feature—"inertia ride control"—automatically adjusts the shock-absorber to all types of road conditions. Oilite springs with metal covers are squeak-proof.

Driving is easy . . . effortless. Shifting is quiet in all speeds, including reverse. Starting is simple . . . turn on the ignition, step on the accelerator and presto! the engine is running.

This new Dodge "8" is speedy . . . and safe! Mono-piece steel body. Hydraulic brakes, with centrifuse drums. Double-drop X bridge-type frame. Low center of gravity. Duplate Safety Plate glass in windshield.

Go to a Dodge dealer and take a look at this new Dodge "8". You'll see why most Dodge owners, when buying a new car, un-hesitatingly buy another Dodge!

NEW DODGE "8"
WITH FLOATING POWER
An Aristocrat from bumper to bumper

Dodge "8": Coupe with Rumble Seat $1115 ... Sedan $1145 ... Five-Passenger Coupe $1145 ... Convertible Coupe $1185
Convertible Sedan $1395 ... Dodge "6": $595 to $695 (All Prices F. O. B. Factory, Detroit)

DODGE BROTHERS
SIXES AND EIGHTS

UPHOLDING EVERY TRADITION OF DODGE DEPENDABILITY

At its astonishingly low price, the Dodge Six costs less and offers more than any other closed car in Dodge Brothers history. It gives you smooth, vigorous, economical performance. It gives you a Mono-Piece Steel Body — squeakproof, rattleproof and strong, with a low center of gravity that makes the car hug the road under even the most difficult driving conditions. You get good looks, too, and surprising roominess, and safe, positive, weatherproof internal hydraulic brakes. Above all, you get Dodge Brothers dependability — insurance of long and satisfactory service.

DODGE SIX
$835
AND UP, F. O. B FACTORY

An outstanding triumph
of a pre-eminent firm

JUDGING by its appearance, you would instantly classify the Dodge Senior as a car selling for well over $2,000. Yet the unique facilities of Dodge Brothers, fortified by the well-nigh unlimited resources of Chrysler Motors, make it possible to produce this marvelous car to sell in the $1,500 class. The Dodge Senior is undeniably one of the greatest manufacturing triumphs just as it is one of the most impressive values of all automotive history. Three or four-speed transmission.
Convenient Terms

DODGE BROTHERS SENIOR

 CHRYSLER MOTORS PRODUCT

DODGE SENIOR BROUGHAM (*wire wheels extra*)

DUESENBERG

Because of its timeless beauty, immense size, super power and high price, the classic Duesenberg has the distinction of being one of the most admired American cars of all time. It was built at Indianapolis from late 1920 until early 1938. Before the introduction of their 1921 car, the Duesenberg Brothers (Fred and August) were building racing engines.

The original Duesenberg of 1921 had the distinction of being America's first straight-eight; it was also the first with 4-wheel hydraulic brakes. The Duesenbergs in the 1920s were known as the "A" series. They were luxurious for their time, but did not compare with the superb Duesenberg which was to follow. The all-new Model "J" was presented December, 1928, for 1929. More powerful, advanced in design, and fantastically long, the Model "J" (and supercharged "SJ") Duesenbergs built and sold, from 1929 on, were the ones which made the name truly famous among auto buffs.

During the 1930s, Duesenberg made no annual model changes, though radiator shutters were chrome-plated, as of 1931. There were minor changes from time to time on the elaborate instrument panel, and other improvements were made when the manufacturer thought it necessary. No further Duesenberg-Lycoming straight-eight engines were manufactured after 1932. By that time, a considerable stockpile of excess parts had accumulated at the factory, enough to last a few more years, even though the demand for luxury cars was dwindling in the thirties.

With the exception of a few custom-streamlined late models, most of the Duesenberg "J" and "SJ" beauties had the classic V-grille, massive long hood and fenders of the '29 model. However, Duesenberg did not build bodies; they were built to order by various high-class custom coachbuilders. Among the dozen and a half companies that built bodies for Duesenbergs were Murphy, Le Baron, Weymann, Judkins, Rollston, Bohman and Schwartz. Also, Willoughby, Van Den Plas, Graber, Gurney Nutting, Saoutchik, Letourneur and Marchand, Derham, Walker, and Walton. A few Duesenbergs were eventually remodeled to suit their owners, in later years. The Murphy-bodied roadster was one of the most popular and, perhaps, the most typical.

The f.o.b. price of a new Duesenberg chassis, *without the body,* ranged from $8500 to above $9500! And because many custom bodies could easily cost $5000 or more, the price of a new Duesenberg in the 1930s was at least $14,750 (usually about $19,000) and, sometimes, as much as $50,000 for the most elaborate models, painstakingly handcrafted over a period of months to suit the desires of those who wanted "the works." Imagine these prices, especially during depression days, when a dollar would buy a whale of a lot more than it will today! Then picture what it would cost to duplicate this workmanship *now!*

In sheer length, the Duesenberg "J" could hardly be exceeded; the wheelbases were usually 142½" or 153½"! The gasoline tank held 26½ gallons.

And what about performance? It was fantastic for its day, as the Duesenberg "J" boasted an honest 265 horsepower, and 320 horsepower with a supercharger! It was capable of doing well over 115 miles an hour in an era when only the mighty cars could exceed 80 (and many could not reach 70!) In *second gear,* the Duesenberg would do 88!

The magnificent engine had overhead valves (4 valves per cylinder) and dual overhead cams. The 420 cubic-inch straight-eight was covered with all sorts of chrome-plated "goodies." A Warner three-speed transmission was standard, and gear ratio choices were 3.8, 4, 4.3 or 4.7. Hefty 7.00 x 19 tires were used on most "J" models, and total weight was nearly three tons . . . sometimes more, depending on the body.

How about a description of the elaborate dashboard? It was an aviator's delight, and contained the following instruments as standard equipment; brake-pressure gauge, clock (with split-second hand and timer), oil-pressure gauge, altimeter, ammeter, tachometer, gas gauge, speedometer and water temperature gauge. In addition, there were red warning lights for "chassis lubricator operating," "oil change needed," or "add battery water." A green warning light was the lubricator pressure and oil reservoir signal. Some models even had a compass. In addition, there were numerous other switches and controls in the cab of a "Duesie," so many, in fact, that the competent operation of this fabulous car was a skill which had to be learned.

Duesenbergs were owned by many prominent show business personalities such as, Gary Cooper, Clark Gable, Ben Blue, Paul Whiteman, etc. And every so often, some collector offers for sale "one of Mae West's Duesenbergs."

Duesenberg fans claim that fewer than 500 "J" and "SJ" models were built, and more than half that amount remain today. At one time, it was possible to buy a good Duesenberg, used, for about $500. However, since the fifties, classic car fans have been on the increase, and a Duesenberg today can bring a price of several thousand dollars, if in reasonably good condition. Who knows how high the value will go in the future??

DU PONT

Du Pont automobiles were produced from 1919 until 1932. Among the most interesting, though least luxurious, were the 1930 speedsters. They had a curved radiator shell, with a split grille having one vertical bar in the center and many horizontal members. The Du Pont, no doubt, inspired the grille that attracted so much favor for the 1932 De Soto. The Du Pont speedster had a very long, smooth hood. However, outlandish, combined fenders and running boards were set high above the wheels and the ground, making the otherwise good design look peculiar. Narrow Wood-lite headlamps were used, as on the 1930 "Ruxton" and several custom-built cars. Although they didn't throw much light on the road, they helped to set the front end design apart from the commonplace. The windshield was unusually low, its small size accentuated by a high cowl and cut-down side doors. The top was skimpy, barely more than a kerchief when raised.

Wheelbase of the 1930 speedster was 126 inches. The Du Pont of 1930 was driven by a straight-eight engine that developed 140 horsepower, and prices were usually above $4000.

Individual coachwork and exclusive body styles, such as town cars and

Victoria cabriolets, were typical "Du Pont offerings to the successful man," and the company occasionally took advertising space in that new dollar magazine, *Fortune*.

Outlets for the machines were limited. Du Pont motor cars could be purchased at 502 Park Avenue in New York, 901 North Broad Street in Philadelphia, 10 West Eager Street in Baltimore, and 3733 Wilshire Boulevard in the swank new section of Los Angeles. Surely there must have been a distributor in or around Chicago.

According to various sources, only 175 Du Ponts were built during 1929, and the number fell to 125 in 1930. The number decreased each year afterward, and 1932 marked the end of the road for a rare marque, which (like the Brewster and Cunningham automobiles) was built in the East for the wealthiest of clients.

Today, Du Pont automobiles are understandably rare, though Harrah's Automobile Collection in Reno, Nevada, has a few Du Ponts on display to the public, and a handful may be found elsewhere.

DURANT

The 1930 Durant was a very attractive model, completely restyled and sturdier in appearance than before. The new bodies looked heavier and lower, and the radiator was plainer than that of the '28–'29 models which had been trimmed with vertical and horizontal chrome strips. There were five, horizontal, dart-shaped louvres on each side of the hood. Wood wheels appeared on cheaper models, but de luxe models had wire wheels, and also had a small parking lamp on each front fender.

The 1930 Durant "614" had 58 horsepower, and the "617" had 70. Both had 6-cylinder Continental engines and 19-inch wheels. The "617" series had an unusually high (for 1930) gear ratio of 3.73 to 1, exceeded only by certain models of Graham and Chrysler.

Durant offered an unusual feature in 1931, described in this advertisement: "In the Durant of 1931 you will find a special Pullman lounge arrangement. The mere pressing of a convenient lever instantly converts the sedan interior into pleasant, comfortable resting or sleeping accommodations." The front seat folded back flat, to join the lower cushion of the rear seat, thus making a bed. This was a feature which became much better known in the Nash of a few years later.

The Thermostatic Motor Temperature Control Shutters (vertical) on the radiator were also new. Hood louvres were the conventional, vertical type.

The larger "617" series was not continued into 1931, but the "614" was still offered. The "614" sedan was priced at $995, and, for $200 less, one could buy the new Standard "612" model with the same engine. That year, Durant returned to the 4-cylinder series (now with 50 horsepower) known as the "610," which sold for $765, but few of these cars found buyers. (The 1931 Durant "610" is among the very scarcest of old cars.) All 1931 Durants had a 112-inch wheelbase, and only 6781 of them were sold by November of that year. Another good car was about to leave the scene.

Durant struggled into 1932 with just one series that was the 71-horsepower "619" model, a six with the sedan price cut to only $600. It was powered with the same Continental 22-A engine as the '31 model, but more horsepower was derived by speeding the RPM to 3300. A shorter car than before, the final Durant had a 109-inch wheelbase, on sedan or coupe.

Body lines were similar to 1930 and 1931 Durants, but the 1932 series had a slightly V-shaped radiator grille and five new, vertical ventilating doors on each side of the hood. But, despite mechanical improvements, this appeared to be the same old car with just a "nose job," and only 1132 of the 1932 Durants were built before the once-popular make was discontinued for good. Sales made a sorry comparison with those of the boom year of 1923, when some 178,000 Durant and Star cars had been produced!

ELCAR

Though never a seller in volume, the Elcar was an automobile with a good reputation, produced in Elkhart, Indiana. Like the Indiana-built Auburn, the Elcar was powered by a Lycoming engine. As the twenties moved along, times grew increasingly difficult for small automakers and, by 1930, Elcar, as well as many another low-quantity producer, was in serious trouble.

For 1930, the 61-horsepower, 6-cylinder "75" series (sedan, $1095) was continued, as well as the 8-cylinder "95" and "96" models with 90 horse-power. But there was an even finer Elcar buy that year. The $2295 Elcar "120" model of '29 became the $1995 "130" model for the new year and its large straight-eight engine was boosted to one hundred forty horsepower! With the exception of the Cadillac V-16 and the Duesenberg, no other 1930 car was more powerful than the big Elcar, which had a 130-inch wheelbase and an easy-cruising 3.80 gear ratio. Certainly, no other automobile offered so much power for the money!

Elcar managed to remain in business for the early part of 1931, with models similar, in most respects, to the preceding series. However, the "95" model was discontinued, and a "140" model was added. The new "140" had the same 322 cubic-inch displacement and 140 horsepower as the continued

"130" series, but the "140" cost $700 more and weighed nearly 400 additional pounds (sedan weight, 4375 pounds.)

Elcar was a maverick when it came to tire size; the "130" and "140" models, and one model of the Stutz, were the only cars still to use oversized 20-inch wheels in 1931, a size more commonly found on heavy trucks.

One modern feature was the Lockheed hydraulic brakes, offered on all Elcar models.

Though 1931 marked the last regularly produced Elcar automobile, the company did not throw in the towel. Instead, an unusual new idea was tried. For 1933, Elcar attempted to produce another car, using the novel Powell-Lever engine. This engine was a double-jointed affair with two-piece connecting rods (so designed to deliver a more powerful "lever" thrust to the crankshaft.) Though pilot models were built, the car never got into full production. But, despite this problem, Elcar managed to find success in another field.

The company began to build travel and camping trailers. As the small trailer industry of the early '30s developed into the booming field of mobile homes, Elcar held on, and prospered.

ERSKINE

For 1927, Studebaker had introduced a lower-priced companion car, named "Erskine" (after Studebaker's president.) Though the early Erskines had more advanced, European styling than the parent car, they were flimsy and not very reliable. The poor reputation of the Erskine spread rapidly, and hindered future sales.

The 1929 Erskine was closer to Studebaker's low-priced "Dictator Six" series, both mechanically and in styling, except that the '29 Erskine had a smaller 6-cylinder engine of only 43 horsepower. Most buyers preferred to pay a little more and get the model with the Studebaker nameplate.

The Erskine for 1930 had a new, 70-horsepower 6-cylinder engine, with piston displacement raised from 160 to 205.3 cubic inches. Wheelbase was also increased from 109 to 114 inches. Lower bodies were made possible by the use of a double-drop frame. The 1930 Erskine was certainly similar to the Studebaker "Dictator" model, which had a ⅛" larger engine bore and only an extra inch in wheelbase. 5.25 x 19" wood wheels were standard, except on de luxe models.

Seven models were available, priced from $895 to $1095, f.o.b. The Erskine sedan sold for $995, whereas the more popular Studebaker "Dictator" sedan cost $200 more. Strangely, the '30 "Dictator" had 2 less horsepower than the Erskine, even though the Studebaker had larger pistons. This was because the compression ratio was only 4.80 in the Studebaker, as compared to Erskine's 5.20. Both cars had a 4.78 to 1 gear ratio and 19-inch tires. The "Dictator" sedan weighed 180 lbs. more than Erskine's 2900. The new Erskine was billed as having "more power per pound than any car under $1000."

Studebaker dropped the Erskine. The replacement was the new Studebaker "Six," basically the same car with another name, priced from $795 to $995. As of 1931, the "Dictator" model became a straight-eight.

Yet the Erskine was not the last low-priced subsidiary car to be offered by Studebaker. Another new companion was introduced for 1932, the "Rockne."

ESSEX

The Hudson Motor Car Company of Detroit first introduced its new, low-cost Essex car in 1919, ten years after the debut of the Hudson. The first Essex had a 4-cylinder engine with a great deal of pep. Most owners agreed that the Essex was a better car during the years that it had the large 4-cylinder power plant. In 1924, Essex became a "Super Six," but the 6-cylinder engine placed in the Essex was much smaller than the Hudson version. The Essex "Six" was undersized, and hampered by an excessively low gear ratio.

By 1930, the Essex "Six" had been considerably improved, and had 60 horsepower at 3600 RPM, with a modest displacement of 161.4 cubic inches. The Essex engine was still fighting a 5.40 to 1 gear ratio in high, however, and the car was overworked at higher speeds. Essex was lower-geared than any other 1930 car.

The Essex "Challenger" for 1930 had a new radiator design, with the motif of the vertical shutters carried all the way to the top. The new front bumper was connected by *two* vertical guards (instead of the former *one*) and dipped slightly at the center. Correspondingly, the headlamp tie-bar also dipped in the middle, and the front license plate was supported above it.

The hood louvres were in two vertical rows, one above the other, and, for 1930, they were set in an oblong, ovalled panel. Cowl lamps were moved

ESSEX

NEW CARS TODAY
BECAUSE OF OWNER MANAGEMENT

THE NEW
ESSEX
SUPER SIX

...tigue. Ease of steering and extraordinary roadability add to driving pleasure. ...ecial spring suspension and a positively rigid frame with four hydraulic ...ock absorbers take up road shocks. The body, of airplane type construction, ...insulated against drumming and its quietness increases riding and driving ...joyment. Deep-sprung cushions make all seats unusually comfortable.

...rformance, as always in Hudson-Essex, is outstanding. You remember how ...th Hudson's Great Eight and the Essex Challenger won first honors in the ...mous Tour de France, that annual 8-day event in which cars from all countries ...mpete in speed, reliability and economy. That is but one of many interna-...nal victories these cars won this year, proving dependability and perform-...ce in highest degree.

...ith such distinguished forerunners, these two cars irresistibly appeal to all ...o seek brilliant performance. Here you find it—in larger motors that give ...urplus of power for mountain or mud, for acceleration in get-away or road ...ergency. You find it in roadability, riding and driving ease, smoothness, ...d in definite advantages of economy.

...every wanted particular of appearance, performance and comfort, both ...rs possess qualities that make them outstanding.

...ney are priced to make them Value Sensations.

GET THE PRICES FROM TODAY'S NEWSPAPERS

back, almost to the windshield posts, and were connected to the belt moulding.

On sedans, the doors now opened at the center-post, where formerly all four had swung open at the front.

Particularly interesting was a new body-type. *Motor* magazine of January, 1930 said: "The high spot in the new product is a sun sedan, a convertible five-passenger body at a moderate price which is offered on both the Hudson and Essex chassis. Hudson, years ago, it will be remembered, initiated the present popularity of the closed car by bringing out the coach, at the price of an open car. It will be interesting to see if this newest Hudson-Essex body type starts a popular trend to convertible cars. Convertible cars, of course, are not new but five-passenger moderately-priced convertible cars are distinctly new.

"The sun sedan is a two-door design with folding front seats. Special precautions have been taken to render the disappearing windows silent and satisfactory. Each window glass is set in a sturdy, chromium-plated metal frame. Grooves in the side members of this frame fit into vertical tongues concealed within the door so that the window is adequately supported whether up or down. Attached to the collapsible fabric top are hinged pillars which fit between front and rear windows to close the opening at this point."

The 1930 Essex had a 113-inch wheelbase and double cowl ventilators. Body hardware, upholstery and trim were "modernistic." The sedan cost $825.

Represented by six thousand dealers in the United States and Canada (and others abroad), Essex sold 59,152 cars between January and the end of October; not a bad figure for an "independent," but far less than the 179,491 units sold during the same period a year earlier. And in 1930, Essex fell from third to sixth place in sales, despite its many improvements. The unusual "sun sedan" did not sell well, yet the body-type was imitated shortly thereafter by Chevrolet, Ford and others.

Essex fared worse in 1931. The car dropped from sixth to tenth place in sales, with 40,086 units sold by November. Yet the new Essex was restyled again, now having a chrome-plated screen in front of the radiator (a la Cadillac), a horizontal tie-bar between headlamps and one large group of vertical louvres on each side of the hood, like most other cars. The new price was only $595 for the coach or two-passenger coupe.

Available at additional cost was selective freewheeling (pioneered on the late '30 Studebaker) and "Startix," the device that automatically cranked the engine when ignition switch was turned on. "Startix" also recranked the engine should it happen to stall.

Essex returned to sixth place in sales during 1932, though only 26,108 cars were sold in ten months of that year. Body designs were entirely new, with styling by Frank Spring, formerly chief designer for California's Murphy Body Company which had previously built certain custom models for Hudson and other manufacturers.

A new, trim, slightly "veed" radiator shell and grille were featured. Headlamps were mounted separately, on the front fenders, without the previous tie-bar. New bumpers were one-piece, and parking lamps were mounted further down the side of the cowl. Bodies were more rounded, and each closed model had a very shallow visor built in over the windshield.

The new engine had 70 horsepower at 3200 RPM, and would carry the car more than 70 miles per hour, thanks to an improved gear ratio of 4.63. A syncro-mesh transmission with silent second was a part of the 1932 model, as was the cork-faced, "wet" clutch which was long a characteristic of both Essex and Hudson. Freewheeling and Startix were now standard equipment. Also incorporated was "ride control," the new type of adjustable shock absorbers which could be set to proper position by a pull-out knob on the dash.

Upholstery came in new pastel colors, and an interesting crisscross (diamond-checked) pattern was printed on seat cushions.

The Essex was replaced in '33 by Hudson's new "Terraplane." The early model was referred to as the "Essex-Terraplane." It was continued as a lower-priced companion to the Hudson until 1938.

The Difference is

1932 ESSEX SUPER-SIX STANDARD SEDAN   •   FIVE PASSENGERS   • $775 F. O. B.

INFORMATION

70 HORSEPOWER AT 3200 R.P.M.   ESSEX SPEEDS BEYOND 70 MILES   SILENT SECOND SPEED 50 MILES

COMPENSATED INHERENTLY BALANCED CRANKSHAFT   POWER DOME ANTI-KNOCK COMBUSTION CHAMBER

FULLY ADJUSTABLE SILENT CHAIN DRIVEN TIMING GEARS   INTAKE SILENCER AND AIR CLEANER   SUPER ACCELERATOR PUMP

ANTI-FLOOD CHOKE   ROLLER VALVE TAPPETS   DUOFLO AUTOMATIC ENGINE OILING   THERMOSTATIC CARBURETOR HEAT CONTROL

LABYRINTHIAN OIL COOLING   TRIPLE-SEALED OIL-CUSHION CLUTCH   SIMPLIFIED SELECTIVE FREE WHEELING   SYNCRO-MESH TRANSMISSION

SILENT CONSTANT MESH SECOND GEAR   DIAGONAL TRUSS FRAME   SPLAYED REAR SPRINGS   TWIN NEUTRATONE MUFFLERS   DEMOUNTABLE WOOD OR WIRE WHEELS

QUICK-VISION INSTRUMENT PANEL   STARTIX, AUTOMATIC SELF-STARTER AND ANTI-STALL

"TELL-TALE" OIL AND GENERATOR SAFETY SIGNALS   RIDE CONTROLS   TWO-WAY SHOCK ABSORBERS

NATURAL GRIP STEERING WHEEL   ARC-SLIDE FASTENER POCKETS   LATERAL SPRING SEAT CUSHIONS   ADJUSTABLE SEATS BOTH FRONT AND REAR

FULL OPENING WINDSHIELD WITH TWO-FINGER CONTROL   FOOT-OPERATED HEADLIGHT DIMMER

9 SPARKLING NEW MODELS WITH GEM-LIKE BODY COLORS AND UPHOLSTERY IN NEW PASTEL SHADES   FITMENTS IN EBONY AND SILVER FINISH   WHEELBASE LENGTH 113"

These, and an impressive list of other exclusive features at no extra cost, illustrate the completeness of Essex 1932 standard equipment

PRICES LISTING FROM $695 F. O. B. DETROIT

it's BIG CAR *Value*

...ANY cars bid for your choice at or near the Essex price
level—some at a few dollars less—some, hundreds
...lars more.

...e real appeal then that the new and greater Essex
...Six makes to you and to every motor car buyer is
...lid appeal of greater value.

...hat has this new Essex Super-Six to offer which
...it Big Car Value?

...g Car Power, for one thing—full seventy horsepower
...0 r. p. m. Smooth, swift and *vibrationless,* using ordi-
...el for premium performance.

...g Car Features for power transmission (Full Range
...ve Transmission, including Free Wheeling, Con-
...nal Drive, Silent Syncro-Mesh, and Silent Second
...for luxurious riding (Essex Ride Controls, Essex
...pe lateral seat cushion springs, Essex splayed rear
...s), and for safety and convenience (Essex Startix, Essex
...-Vision Instrument Panel, Essex 30 times stronger
...nal Truss Frame).

...d Big Car Qualities of ampler roominess, deeper,
...upholstery, the luxurious silence of Essex solid-unit
...odies, and the new-color, new-line beauty of Essex
...ance.

...eigh these features and qualities on whatever scales
...ill, and you are bound to see the balance tip in favor
...new and greater Essex—the yardstick of motor car
...for 1932.

...SON MOTOR CAR COMPANY, DETROIT, MICHIGAN
...HUDSON-ESSEX OF CANADA LIMITED, TILBURY, ONTARIO

ESSEX
SUPER-SIX PACEMAKER

Comfort in all weather is assured by the weatherproof solid-unit steel body of the new and greater
Essex Super-Six, insulated against heat, cold and noise

Look at the inviting width of the new Essex seats; note the
contoured roll-top and back design; then try out for yourse...
the pillowy luxury of their new-type lateral seat cushio...
springs — steady, jounceless and bounceless on any roa...

FORD

The 1930 Model A Ford was noticeably different from earlier models, with a larger and better radiator (featuring "rustless" steel brightwork,) a higher, more streamlined hood which blended with cowl and body, and smaller wheels (19-inchers instead of 21s).

Motor magazine mentioned other changes in the 1930 Ford, such as redesigned fenders, an improved gas tank (still built into the cowl) with a less conspicuous filler cap, longer and roomier bodies, and new engine mountings designed to reduce vibration. Top speed was usually found to be 65.

With proper handling, the Model A could get 25 miles from a gallon of gas, and the car was so simple and well-planned that it was virtually trouble-free.

As before, the 1930 Ford had 40 horsepower. Wheelbase was 103½ inches, which gave the car a rather stubby appearance. The Model A Ford outsold Chevrolet in both 1929 and 1930; the sales figures for the two cars, during the first ten months of 1930, amounted to 989,626 Fords and 566,706 Chevrolets. With the Model A standard roadster priced at only $435, f.o.b., no other full-sized car could match the bargain.

Of all vintage cars remaining today, the '30 Ford coupe is, by far, most fre-

ALOFT IN LUXURY!

Like an albatross of burnished silver . . . the new Ford de luxe club plane

THE NEW Ford all-metal, tri-motored club plane meets delightfully all the demands of the most exacting yachtsman of the skies. Fundamentally it is designed as close to mechanical perfection as possible, with all the strength and extraordinary performance ability for which Ford planes are famous. This great new plane permits you to forget the mechanics of flight. It gives you the freedom, the exhilaration, the full joy of sailing at will across the skies in club comfort.

Beautiful as a jewel, it spreads its wings like burnished silver, to fly with the grace of an albatross over sea, over land, over deserts or arctic wastes. Here, truly, is a yacht to be proud of! Here, above all things, is the worthy vehicle of the modern man of spirit and imagination!

FORD MOTOR COMPANY

Visitors are always welcome at the Ford Airport at Detroit

New de luxe club plane

Mechanical features are similar to those of the famous Ford 5-AT: Built of aluminum alloys, lighter than wood; powered with three Pratt & Whitney air-cooled motors, with total of 1275 horse-power; a capacity of nine passengers plus a pilot and mechanic. Cruising speed over 115 miles an hour, for hundreds of miles!

In addition, the de luxe club plane contains kitchenette, folding berths, radio cabinet, writing desk and book case. Seven overstuffed chairs and a two-place divan. Card tables and serving trays. Refrigerators and thermos cases. A lavatory with toilet, running water, towel racks, and closets for luggage, guns, fishing tackle or golf sticks.

Walls and ceiling are sound-proofed.

The entire interior is beautifully trimmed and decorated in choice fabrics. Individual ventilation at each window. Dome and wall light and heat register in floor add to the comfort and luxuriousness of the plane. Tile walls in kitchenette and lavatory.

The pilot and mechanic in their forward control cabin have every mechanical device necessary for day or night flying in all seasons under all conditions.

Price on request.

quently in evidence. It remained in greater numbers because more were built in the first place. But, the 1930 Ford also had much better cooling than the earlier Fords, was considered more attractive, and was so simple and durable, so ideally suited for a "work" or "transportation" car (the coupe could be adapted easily to a "pick-up") that it remained popular long after it had been replaced by the Ford V-8.

On June 3, 1930, production was started on a very interesting Model A, the "De Luxe Phaeton." This differed from the ordinary Ford phaeton (or touring car) in that the "De Luxe Phaeton" was a two-door rather than a four-door car. This became a rare model, only 7281 De Luxe Phaetons being produced in '30 and '31.

In 1931, Ford adopted a new radiator shell, with the top pan portion indented and painted. The Ford emblem, formerly of blue-and-white glazed enamel, was now of unpainted stainless (or "rustless") steel.

Most noticeable change in the 1931 Ford Model A was in the four-door sedan. The windshield was slanted at 10 degrees, and the external visor eliminated. Also new was the attractive Victoria, a two-door, five-passenger coupe with an abbreviated rear deck section. The Victoria was available either with padded or metal-surfaced rear quarters. Both Briggs and Murray bodies were used on these models, as on other Fords.

On May 22, 1931, production began on another new body type, the "Convertible Sedan." This was a two-door coach with solid panels around side windows, but with a sloping windshield and convertible top. Though the side panels were stationary and could not be lowered, this car was apparently Ford's answer to the Essex "Sun Sedan" of the preceding year. Only 5,085 Fords of this body-type were built in 1931, and they are of considerable interest to those who collect and restore the Model A.

Another model frequently hunted by collectors is the Ford wooden-bodied station wagon. This was offered by the factory since 1929, though earlier, custom-built "estate wagons" (by independent body manufacturers) had been available.

On April 14, 1931, Henry Ford produced his twenty-millionth car. It was a Model A town sedan, boldly labeled, "THE TWENTY-MILLIONTH FORD," and was frequently photographed. This car was kept by the company for publicity purposes.

Roughly speaking, *one million* of the five million Model As built still are in service. This is a remarkable record, considering the present age of the Model A!

For 1932, Ford introduced an all-new car. A V-8 was offered, in a companion series to the 4-cylinder Model "B." Because of the necessary retooling, the Ford V-8 was late in arriving for the new season; it was introduced after other 1932 models already were on the road. The '32 V-8 was later to be prized among "hot-rodders" for its clean, curvy lines and its adaptability for street racing. The '32 Ford body was a complete change from the Model "A" styling. The outside sun visor was banished for good, and the top was lower and semi-streamlined, with curves above the windshield, and, on the V-8, a wider rear window. Two coupe models were built; the 3-window and the 5-window variety, in addition to Victorias, sedans, convertibles, etc.

Ford production was slow in the early months of 1932, as these figures show:

January	3858 units
February	3198 units
March	3434 units
April	9627 units

In May, 63,188 Fords were built; in June, the figure was an even healthier 82,263! By midyear, the V-8 Ford was selling well, and the 4-cylinder Model "B" was preferred by some who had liked the Model "A."

Though the Model "B" was a 4-cylinder car, unlike its predecessor it had a gas tank located at the rear, with a fuel line and mechanical fuel pump on the engine. The Model "B" engine had an automatic spark advance built into the distributor, a feature seen on other cars before, but new to Ford in 1932. The Ford Model "B" resembled the V-8 in appearance, but when it came to performance it was quite different.

Late in 1932, in an economy drive, Ford shut down assembly operations in the Louisville and Oklahoma City plants.

In 1933, Fords were again restyled, with larger, lower bodies and a longer hood with a more sloping, V-shaped grille. The V-8 was Ford's most popular model, though a few 50-horsepower "fours" were offered. The 4-cylinder 1933 model shared the V-8's body design, and was known as the Model "C." Hampered by its heavy body and chassis, the Model "C" had little pep.

On a 112-inch wheelbase, the 1933 Ford was an entirely different breed from the diminutive Model "A" of two years earlier. As before, safety glass was included on all Ford windshields; it was optional on the other windows. Safety glass however, was offered throughout on De luxe models.

Tire size was 5.50 x 17 inches, and the V-8 was rated at 75 horsepower. F.O.B. price range was from $410 (Model "C" standard roadster) to $610

New Beauty for the New Ford

THE NEW FORD TOWN SEDAN

NEW ROOMY BODIES . . NEW STREAMLINES . . NEW COLORS . . NEW RADIATOR

. . NEW FENDERS . . NEW WHEELS . . NEW RUSTLESS STEEL . . NEW UPHOLSTERY.

NOW, MORE THAN EVER, THE NEW FORD IS A "VALUE FAR ABOVE THE PRICE."

(Fordor De Luxe V-8 sedan.) Though movie stars usually bought expensive automobiles, both Johnny Weissmuller and Franchot Tone chose '33 Fords.

An increase to 85 horsepower was made possible on the 1934 Ford V-8 by the use of a dual, downdraft carburetor and dual manifold. However, a limited number of '34 Fords were scheduled to be built with a single manifold, as well as with a *self-feeding carburetor* that drew fuel from the rear tank *without the use of a fuel pump*. Had this idea taken hold, early Ford V-8s would have been relatively trouble-free (one of Ford's worst faults in the 1930s was fuel pump failure.) Many Ford V-8 owners had to replace faulty or worn-out fuel pumps as frequently as five times in one year!

Steering ratio was improved on the 1934 model, from 13 to 1 to 15 to 1. Body design on the '34 Ford was similar to that of the '33s. However, the grille was slightly modified, with a straight front edge, a broader shell, and a generally heavier look. There were also two handles provided on each side of the hood, instead of one as in 1933. No 4-cylinder models were offered.

New for 1934 was "clear-vision ventilation," the glass in the doors made to slide back an inch in front doors and two inches in side windows, as a means of drawing stale air from the interior. In addition, these windows also could be rolled up and down the usual way. The bottoms of the side doors were drilled, so that fresh air could enter through the holes and then rise to the window frames, from where it would be transferred to the car interior.

On de luxe models, instrument panels were finished in an attractive, imitation walnut grain.

Ford's early 1934 body colors were Black, Dearborn Blue, Cordoba Gray, Coach Maroon, and Vineyard Green. The latter color (for reasons known only to the manufacturer), was *not* to be included on any Standard models *except* those that were to be sold on the West Coast or in Florida. Also, contrasting black fenders and running gear were found only on Standard models, de luxe Fords all being finished in one solid color. One would think it would be the other way around, since two-tone paint jobs are generally more expensive!

Top speed of the 1934 Ford was in excess of 85 miles per hour, which made it readily adaptable for police use. Because the Ford V-8 was light, fast, and had the ability for fast "getaway," it was also appreciated by elements of the underworld. None other than the notorious John Dillinger took time out from his busy bank-robbing schedule, to write a note of appreciation to Henry Ford. Dated May 16, 1934, Dillinger's whimsical message to Mr. Ford read as follows:

"Hello Old Pal:-

Arrived here at 10 A.M. today. Would like to drop in and see you.

You have a wonderful car. Been driving it for three weeks. It's a treat to drive one.

Your slogan should be.

Drive a Ford and watch the other cars fall behind you. I can make any other car take a Ford's *dust*.

Bye-Bye,

John Dillinger"

The "wonderful" Ford V-8 mentioned in the letter was a stolen car. John Dillinger was shot to death in front of a theater later that year.

RICHLY COSTUMED FOR A LEADING ROLE

UPON the roadways of the world, the new Ford plays an important part in the widening activities of the modern woman. Its distinctive beauty of line and color is apparent at a glance. Through many months of constant use you will develop a sincere pride in its reliability and faithful performance.

The high quality of the new Ford is revealed also in every detail of its interior finish — in those all-important little things a woman's discerning eye is quick to note and remember.

The richness of the upholstery and the carefully tailored trimming — the excellent taste in appointments — the ease with which the windows go up and down in the substantial doors — the deep, well-sprung cushions in the restful seats — the pleasing harmony of color . . . all of these bespeak the care and craftsmanship that have gone into the building of the Ford car.

In addition to the Convertible Cabriolet, illustrated above, there are twelve other Ford body types in a variety of attractive colors. The first cost of the new Ford is low and you may purchase on convenient, economical terms through the Authorized Ford Finance Plans of the Universal Credit Company.

A distinctive beauty of line and color

THE BEAUTY of the new Ford, so apparent in line and color, extends also to the upholstery and appointments. You note it as you open the doors and see the attractive interiors. You find it also in those important little details of trim and finish which a woman's practiced eye is quick to catch. There is about the car a distinctive style or tone which reflects the substantial quality that has been built into it. In external things, as in mechanical construction, the new Ford has been built to endure.

THE NEW FORD SPORT COUPE

FRANKLIN

The Franklin Automobile Company of Syracuse, New York, built passenger cars from 1902 until 1934, after which Franklin went into the manufacture of aircraft engines. Franklin cars were unusual in many respects but, principally, because they had air-cooled engines.

During the 'twenties, Franklin was not noted for speed, yet the 1930 Franklin was advertised as able to attain 80 miles per hour in fourth gear with its new horsepower rating of 87 (later boosted to 95.) The Franklin engine was a six, with overhead valves and a heavy shrouding of air passages that hid the cylinders from view. Bore and stroke were 3½″ x 4¾″. Franklin advertised its 1930 model as, "America's first motor car with an AIRPLANE TYPE ENGINE."

The 1930 Franklin achieved greater power than before mainly because of the new, detachable cylinder head made of "Y" alloy aluminum. The new head was cooled more efficiently by generously sized fins which were swept by a heavy blast of air coming through the wind-tunnel shroud that covered the engine. This cooler engine made feasible a higher compression ratio of 5.3. Also, power was increased by the use of larger valves and a larger intake manifold.

"Radiator shutters" gave the front end a new dignity, and the new, horizontal hood louvres were shaped like long darts. Standard bodies were built by Walker, and various custom bodies for the Franklin were available from Dietrich, Locke, Derham and Holbrook. One of the sportiest models was the "Pursuit" phaeton, a saucy, dual-cowl model with sloping rear, wire wheels and side mounts.

Most of Franklin's standard models were priced between $2500 and $3000 during 1930.

Wheelbase was 125 inches on the "145" series, and 132 on the "147s."

New Franklin cars for 1931 were unveiled in December, 1930. Prices were down (beginning at $2295, f.o.b.), for Franklin, like many other independents, was hit hard by the depression. Sales declined from 6819 units (January to November, 1930) to only 3267 in the corresponding 1931 season. Furthermore, Franklin declined to twenty-eighth place in sales for '31. Even a limited-production newcomer, the De Vaux, was able to crowd ahead of Franklin and take twenty-sixth place.

In spite of the sales decline, Franklin had its loyal supporters. One was the famous aviator, Captain Frank M. Hawks who, on January 2, 1931, wrote a testimonial to the Franklin Automobile Company, addressed to Mr. H. H. Franklin. In part, the letter read:

"My experience with aircraft has proved the superiority of air-cooled power plants, and it is this feature in your car, more than anything else, which influenced me in my purchase of a new 1931 FRANKLIN DE LUXE CONVERTIBLE SPEEDSTER.

"I consider the progress of aviation owes a great deal to you, Mr. Franklin, for sticking to the principle which you knew to be right; your new engine, which develops more horsepower for size than any other engine, is a tribute to American engineering brains. This air-cooled principle, applying an air stream directly to the heated parts of the engine, will cool the engine more effectively than the indirect methods which embody unnecessary fluids and attachments.

"Not only this perfection of cooling, but also the trouble-free operation which goes with it, the lighter weight, increased riding comfort and the ability of the Franklin to stay at wide open throttle without loss of power, are all reasons why I am extremely enthusiastic about my new Franklin speedster.

"With best wishes for your continued success, I am

Yours very truly,
Frank M. Hawks"

The new Franklin purchased by Captain Hawks was a classic creation with body by Dietrich. It was a close-coupled convertible sedan with a very high hood line, small, sloping windshield, a large trunk placed at the rear, and a spare tire, fabric-covered to match the top. It had wire wheels, though other models came with wood wheels, if desired.

As before, air-mindedness was the theme of Franklin, with such descriptions as "airplane-type engine," "airfoil fenders," "airplane windshield," and "airplane instrument panel." However, the interior featured what Franklin chose to call, "library upholstery." Perhaps, in those days, "aircraft upholstery" might have sounded a bit too Spartan for advertising copy.

There were two models in the Series 15 for 1931: the Transcontinent, or the higher-priced de luxe model, priced at $2695, and up.

Hood ventilators distinguished the 1931 from 1930 models. The 1931 Franklins had three vent doors in each side of the hood, the first door placed well ahead of the other two, making it appear that a fourth door could have been included in the gap. Also, parking lamps were now located at the rear of the cowl, rather than on the fenders, as in 1930. This was the reversal of a popular trend, as many 1931 models were moving parking lamps to, rather than from, the fenders.

Franklin cars for 1931 were equipped throughout with Libbey-Owens-Ford safety glass. Four-wheel Lockheed hydraulic brakes with 14-inch drums were standard, with emergency brake contracting on the driveshaft. Horsepower was boosted to 100 at 3100 RPM.

To combat the effect of lagging sales, a Franklin dealer in Akron installed a miniature golf course right inside the automobile showroom. As a hard-times source of added revenue, it brought in twenty dollars a day. Golfers saw pictures, under glass, of the new Franklins, conveniently located near each hole. And at least one car was kept in the showroom, safely out of the reach of golf clubs. A popular fad that took hold of the country in 1930, miniature golf was played in several automobile showrooms during 1931, as a money-making gimmick. In fact, there were many serious thinkers in America who proposed that miniature (or "pee-wee") golf might be a means to bring the nation out of the Depression!

For 1932, Franklin added a fourth ventilating door on each side of the hood, to fill the noticeable blank space on the 1931 models. Radiator grilles became more noticeably sloped, and closed bodies were rounded at the corners.

However, Franklin's biggest features for 1932 were the addition of an optional supercharger, and a brand-new V-12 engine of 150 horsepower. The mighty "Franklin Twelve" on a big 144-inch-wheelbase chassis, was introduced in the spring of 1932. It was the new companion to the regular 6-cylinder Franklin, and both models featured air-cooled engines. Because of the larger size of the "Twelve," it had *six* ventilating doors on each side of the hood.

Other 1932 improvements were a syncro-mesh transmission with silent second gear, free-wheeling, Startix, and two-way Delco-Remy shock absorbers which could be adjusted by the driver.

Benefits of the new supercharger were explained to the public in a Franklin advertisement of February, 1932:

"Without taking additional power to operate, the Franklin Supercharger packs the ingoing charge of gas into every cylinder EQUALLY, and in maximum quantity. Rather than sucked in, gas is forced in. No starved cylinders. No gasping acceleration. A smooth, even flow of turbine-like power, etc."

Franklin further stated that . . . . "now, also, comes 'Spot-Controlled Temperature.' Each spot on each cylinder is the same temperature as the corresponding spot on all other cylinders—possible only with air-cooling. As a typical result, valves in Franklin are the coolest of all automobile engines.

"In the new Franklin engine a torrent of air is forced under *pressure* to the exact spots to be cooled. Now, uniform cylinder output, maximum power and longer engine life are achieved with astonishingly improved performance."

Despite a minimum price of $2250 (including supercharger), Franklin's sales for 1932 were dismal. Only 1577 cars were produced in ten months, and Franklin suffered a decline of 51.7% in 1932 sales. But Franklin wasn't licked yet.

In 1933, Franklin presented a third model; the "Olympic Six," with sedan or coupe priced at only $1385, f.o.b. The "Olympic" had a 118-inch wheelbase, and the highest gear ratio of all three models (4.30 to 1.) The "Olympic" had the same 274 cubic-inch, 100 horsepower engine as the regular 6-cylinder series, but with the elimination of various unnecessary extras, the new car sold for nearly $1000 less than other Franklin models; truly a "break-through" so far as cost was concerned. Yet, Franklin's advertising stated that: "all cars have superchargers." It was little short of a miracle that Franklin was able to offer so much as it entered the lower-middle price field!

Styling was similar to '32, though the new models had a windshield that was curved at the top edges, and the group of four ventilating doors on each side of the Olympics hood was not framed by a raised panel as before.

The big twelve-cylinder series offered the sedan at $2885, f.o.b.

However, though new features and the introduction of the "Olympic Six" made the Franklin a terrific "buy," only 1180 Franklins were sold between January and November, 1933.

From *Motor* magazine: "The Franklin Airman Six for 1934 has been restyled to resemble the Twelve. The 'radiator' grille is Vee-shaped and slopes sharply. The hood has been lengthened so that it extends completely over the cowl. The windshield is built in and slopes at the same angle as the grille. Front and rear fenders have skirts. As on the Twelve, the doors are wider and carried down (closer) to the running board."

Base price of the "Airman" was $2185 for the five-passenger sedan. A seven-passenger and club sedan were also built. Manually-controlled (ride-control) shock absorbers were included for the third successive year.

The "Olympic" six had a 119-inch wheelbase, semiskirted fenders, and a box-type X-frame, as well as several other mechanical improvements. By now, the manufacturer was in a tight spot, so "Olympic" prices had to be raised slightly, with sedan and coupe priced at $1435, and a convertible coupe (rare) selling for $1550.

The "Twelve" was continued, virtually unchanged from the previous year's model.

Sales figures were so miserable, however, that Franklin did not continue its line of automobiles after 1934. Instead, the Syracuse manufacturer devoted its major efforts to aircraft engines.

Thirteen years later, Franklin again entered the automobile business, in an indirect way . . . . by building the revolutionary, air-cooled "pancake" (horizontally-opposed cylinders) engines for the all new automobiles, designed and promoted by Preston Tucker. Nevertheless, the 1948 Tucker car was not a success, even though it was packed with wonderful features. Preston Tucker was not a shrewd financial manager, and only four dozen of the Tucker cars were built and sold between 1947 and 1949.

GARDNER

Built in St. Louis, between 1919 and 1931, the Gardner was an "assembled" car (built of components from various specialized companies.) The Gardner never sold in great numbers, yet it was an impressive vehicle during its later years on the market.

Starting out after World War I as a light, Chevrolet-sized 4-cylinder car, Gardner's early slogan was, "it speaks for itself." The founder of the company, Russel E. Gardner, announced that during the first year of business, "many thousands" of Gardner cars were sold. Gardner progress was moderately steady throughout the twenties.

By 1930, Gardner was in serious financial trouble, even though a much-advanced model was introduced that year, the daringly different *front-drive* model.

Advertised as, "The only front-wheel drive car in the $2000 field," the special Gardner was rakishly long and low, with a unique, sloping front end, unlike that of any other American car. The French Renault of that era had a sloping front end, but the Gardner differed in that it had a striking new grille bisected down the center. Headlamps were attached without tie-bars, and the visorless windshield section sloped considerably. The wheelbase was 133 inches.

Yet, when lifting the hood of this elegant-looking new model, one was amazed to discover a modest 6-cylinder engine of 80 horsepower, practically lost in all that space beneath the bonnet. The distance between the engine and the radiator was almost as great as the length of the block itself! An awkwardly long water pipe stretched a great distance between the top radiator pan and the *rear* of the engine, and other such peculiar-looking arrangements under-hood gave the entire mechanism a "jerry-built" look.

The belt moulding was unusual in that it curved up over the cowl and did not follow along the sides of the doors. The running boards were of "mahogany-finished" wood, fluted and inlaid with chrome-plated strips. The car had a definite foreign look, despite its Missouri origin. Overall height was only 65 inches!

Inside the front-drive Gardner, the gearshift control extended out from the instrument board. Describing the "power train," *Motor* magazine stated that the clutch, transmission and differential were placed ahead of the engine, and all were bolted together to form a single unit. "A shaft issuing from either side of the differential housing drives each wheel," concluded *Motor's* automotive writer in the January, 1930 issue.

All these cars were equipped for easy installation of a radio with an aerial built into the body.

In addition to the front-drive model, Gardner built one other 6- and two 8-cylinder cars. These conventional models were similar in most respects to their 1929 predecessors.

1931 was Gardner's final year. The front-drive car had failed, most buyers being afraid of anything too different. The sedans of the 70-horsepower "136" 6-cylinder series were priced at $1270, f.o.b. Sedans of the 8-cylinder "148" and "158" series were priced, respectively, at $1790 and $2170. All three models used Lycoming engines, and the eights had 100 and 126 horsepower, the largest engine having a piston displacement of nearly 300 inches.

Wheelbases for the last three models were 122, 125 and 130 inches. Needless to say, the 1931 Gardners are as scarce as the 1930 front-drive models.

GRAHAM

The Graham car of 1930 was the descendant of the old Paige. The three Graham Brothers (Ray A., Robert C. and Joseph C.) had given up their truck-building association with Dodge Brothers in 1927, and had bought into the Paige-Detroit Company, which they promptly reorganized. The new "Graham-Paige" car was introduced in 1928, but early in 1930, the name was shortened to Graham. A few "Paige" taxis and commercial cars were also built that year.

The *early* 1930 models, however, were still known as Graham-Paiges. Appearing late in 1929, they were similar to the models that had preceded them.

Then, early in 1930, the new Graham cars appeared. There was the 66-horsepower Graham "Six," with 207 cubic inch, seven-main-bearing engine and the 100-horsepower straight-eight. Sedan prices were $845 and $1595.

Graham de luxe models came with a four-speed transmission (3.92 to 1 in high gear), and the Graham "Eight," so equipped, was able to reach 80 miles per hour.

The new radiator contour was deeper than before, with curved top and bottom core lines, and came forward in the middle to a slight point. Curved radiators had long been an expensive feature of both Graham-Paige and the earlier Paige cars.

Four-speed models came equipped with thermostatically-controlled radiator shutters, and, on each 1930 Graham, the emblem was carried in the middle of the headlamp tie-bar, instead of on the radiator, as previously.

Fender parking lamps were included, and the four-speed models sported glass visors in chrome-plated brackets. Standard models had inside visors, only.

The 8-cylinder models had four ventilating doors on each side of the hood, while the 6s had vertical louvres set well back toward the cowl in one, long group.

Hydraulic brakes were standard in all models. The eight would reach 60 m.p.h. from a dead stop in 19 seconds. Safety glass was optional, "at lowest additional cost ever placed on such equipment."

Leather upholstery was available in closed models, if desired.

For 1931, all Graham cars had a new, built-in grille connected with the radiator shell. Ventilating doors appeared on the hoods of some sixes, as well as on eights. There were, also, twin vents atop the cowl.

Standard and Special "Sixes" had a wheelbase of 115 inches, and 76 horsepower. The Special "Eight" was a new model, replacing both Standard and Special "Eights" of 1930. The Special "Eight" for 1931 had a 248-cubic-inch engine which developed 85 horsepower; wheelbase was 120 inches. On a 134-inch wheelbase, the big "Custom Eight" had a 100-horsepower engine.

There were new single-bar bumpers, also two headlight tie-bars. The upper one featured an ornamental nameplate in the center which bore the name "GRAHAM," and a stylized picture of the three Graham Brothers.

The "Standard Six" had a three-speed transmission with a 4.3 gear ratio, but all other 1931 Grahams had the four-speed gearbox (synchro-silent) with a 6.11 ratio in third and 4.1 ratio in fourth gear.

Roadsters were available only on the "Standard Six" chassis, and no touring cars or phaetons were offered. Twelve closed models were available (mostly various types of sedans) a rumble-seat coupe and a seven-passenger "Custom Eight" limousine.

Prices for 1931 were reduced from as much as $190 to $400.

Graham's finest year, where styling was concerned, was 1932. The Graham "Eight" was thoroughly remodelled, with considerable streamlining. For the first time on any production car, skirted front fenders were offered. At the rear, a sloping apron hid the gasoline tank and chassis components, as it followed the sweep of the rear fenders. Headlamp shells were painted to harmonize with body color, and dual equipment (twin taillights and windshield wipers) was much of a novelty.

Under the car, a new "banjo-type" frame was used: the side-rails had no "kickup" in front, and at the rear the axle housing was placed in banjo-shaped openings in the side-rails making the rear "kickup" unnecessary. The springs were placed outside the frame instead of under it. This provided a lower center of gravity and a more stable ride.

The "Eight" had 90 horsepower, a 123-inch wheelbase, 4.3 gear ratio, and 17-inch tires with either demountable wood or wire wheels. It was known as the "Blue Streak" model, and though it could be had in various colors, the most typical was blue.

Especially unique was an optional paint job with a special base of *powdered fish scales*. Light blue in color, this special paint cost Graham owners $100 extra. When the sun shone on it, it appeared to be several different colors at once. This remarkable paint was called *Pearlessence of Blue*. Graham also offered a lower-priced coating named *Opalessence of Blue,* but the Pearlessence was superior. A former owner of a '32 Graham relates that he had ordered the $100 paint job and was certainly pleased with the results. "When I would park it along the curb," he writes, "people would crowd around the car, endeavoring to figure out what color it was. It was really luxury in 1932."

Prices of the Graham "Eight," minus extras, ranged from $995 for the business coupe to $1170 for the deluxe convertible coupe. A 70-horsepower Graham "Six" was available, too (sedan priced at only $795), but the "Eight" was the star of the show.

The instrument panel was an arched silver panel, containing three circular gauges including a pointer-type speedometer. The success of the Graham car in 1932 was marred only by the death at age 45 of one of the three Graham Brothers.

For 1933, the conservative instrument panel in the Graham was further simplified. All gauges were enclosed within the 6¼-inch dial that contained the sweep-hand speedometer, and the surrounding panel was finished in imitation walnut grain.

Both sixes and eights shared the semi-streamlined body in 1933, the "Six" having made the switch in mid-1932. A few exterior details were new, such as the V-type split front bumper, and a chrome strip which ran into the lower fender panels from the running board.

The banjo frames on the "Six" and smaller "Eights" had improved cross-members with diagonal "K" bracing at the front and other strengthening members added. The body floor was steel, permitting lighter body sills. Steel brake drums with improved lining were also featured. The weight of the Graham "Six" was cut from 3500 to 3200 pounds, making improved performance possible.

F.O.B. prices of sedans were $795 for the new "Six," and $895 for the Standard "Eight." The "Six" had 85 horsepower; the Standard and Custom "Eights," 95.

Because of a new supercharger, horsepower was increased to 135 at 4000 RPM on the Graham "Custom Eight" for 1934, and the car would do better than 90 miles per hour. Horsepower on the other models remained the same as before. Wheelbase was still 116 inches for the "Six," 123 inches on "Eights." For the second year, standard gear ratio on all Grahams was 4.27 to 1.

Price of the 6-cylinder sedan was trimmed to $745, but the two "Eights" were boosted to $1015 and $1295.

New 16-inch steel artillery wheels were featured, and a new hood ornament made its appearance. Otherwise, the body lines were similar to the original "Blue Streak" which had been so much in favor in 1932.

The interior of the '34 Graham was inviting, with ash trays and storage compartments built into the comfortable rear seat arm rests. The steering wheel and gearshift knob were done in an attractive, new, light color, and the instrument panel contained a long, ribbed aluminum section which concealed storage compartments.

During the course of the 1934 season, the minimum price of the "Six" was cut to $695. But the biggest news for '34 was undoubtedly the "Eight's" new supercharger, with a centrifugal blower placed between the downdraft carburetor and intake manifold.

Graham cars were built until 1941. After World War II, Kaiser-Frazer, having bought up the Graham interests, built new cars which had much in common, mechanically, with prewar Grahams. Moreover, early post-war Frazer cars were described in advertisements as, "a product of Graham-Paige."

HUDSON

Hudson cars were produced from 1909 until 1957. And Hudson, from 1919 to 1933, also produced its low-priced subsidiary car, the "Essex" which was succeeded by the "Terraplane."

Late in 1915, Hudson presented its new "Super Six" models. The Hudson "Super Six" became a popular car, and was continued for many years with few major changes. But for 1930, Hudson made a dramatic change. The "Super Six" (so well thought of in 1929 that the California Highway Patrol had purchased a large fleet of Hudson coupes) was dropped. All 1930 Hudsons were powered by straight-eight engines, and were known as the "Great Eights."

The new engine developed 80 horsepower at 3600 RPM (a faster "turn-over" than most 1930 engines) and the top speed was well over 75; 119 and 126-inch wheelbases were available.

A new model for 1930 was the "Sun Sedan," the convertible two-door sedan with folding front seats (also featured by Essex). It was hoped that this new model would be a great seller, especially in warm climates, but Hudson's greatest sales continued to be among closed models. In fact, Hudson and Essex had popularized closed bodies during the early 1920s, when they were able to cut the prices of their coaches (2-door sedans) to those of open cars.

The 1930 Hudson "Great Eight" had a top pan on the radiator which blended with the vertical shutters, and each side of the hood contained a panel with five ventilating doors.

Weight of the new Hudson sedan was 3316 pounds; lighter than the 1929 model, but considered substantially stronger because of improved construction.

A special creation, the Hudson Club Sedan, with body by Le Baron, had wire wheels, side mounts, covered trunk, sloping windshield, and enclosed rear quarters done in a contrasting, light color. Most of Hudson's custom models, since the middle twenties, had featured bodies by Murphy of Pasadena.

As in the Essex, modernistic design was artfully applied to the Hudson instrument panel and interior fittings, creating a pleasing effect. Both Hudson and Essex won the annual Tour de France in 1930. This was an eight-day endurance event in which cars of all nations competed for "speed, reliability, and economy." Moreover, a Hudson "Great Eight" sedan delivered 25.5 miles per (Imperial) gallon in a 480-mile run through New Zealand, in August, 1930.

Advertisements in 1931 claimed that Hudson and Essex had the highest-compression engines that would operate on standard fuel. These engines had a 5.80 compression ratio; not much by later standards, but higher than average in 1931. Lowest compression, that year, was to be found in the Buick "80" and "90" series (only 4.50, which could be the reason why the Buick engines seemed to last so long.) And highest compression of 1931 was an optional 6.30 on the Chrysler 8, also a durable engine.

The 1931 Hudson developed 87 horsepower at 3600 RPM, and, for the second year, only a 233.7 cubic-inch eight was available. As in 1930, standard tire size was 5.50 x 18.

A new feature of the 1931 Hudson was the attractive mesh grille (or "stone guard") on the radiator, and the double X-type tie bar which connected the headlights and also supported a disc-shaped vibrator horn at the center. Placed low, this tie-bar assembly emphasized the height and massiveness of the radiator.

A graceful, bird-like figure on the radiator cap enhanced the front view of the car.

Bumpers were similar to those on '30 models, except that they no longer carried a third vertical clamp in the center.

On closed models, the rear window was now rectangular, and not curved at the edges as on '30 models.

Although wood wheels were standard on both the 1930 and 1931 Hudsons, wire wheels were available. Strangely, most 1930 advertisements pictured the Hudson with wire wheels, while in 1931 a majority of wooden-wheeled Hudsons were illustrated.

Hudson continued to feature its "wet" cork-faced clutch, a novelty found on Hudson-built vehicles since 1910. Hudson engineers believed that their unusual type of clutch, immersed in a bath of oil, was superior.

Later in 1931, Hudson featured a new accessory, "Startix" (described earlier.) Also, a remodeled "Club Sedan" made its appearance. The new 4-door version had a modernized body, with rear quarter windows, special sloping windshield with no visor and body lines much curvier than before. It also featured doors that were hinged at the center post. For a 1931 model, it looked much more modern than many of the 1932 Hudsons that followed!

An experimental but most attractive model was the special 4-door convertible sedan, with Murphy body. It had wire wheels and sidemounts, long, arching fenders, and special, Wood-lite headlamps (as on "Ruxton" cars.) Also it had a most unique, custom V-shaped radiator shell and grille unlike those on any other Hudsons. Tubular bumpers were also indicative of the "Special."

In mid-1931, selective freewheeling was also available. As of April, Hudson prices ranged from $875 to $1450, f.o.b.

58,545 Hudson and Essex cars were sold in 1931.

Have you ever heard of an eight-wheeled Hudson? It sounds incredible, but, in 1932, Hudson built and sold *six* such cars. These unusual 2-door touring cars were built for shipment to Japan. They had *four wheels on each side* though, under most circumstances, only six wheels touched the ground at one time. The two additional wheels hung suspended below the specially-built fenders, just behind the front wheels; the "idler" wheels were for use on particularly rough terrain. These cars were designed for use in the Manchurian campaign. The eight-wheeled Hudsons were reminiscent of the earlier Reeves "Octa-Autos." Any of these special Hudsons that might have survived those long-ago battles would certainly be of great interest to automobile collectors!

Only 7,777 Hudsons were built in 1932, more attention being given to the lower-priced Essex. In 1932, Hudson featured two new types of closed cars, one with a shallow exterior visor and the other without the visor. Both had sloping windshields and more body curves. Styling was by Frank Spring, the former chief designer for Walter M. Murphy Body Company. A new V-type

HUDSON
IS SHOWING TWO
PRODUCTS OF AN ORGANIZATION UNIQUE

These cars are designed, built and priced to continue Hudson-Essex leadership—a position established over 22 years and confirmed by a million and a half users.

The ability to furnish such values to the public is due to the unique position Hudson-Essex holds in the industry. The men who are now guiding its destinies have been with the company practically since its inception. Its department heads and principal distributors are its controlling owners. For the most part they have devoted their entire business life to Hudson-Essex. They have always built cars of outstanding quality and delivered them to the public at distinct price advantages.

In both cars, beauty includes more than their smart up-to-date bodies and tasteful combinations of color and chromium plate. It is evident in every detail of their interior trimmings, fittings and appointments.

Special attention has been given to comfort and convenience. The starting button is located on the dash. The steering wheel and both front and rear seats are adjustable. Head-room is higher, seats are roomier, doors are wider and leg-room is greater than usual.

Exceptional riding ease is characteristic of Hudson and Essex. Genuine comfort is so important that these cars are especially engineered for easy riding even over cobblestone pavements or rough roads. Motor smoothness eliminates

THE GREATER
HUDSON
EIGHT

GET THE PRICES FROM TODAY'S NEWSPAPERS

radiator grille was an improvement, and new one-piece bumpers were used. Headlights were of a new shape, and were no longer joined by tie bars.

The 1932 Hudsons offered a great deal, including these features:

101 horsepower at 3600 RPM
85–90 miles per hour
55 miles per hour in silent second gear
Intake silencer and air cleaner
Labyrinthian oil cooling (new baffles in oil pan to give a longer, cooler path for circulating oil)
Freewheeling and syncro-mesh transmission
Diagonal truss frame with splayed rear springs
Twin "neutratone" mufflers
"Startix," automatic self-starter and anti-stall
"Ride control" adjustable shock absorbers
Lateral spring seat cushions
Adjustable seats both front and rear
Full-operating windshield (swing-out) with two-finger control
14 new models with new pastel upholstery colors and fittings in ivory and silver finish

Hudson's 1932 instrument panels were simple, with only two, large dials set in a walnut-finished dashboard. The early use of "idiot lights" * should be noted, because the '32 Hudson had only a warning light to indicate lack of oil pressure or generator output.

One very interesting novelty was the zipper fastener on each door pocket inside the car. Zippers were a novelty in the early 1930s, and were known then as, "slide fasteners."

There were three new 8-cylinder series in Hudson's 1932 line; the "Standard" series ($995 to $1095) on a 119-inch wheelbase; the "Sterling" series ($1275 to $1295) on a 126-inch wheelbase; and the big, 132-inch-wheelbase "Major" series which offered a beautiful "Pacemaker Brougham" sedan for only $1495 (and other models ranging from $1445 to $1595.)

Unlike many other cars, which had a freewheeling control on the dash, Hudson's freewheeling was actuated by a button in the middle of the gearshift knob.

---

* Years later, in the 1950s, other automobile manufacturers began to replace gauges with telltale warning lights, this being a simple system but one which left too much to the driver's imagination. Many motorists prefer to know just *how much* oil pressure prevails, etc., and would choose specific gauges rather than vague warning lights. The excuse for the lights is that "nobody looks at the gauges." Fortunately, some manufacturers have heeded our demands and have turned away from "idiot lights."

Hudson began the new, 1933 season with an interesting development, the return of a 6-cylinder model. Though Essex cars had been sixes ever since 1924, the Hudson six had been replaced with an eight from 1930 to 1932. But, for 1933, Hudson offered a choice of 6- or 8-cylinder engines, and, quoting from a catalog:

"Since we discontinued the "Super-Six" in 1929, Hudson owners have written to us. Hudson owners have talked to us. Hudson owners have asked us, again and again, to give them a new "Super-Six.""

The new six had 73 horsepower, and the displacement was 193.1, the same as the 70-horsepower "Essex-Terraplane" engine. However, the old Hudson "Super-Six" engine of 1929 had been much larger, boasting some 288 cubic inches.

The new six, moreover, had only a 113-inch wheelbase, which was the same as that of the larger "Essex-Terraplane" for 1933. So the new Hudson "Six" was little more than an Essex with a new name, though it had pleasingly different lines, with a modified radiator grille, vertical hood louvres, front doors that were hinged at the rear (except on phaetons) and new semi-skirted fenders. Headlights were restyled, having deeper shells than before. Bumpers no longer dipped in the center.

Safety glass and an automatic clutch were available options, and the new dashboard featured two symmetrical panels, the left containing the gauges and warning lights, and the right a glove compartment.

The 8-cylinder Hudsons and Essex-Terraplanes had four ventilating doors on either side of the hood. Interestingly, a vacuum tank was still used for fuel feed on the 1933 Hudson "Eight," although most other cars had long since switched to mechanical fuel pumps.

Inspired by Greek mythology, a winged griffin figure crowned the radiator shells on 1933 Hudson products.

Big changes were featured by Hudson in 1934. As a result, Hudson sales doubled over 1933's output, and a total of 85,835 Hudson-built cars were sold. All 1934 Hudsons were straight-eights, and all 1934 Terraplanes were sixes. This simplified matters considerably, though long-time admirers of the Hudson "Super Six" began to howl again.

The new Hudson looked much larger, with a massive, new, checkerboard grille, new ribbed headlights with twin horns adjacent, and horizontal ventilating doors in the long hood. Flanged fenders with parking lights on top were also new, as was a bumper with a sharp dip in the center. Steel artillery wheels with 6.00 x 16" tires were introduced, and the 116-inch-wheelbase "Eight" had an engine of 108 horsepower with an additional 5 horsepower in 123-inch-wheelbase models.

A *radio* was *standard equipment* in all 1934 Hudson de luxe models, and sedans included a built-in trunk door at the rear, where either the spare tire or a small quantity of baggage could be carried. All Hudsons and Terraplanes had butterfly ventilating wings in the front door windows, a decided improvement over the 1933 models, in which the rear quarter windows slid sideways an inch.

As optional equipment, a hill-hold device was available, which prevented backward rolling on inclines.

An automatic choke was controlled by engine temperature.

Rear windows in 1934 Hudson sedans were broad, and somewhat arched. From the deep, wide grille capped by its new winged mascot to the gently sloping rear deck, the Hudson for 1934 * was a conservatively modern, luxurious motor vehicle. The general body lines were carried on, to some extent, in Hudson's 1935 offerings, which featured only minor styling changes. The next big styling switch came for Hudson and Terraplane in 1936.

* Strangely enough, though Hudson and Nash did not merge to form American Motors until 1954, the designs of both Hudson's and Nash's '34 models were strikingly similar, so much so that one might mistakenly think that the two companies were connected back in the thirties.

HUPMOBILE

Hupmobile's finest and largest 1930 model was the Murray-bodied, 133-horse-power Model H. It was a straight-eight beauty that would reach an honest 90 miles an hour! Describing the car in 1930, an automotive writer declared that its acceleration "gives you a real kick between the shoulder blades!" (Despite this violent promise, many prospective buyers were anxious to learn what the writer had been talking about.)

The Model H had a 4.07 to 1 gear ratio in high, and could easily pass 60 miles an hour in second gear. Its 365.6 cubic inch engine was surpassed in power only by the Duesenberg, Cadillac V-16, and the largest Elcar. The Model H was the first American car to offer an oil cooler. The device was unique in that oil was pumped through a separate left-hand section of the radiator core in order to be cooled. An oil filter was included.

"Steeldraulic" Midland mechanical brakes and 6.50 x 19″ tires were standard, with a choice of wire or disc wheels if the standard wood wheels were not preferred. The "Model H" sedan sold for $1985, which was a bargain for such a car. Unlike most 1930 offerings, the "Model H" had no external visor, and the metal panel above the windshield was somewhat V-shaped.

In addition to the "Model H," there were two new "Century" models; the 100-horsepower, 8-cylinder Model C, and the 70-horsepower, 6-cylinder "Model S." The standard business coupe in the latter series sold for just $995.

Top speeds of the "Century" sixes and eights were, respectively, 70 and 75 m.p.h.

What was new for 1931? Hupmobile featured freewheeling, controlled, as with Hudson, by a button on the gear-shift knob. The following lines were available:

70-horsepower Century Six	$1145, and up
90-horsepower Century Eight	1345, and up
100-horsepower Eight	1695, and up
133-horsepower Eight	2080, and up
133-horsepower Custom Eight	2645, and up

In March, 1931, all Hupmobile prices were reduced, and a standard, wood-wheeled "Century Six" sedan could be had for $995.

On a 7000-mile torture test, a 1931 Hupmobile known as "The White Ghost" was put through its paces to demonstrate the merits of Hupmobile's new freewheeling unit. This enabled the driver to use the clutch pedal 67% less frequently. Along the test route, in St. Louis, Kansas City and New Orleans, public officials rode in, and even drove, the "White Ghost" test car, and lauded its good features. By November, 16,010 1931 Hupmobiles had been sold. But, Hupp had something much more interesting in store for the following season.

"A NEW CAR FOR A NEW AGE." That was the slogan for the 1932 Hupmobile. The "Eight" was completely restyled, and came out far ahead of the competition, in appearance! The grille was slightly "veed," with vertical fins, and there was an attractive new radiator ornament on top, in the form of a stylized, encircled letter "H."

Front fenders were very short, each with a covered spare tire mounted directly behind. The hood was long, and there was a decided slant to the visorless windshield; this line was carried down in the slanting of the front door and cowl moulding.

Inside the new car, the modernistic motif of grouped parallel lines was carried through in the upholstery, window sills, etc. The dash panel was simple but pleasing, with four, circular black gauges in a trapezoid aluminized panel. The only feature which could have been improved upon was the plain, black 3-spoke steering wheel. But, in general, the car had beautiful classic lines, and was only 5½ feet in height.

Hupmobile "Aerodynamic" sedan which is 6 inches wider than the victoria and coupe below

Smoothly curved surfaces distinguish the front view

Aerodynamic Victoria

Coupe

Aerodynamic

Hupmobile

Six and Eight and Low-Priced Six

Pleasing interior view of Aerodynamic sedan

TWO CENTURIES
AHEAD
OF THEIR TIME

•

THE • NEW • CENTURY • SIX

70 HORSEPOWER . . . . 70 MILES AN HOUR

The sweetest Six you've ever driven . . . the greatest Six in Hupmobile history.
Twenty-five per cent more power than its famous Century predecessor. Faster, roomier,
smarter . . . with many new refinements in design, upholstery, and fitments.

Yet priced at $200 less.

THE • NEW • CENTURY • EIGHT

90 HORSEPOWER . . . . 75 MILES AN HOUR

This newest addition to the great Hupmobile line of Eights again reflects Hupmobile's
mastery of eight-cylinder engineering, the product of its six years of pioneering
experience in the eight-cylinder field. More powerful than the previous Century Eight.
Faster, smarter, more luxurious.

Yet priced at $400 less.

•

CENTURY SIX, 70 H. P. . . . . FROM $1145
CENTURY EIGHT, 90 H. P. . . FROM $1345
100 H. P. EIGHT . . . . FROM $1695
133 H. P. EIGHT . . . . FROM $2080
PRICES AT THE FACTORY

Hupmobile
SIXES AND EIGHTS

There were eight 1932 series, from the $795, 6-cylinder "Model 214" to the 133-horsepower, straight-eight "Model 237," reasonably priced at under $2000. The last two digits of the various model numbers indicated the wheelbase (the only exception being the "214" which actually had a 113½-inch measurement.)

Hupmobile's inexpensive sixes did not have the "new look," but bore a general resemblance to the 1931 versions; one exception was the new grilles on *all* models.

Amazingly, there were *seven* different engines to choose from in the 1932 Hupmobile line and, for a depression era, this policy was extravagance to the point of being senseless! It's a wonder that the Hupp Motor Car Corporation could have priced their cars as reasonably as they did and still have survived!

Other features of the 1932 Hupmobile were freewheeling, synchro-shift, silent-second transmission, X-braced frame, underslung springs, hypoid rear axle gears, needle-bearing universal joints on driveshaft, and a disappearing top which folded neatly into a well in the cabriolet roadster.

For the good of the company, Hupmobile offered a narrower selection of models for 1933. There was the 90-horsepower "321" six, and the "322" and "326" eights with 93 and 109 horsepower, respectively. Price range was also contained, with the 6-cylinder sedan going for $995, and the "326" sedan priced at only $1445, f.o.b.

Styling was similar to 1932, with 6-cylinder cars now having the new body. The grille was more pointed at the lower edge, and twin trumpet horns appeared below the headlights. Running boards now had a chrome moulding.

On the eights, a new sidesway eliminator consisted of a spring steel rod mounted to the frame, with the ends linked to the rear axle. This tended to prevent the body from rolling outward in rounding a turn, and also made it possible to use softer rear springs.

New "kingpin oilers" were activated whenever the front wheels were cramped, causing a tiny drop of oil to be squeezed from a wick and delivered to the kingpin.

The 1933 models were known as the "Silver Anniversary Hupmobiles," and the manufacturer reported that, as of December 27, 1932, the Hupp Motor Car Corporation's balance sheet showed, "no bonded indebtedness, no borrowed money, and a 7 to 1 ratio of current assets to liabilities."

Five engines were offered by Hupmobile in 1934, but the most dramatic development was the "Aerodynamic" model, offered with either 6- or 8-cylinder engines. The "Aerodynamic" had broad, skirted fenders, a wide sloping grille, and unique headlights *built into the sides of the hood!* Most remarkable of all was the three-piece "bay-windshield," a panoramic novelty with a broad front panel and two, diagonal side panels. This windshield design was as "far out" as any could be, and was used by no other car. It was an identifying characteristic of the "Aerodynamic" Hupmobile.

The rear quarters were also streamlined, with divided rear window that somehow had a droopy, mournful look. The spare tire cover was built into the sloping trunk.

The "Aerodynamic" was a real departure in auto design, but looked somewhat like a Chrysler "Airflow" with a case of indigestion. Its design was too, *too* radical . . . striking as it may have been. A $795 6-cylinder model, with a conventional body, was available for those who didn't like to see raised eyebrows as they drove by. The low-priced six had pontoon-type fenders, a grille similar to the '32 model, and horizontal louvres on each side of the hood. The windshield resembled that of a '34 Ford, but the rear end of the body bore a resemblance to the design that Plymouth and Dodge were to offer the following year. The radical body-style was used for another year, but '36 models looked more like other cars.

JORDAN

The Jordan Motor Car Company of Cleveland lasted only fifteen years, and its yearly output was less than 5,000 cars. Jordan prospered for a time, especially during the early twenties, because of some wonderfully well-written advertising; refreshingly new and different copy, which called attention to the romantic thrills of driving Jordan cars especially the "Playboy" roadster.*

Later in the 'twenties, Jordan specialized in a new line of small but attractive cars with L-head, straight-8 engines . . . though a Jordan Six was available again in 1928 and 1929. Continental engines were used. By 1929, Jordan was building less than 3000 cars a year.

The 1930 Jordan came in two basic models; the "80" (or T series) with a wheelbase of 120 inches, and the "90" (or G series) with a 125-inch wheelbase. Respective sedan prices were $1495 and $2295, f.o.b. Cleveland, and both models were eights. The "80" had a Continental "17-S" engine which developed 80 horsepower at 3000 RPM, with a very low 4.90 gear ratio. The "90," powered by a Continental "15-S" with a ⅛" larger bore, developed 85 horsepower at 3200. It had a more favorable gear ratio of 4.45 to 1.

The Jordans had Lockheed hydraulic brakes, and the hand-brake con-

*Text of some of the famous Jordan advertisements is included in *Cars of the Early Twenties*.

tracted on the driveshaft. The electrical system was by Auto-Lite; 18-inch wood wheels were standard.

These body models were offered by Jordan during 1930:

8T SERIES ("80")

Sedan	$2095
Coupe (rumble seat)	2095

8G SERIES ("90")

Roadster (rumble seat)	2695
Phaeton	2895
7-passenger Touring	2995
Coupe (rumble seat)	2395
Sedan	2395
Convertible Coupe	2595
Sport Sedan	2695
7-passenger Sedan	2695
Limousine	2795

Until the mid-30s, roadsters and touring cars were usually less expensive than closed models. If one wonders why the Jordan roadsters and touring cars were priced higher than comparable, closed models, it was because Jordan's open cars were special sport models, on the same special 131-inch-wheelbase chassis as the limousine.

For 1931, specifications of the Jordan remained the same as the previous year, though prices were down. The "80" coupe and sedan were priced at $1795. Similar reductions were made in the "90" models. All eleven varieties offered during 1930 were carried into 1931. A retooling at this point was a financial impossibility. No Jordan cars were offered for 1932.

Though the Jordan Motor Car Company went by the boards, founder Ned Jordan worked as an advertising consultant after the Depression. He had not lost his great way with words, and from 1950 until his death in 1958, Jordan was a writer, with a weekly column in one of the automotive trade journals.

KISSEL

In Hartford, Wisconsin, the Kissel Motor Car Company entered its twenty-third year in 1930, in poor financial condition. Sales had declined in recent years though, during the early twenties, Kissel had been famous for its "Gold Bug" speedsters and other racy models. Kissel had a few automotive "firsts" to its credit, and in 1930 the company advertised a list of features it had originated:

Brougham type body (since 1913)
Low chassis with double drop frame (since 1913)
Bumpers an integral part of frame (since 1924)
Thermostatic control (since 1924)
Lynite pistons and rods (since 1924)
Cushioned-in-rubber chassis (since 1926)

In addition, there were other Kissel "innovations":

Fully stabilized chassis (since 1925)
Form-fitting seats (since 1917)
Wide doors (since 1917)
"All year" body (since 1915)

The 1930 Kissel was available in various sizes, including the 117-inch-wheelbase Model "73," with 6-cylinder, 70 horsepower engine. Also produced that year was the straight-eight version, in the Model "95" and "126" series, the model numbers indicating the horsepower. The "White Eagle" eights, as they were called, were built on wheelbases of 125, 132 or 139 inches.

Sedan prices ranged from $1695 to $3185 on the three different models.

Other Kissel products were National-Kissel funeral cars and Bradfield taxi cabs.

Kissel built the "73," "95" and "126" models again for 1931, though each was lightened by a few pounds.

Kissel was never a volume producer, and its vehicles were virtually hand-built. In fact, the Kissel was once advertised as "the custom-built car." Though 1925 had been a typically "good" Kissel year, during that time only 2881 cars and 62 commercial vehicles were assembled. No wonder, then, that later models are particularly difficult to find, even in museums!

Kissel discontinued its automobiles in 1931, reorganized as Kissel Industries, and built outboard motors.

LAFAYETTE

In 1923, Nash Motors acquired the trade name and the assets of the La Fayette Motors Corporation of Indianapolis, a builder of large, expensive V-8 cars in the early 1920s. In 1924, Nash dropped La Fayette.

Nash thereafter made no use of the exclusive name (for ten years) until they decided to introduce a new lower-priced companion car to compete with Hudson's Terraplane, and other popularly-priced makes. For their new 1934 offering, Nash chose the name Lafayette, a slight alteration of the name they had purchased.

The all-new Lafayette of 1934 had a 113-inch wheelbase and a 6-cylinder, L-head engine of 75 horsepower. Prices of the six body types were as follows:

Standard 2-door Sedan	$595
Standard 4-door Sedan	645
Special 6-window Sedan	695
Special Touring Sedan with trunk	685
Special 2-passenger Coupe	635
Special rumble-seat Coupe	675

Individually-sprung front wheels were available if desired, at no extra cost, on special models.

The 1934 Lafayette was advertised as the *"Jeweled-Movement"* car, in order to point out the quality-construction throughout. Like the Nash, it had a Seaman-built body, with pleasing, unobtrusive lines. The car was less than 16 feet long, a convenient size for the many one-car garages existing then.

Special features included "synchronized springing," X-dual frame, and "draftless clear vision" ventilating windwings.

The 1934 Lafayette had horizontal ventilating doors on the hood which were replaced in 1935 by three long, horizontal louvres. Later in the thirties, the Lafayette ceased to exist as a separate make, and became the lowest-priced Nash. The name was dropped entirely from the Nash line in 1939.

LA SALLE

The La Salle was introduced by General Motors in 1927, as their Cadillac car running mate. Priced below the Cadillac, La Salle was designed originally as a sporty car for those who wanted something "different" just below the Cadillac cost range. The 1927 La Salle was an early effort of General Motors' stylist, Harley Earl, and it had a lot of distinction. By 1929, both La Salle and Cadillac had become quite similar, both in design and in mechanical components.

In 1930, the Cadillac Motor Car Company division of General Motors advertised:

"There is no let-down in La Salle from Cadillac standards– – –instead, a steady measuring up to the highest of manufacturing and decorative ideals. You are not penalized by a 'saving' here and a skimping there, because La Salle is very moderately priced. On the contrary, you are profited and benefited by the fact that Cadillac and La Salle with their two great high grade markets utilize *all* of the resources of the vast plants which they jointly occupy." The advertisement further indicated that La Salle (by 1930) had proven itself "worthy of its Cadillac birthright."

La Salle's selling points in 1930 included the V-8 engine of 90 horsepower, "harmonized steering" (with patented modulator to eliminate wheel shimmy) and a syncro-mesh transmission. Shatterproof glass was included all around.

The 1930 La Salle engine had ⅛" less bore and 5 horsepower less than the nearly identical Cadillac power plant, but there was a considerable difference in price. The 1930 La Salle sedan sold for $2565., f.o.b., some $1130 less than the corresponding Cadillac.

Prices were lower in 1931, with buyers' choice of La Salle hardtop or convertible coupes at $2195 (f.o.b., Detroit) and the sedan, at $2205. For those who preferred luxurious models with Fleetwood bodies, there were La Salles available for as much as $3245. But most of the La Salles that sold well were the lower-priced models with body by Fisher.

During 1931, horsepower was boosted to 95, as the La Salle engine was bored out that extra eighth of an inch to match the Cadillac engine. And, later in the model year, the La Salle sported the chromed "stone guard" in front of the radiator as well as the door-type hood vents seen on Cadillac.

An obvious classic was the La Salle phaeton advertised in *The Spur* for April 15, 1931, and in *Cosmopolitan* magazine for the following month. It was a turquoise color, with darker blue-green fenders and trim and a touch of vermillion striping here and there. A khaki top was typical of the period.

Surprisingly, despite its lower price and boost in power, La Salle fell behind Cadillac in sales for 1931. During 1930, La Salle had been in twenty-second place, and in '31 it sank to twenty-third. On the other hand, Cadillac had risen from twenty-third to twentieth place. In ten months (of 1931), Cadillac produced 9924 cars to La Salle's 6246. It appeared that people of means who could afford a Cadillac would rather *pay* a few hundred dollars more and get the Cadillac *name*.

Improvements in 1932, in addition to new styling included an automatic vacuum clutch with freewheeling, silent helical gears in the transmission, and "ride control" 2-way hydraulic shock absorbers that were adjustable from the driver's seat.

Horsepower was increased to 115 by redesigning the intake manifold, with short passages of equal length to all cylinders. A combined air cleaner and silencer did away with the old-fashioned "hiss" of the carburetor intake. A new muffler with "straight through" passage also helped to increase power by reducing back-pressure, and muffler brackets were insulated from the frame by rubber.

In 1932, both La Salle and Cadillac switched to a diaphram-type AC fuel pump; and a Cuno self-cleaning oil filter was featured.

Wire wheels with 7.00 x 17" tires were standard. The new 1932 bodies (as on all other General Motors products) were gracefully curved, and had large window areas and a sloping windshield with a curved area above where the sun visor formerly was located.

Again, in 1932, La Salle was behind Cadillac in sales. Only 3456 cars were sold by November.

The sum of $2245 could purchase a new La Salle sedan in the spring of 1933. The latest models were adorned with a new V-shaped grille, skirted fenders, and horizontal ventilating doors on the hood.

"No-draft" butterfly window wings were built in, a feature of all General Motors cars for 1933. Wheelbase was 130 or 136 inches and, despite a comparatively low 4.60 gear ratio, the La Salle moved along well on the highway. The 1933 model was really a great-looking car, but greater changes were to come the following year.

The new La Salle bore little resemblance, either in appearance or in mechanical specifications, to its predecessor. The 1934 model featured a brand-new engine, a straight-eight of 90 horsepower. Cadillac continued to use the 353 cubic inch V-8 engine, but the engine found in the new La Salle was the same 240.3 cubic inch variety as used in the Oldsmobile straight-eight. This engine change made possible a dramatic price reduction; suddenly the La Salle sedan was only $1595! Despite the drastic cut in price, the 1934 La Salles now featured hydraulic brakes.

Even more dramatic than the engine change, new brakes or the price cut, was the advanced styling of the 1934 La Salle. The new body, by Fleetwood, was completely streamlined, with a graceful slope to both front and rear quarters. The grille was high and very narrow, and was followed by an unusually long hood which had five bubble-shaped vents on either side. Long pontoon fenders and 16-inch disc wheels added to the ultra-modern effect, as did the new bumpers which were made of two horizontal, back-swept blades. Other niceties consisted of bullet-shaped headlights attached to the sides of the hood, and chrome chevrons on each front fender. Though the low windshield was of the one-piece type, rear windows on closed cars were divided down the middle.

Individual front wheel suspension was another 1934 feature, and the La Salle, though having only a 119-inch wheelbase, had a wonderful ride to it. On a rough road, the luxurious car handled like a speedboat rollicking over gentle waves.

The 1934 La Salle was such a beautiful machine that its styling (except for minor details) was hardly changed in 1935. For example, the 1935 model was the first La Salle to have an all-steel top and a V-windshield.

La Salle used the straight-eight engine in all models from 1934 to 1936, inclusive. In 1937, La Salle returned to a smaller-bore version of the Cadillac V-8 engine. The last of the La Salles was the 1940 model, as Cadillac finally decided not to retain any models that used a different name.

It is a truth, almost without exception, that those who visit the Cadillac plants prefer Cadillac and La Salle forever after. To see these magnificent cars in the process of creation—to watch, with one's own eyes, Cadillac craftsmen at their work—is to have an enduring conviction that no higher standards could be enforced. And such, indeed, is Cadillac's oldest tradition—to build as finely as it is possible to build

CADILLAC MOTOR CAR COMPANY, DETROIT, MICHIGAN, *Division of General Motors*

Built by Cadillac, in the finest Cadillac traditions—
the new La Salle is the first car of its type to be made
available in the medium-price field. Entirely aside
from its Cadillac-born quality and prestige, it represents unusual value—for it serves so well and so
dependably that owners drive it far longer than the
average automobile

$2195 to $3245, f. o. b. Detroit

*The liberal G. M. A. C. payment plan is available
to purchasers of La Salle*

L A S A L L E

When engineers are engaged in perfecting the design of Cadillac or LaSalle, they are never hampered by any restrictions as to cost. Quality is their only concern. Whatever improvements result from their labors, Cadillac incorporates in its distinguished family—and then depends upon the science of Cadillac manufacture to bring the cost within the necessary limits. The value of this policy is strikingly exemplified in the new LaSalle V-8—one of the world's truly fine automobiles, yet priced for the family of moderate income.

L A S A L L E   V - 8

Enriched and refined throughout, and benefiting from the advancements in comfort and performance developed in creating the Cadillac V-12 and V-16 — the LaSalle V-8 is, more than ever, a companion car to Cadillac. Yet it is offered at prices ranging from $2195, f. o. b. Detroit — with the G. M. A. C. Payment Plan available to all purchasers. Coachwork by Fisher and Fleetwood.

CADILLAC MOTOR CAR COMPANY   DIVISION OF GENERAL MOTORS

The silent, smooth performance of La Salle V-8 is admirably reflected in the long, flowing lines of the Convertible Coupe, with body by Fisher, illustrated below. La Salle V-8 prices range from $2195, f. o. b. Detroit. G. M. A. C. terms available on all body styles

So completely is the ideal of fine workmanship ingrained at the Cadillac plant that, no matter whether it be for Cadillac or for La Salle, every detail of design and manufacture is approached with the same meticulous care.

There is only *one* standard of excellence, regardless of the task to be done. As a result, the La Salle V-8 provides a degree of quality and a type of performance far beyond those suggested by its moderate price.

LA SALLE V-8

The Seven-Passenger Sedan, list price $2495, f. o. b. Detroit — 5 wire wheels standard — G. M. A. C. terms available

DON'T HOPE TO EXPERIENCE IT ELSEWHERE
..it is found in La Salle alone!

It would be difficult to imagine a more completely satisfied group of motorists than those who drive La Salles. From the date of its introduction six years ago, La Salle has enjoyed an owner loyalty and an owner enthusiasm unusual among motor cars. Today, it is the rare exception to find a La Salle owner who is other than a staunch and enthusiastic advocate of his car. . . . Some explanation of this is found in the fact that La Salle is a highly individual creation—with qualities and characteristics that are quite peculiarly its own. In its staunchness and sturdiness, its roadability and balance, it reveals its heritage from Cadillac. And so in its quietness of operation and its general mechanical trustworthiness. Yet it has a sprightliness of manner that belongs to no other car on the road; and there is simply no duplication anywhere of the youthful eagerness with which it obeys its driver's inclination. . . . This peculiar combination of staunchness and verve is most intriguing. In fact, once you have experienced it thoroughly, it is practically impossible to find a satisfactory substitute. . . . This extraordinary car is now priced most reasonably for what it provides. The Standard 5-passenger Sedan, for instance, lists at $2245, f. o. b. Detroit.

La Salle V·8

A GENERAL MOTORS VALUE

LINCOLN

During the latter part of 1920, Lincoln cars appeared on the market. They were first produced by a famed engineer, Henry Leland, who was one of the guiding lights behind the early Cadillacs.

The first Lincoln was a large, powerful car with V-8 engine, and, when Mr. Leland was given a ride in a road test and told the throttle was wide open, he was surprised to find that the car was traveling a smooth 70-plus when he thought it was doing a mere 40 miles an hour.

Within two years, Lincoln was sold to the Ford Motor Company. After a few minor squabbles with an equally headstrong Henry Ford, Henry Leland (over 80 years of age) decided to resign from the company. Despite Leland's fears that the Lincoln car would be cheapened, its high quality was maintained and, in fact, improved. (All Lincoln cars had V-8 engines until 1932, when a new V-12 was added to the line.)

Lincoln horsepower for 1930 was increased to 90, and stately, indeed, was the "Two-window Town Sedan," a close-couped model with a fine Willoughby body. Many models (both closed and open), were available, featuring handcrafted bodies by many other custom coachmakers such as Le Baron, Locke, Brunn, Dietrich, Derham and Judkins. A 136-inch wheelbase was the minimum standard.

Despite the variety of models available, Lincoln was not a quantity pro-

The LINCOLN

A WORD, a gesture, the inflection of a lovely voice are scarcely more revealing than some material possessions. A Lincoln, glimpsed across an Autumn terrace or drawn up at the door of a couturière's, can confirm unmistakably an impression of elegance. This, truly, is a patrician vehicle. . . . A swift, powerful car, which wears an authentic beauty, the Lincoln is so singularly well-made that it will function smoothly and loyally for years—as nearly perfect a motor car as humans can build. And it is a thoroughly safe car; under the most trying road conditions, or up incredible hills at an incredible pace, you ride in comfort and security. The new Lincoln V-12 cylinder engine, developing 150 horsepower, is declared the finest that Lincoln engineers have yet designed. In two wheelbases—standard and custom-built body types.

ducer. Only 3967 units were sold between January and November of 1930 and, for the second year, the Lincoln was in twenty-ninth place in sales. Small wonder, however, in consideration of the price. The "cheapest" sedan sold for $4500 at the factory, and most of the various custom-bodied models were priced considerably higher.

Contrary to the Depression trend, the price of the 1931 Lincoln was *raised,* with the lowest-priced sedan at $4600, f.o.b. Horsepower was boosted to 120 at 2900 RPM, and standard wheelbase was lengthened to 145 inches. Free-wheeling was added, and it was possible to shift back and forth between second and high gears without pressing the clutch pedal. Top speed was 85.

Custom models continued to be produced, one of the most interesting being a predecessor to the recent four-door hardtops. This was a Derham-bodied creation with a fixed, fabric-covered roof and center posts between side windows that could be folded down for an "open car" effect.

Another interesting car was the Le Baron custom limousine, with a long hood that extended back over the cowl (as on several 1932 and 1933 cars.) This limousine also had a commodious, streamlined trunk and metal-covered spare tire at the rear. One such car was ordered by the famed cartoonist, Rube Goldberg. Since Mr. Goldberg has long been known for his wacky, complicated cartoon "inventions," one would naturally have expected him to order a less conservative automobile. Nevertheless, it was Rube Goldberg's new Lincoln that inspired Walter P. Chrysler to lengthen the hoods over the cowls of his Chrysler Custom Imperials of the following year.

For 1932, Lincoln developed a new V-12 model, as a companion to the V-8. Price of the V-8 two-window town sedan was reduced to $3100, while the same model with the new 150-horsepower, 12-cylinder engine sold for $4500.

The new Lincolns flaunted restyled bodies that sat very low over the chassis. A new, slightly "Veed" grille replaced the old radiator and vertical shutters. There were five ventilating doors on each side of the hood, followed by an additional vent door on each side of the cowl, a well as (on some models) atop the cowl. For 1932, parking lights were moved from the cowl band and placed on the front fenders.

Wire wheels (7.50 x 18″) were standard. As noticed in 1931, the Lincoln again bore a family resemblance to its little brother, the Ford.

In mid-season, Lincoln V-8 cars could be had for as little as $2900 and the V-8 engine had been somewhat altered, in order to cut production costs in a difficult year.

But the "V-12" was the star of Lincoln's 1932 show. When the new 12-cylinder series was introduced, Lincoln advertising described the engine as being "cast in two blocks of six and set at a V angle of 65 degrees to give out-of-step firing and insure smooth operation." Bore was 3¼″ and stroke 4½″, and there was dual downdraft carburetion with special intake silencer and air cleaner. The exhaust pipe was carried forward and below the engine to keep heat as far as possible from the passenger compartment.

Brakes were mechanical, with a vacuum booster. Both the radiator shutters and the hood vents were thermostatically controlled.

And variety? Twenty-three body types were available in the "V-12" series alone!

For 1933, a new grille with both vertical and horizontal members was added, and vertical hood louvres appeared again (as in '31.) Though bodies were not markedly changed, fenders were semi-skirted in the latest fashion.

Two, basic "V-12" types were available: the 136-inch-wheelbase model, priced at $2700 and up, and the 145-inch-wheelbase Lincoln which ranged as high as $7000 and more, according to what extras the buyer ordered.

The V-8 Lincoln was eliminated during 1933.

For the 1934 model year, Lincoln offered only the 150-horsepower "V-12" models. A V-8 Lincoln was not to be offered again until the spring of 1948 when the 1949 Lincolns appeared, and the Lincoln "V-12" was dropped.

The most notable exterior difference between 1933 and 1934 Lincolns was that the 1934 models returned once again to vent doors in the hood. Prices were up slightly, though they seem reasonable for a multi-cylinder car. The f.o.b. range began at $3200.

An improved ventilating system was applied to all doors and quarter windows. Like those on the Ford, the 1934 Lincoln windows would slide back an inch if the cranks were turned further after they were fully raised. And, on the "145" models, there was a combination roof-vent-and-dome-light.

Aluminum cylinder heads with polished combustion chambers made their appearance, in addition to aluminum alloy pistons with surfaces that were oxidized for hardness and oil adherence. An oil temperature regulator exchanged heat between cooling water and oil; coolant capacity was increased 15%. A single plate clutch was used which required less pedal pressure. Another 1934 feature was the improved two-shoe servo brakes with vacuum boosters. At the higher speeds of 1934, many manufacturers were learning that ordinary mechanical brakes were not sufficient.

The massive "Model K" was continued, with ultra-conservative styling, until 1940. Though admirable automobiles, these truck-like dreamboats looked more at home in Grosse Point or Newport than in Hollywood or Miami. Nevertheless, show personalities such as Fred Waring and W. C. Fields admired them enough to purchase convertible models in 1934 and 1935.

THE TWO-WINDOW TOWN SEDAN

The **LINCOLN**

START out early in the morning, drive five hundred miles, and arrive at your destination so refreshed and relaxed that, if you desire, you can play golf before sundown. . . . Seasoned travelers know best how comfortable and secure the Lincoln is. This car has the power to speed up and across the Great Smokies, without a suggestion of labor from the V-12, 150-horsepower engine. Around hairpin curves, the rear of the Lincoln cleaves to the road. You need not shift gears on the downgrade. Narrow and rocky stretches, full of ruts, pass smoothly and almost unnoticed. Long springs, and shock-absorbers automatically adjustable to road conditions cushion each potential blow. Your grip on the steering wheel is light. Deeply upholstered seats enable you to relax completely. . . . Clear-vision ventilation system. New single-plate clutch. Improved brakes. Faster acceleration, so that you go from 20 to 50 miles an hour, upgrade, apparently without pressing the foot throttle. Two wheelbases—standard and custom-built body types. From $3200, at Detroit.

BRUNN BROUGHAM

The *LINCOLN*

BUILDERS of the Lincoln never compromise with quality. At all times, irrespective of price trends, cost of materials and manufacture, the Lincoln is built to the highest standards of mechanical excellence. . . . The Lincoln factory is a model of efficiency. Skilled craftsmen work unhurriedly. Rigid tests control each step of manufacture within precision limits almost unbelievably minute. . . . The Lincoln of today provides the unsurpassed power and smoothness of the 150-horsepower, V-12 cylinder Lincoln engine. It offers new features of safety, new ease of handling, greater economy of operation, and important refinements of body design and finish that bring to owners a new appreciation of motoring comforts. . . . The Lincoln is today available in two wheelbase lengths, in standard and custom body types, at prices that range from $3200 at Detroit.

LeBARON CONVERTIBLE ROADSTER

The **LINCOLN**

A LINCOLN OWNER in California has driven his car well over 150,000 miles, chiefly over mountain and desert. A 1925 Lincoln has traveled 200,000 miles. . . . These are not solitary examples of the Lincoln's endurance. Staunchness, dependability evoke the loyalty of owners everywhere, even though they may never put their cars to supreme tests. . . . From the laying of the frame to the tailoring of upholstery, the Lincoln is soundly and beautifully constructed. And this, so true of Lincolns in the past, is even more characteristic of today's Lincoln. The new V-12 cylinder engine, developing 150 horsepower, Lincoln engineers deem unsurpassed by any they have thus far designed. Airplane-type bearings, here first used in motor car engines, will withstand excessive temperatures as high as 750 degrees. Other achievements include an improved cooling system, aluminum cylinder heads, and a single-plate clutch, which at a touch fairly animates the car. Two wheelbases—standard and custom-built body types. From $3200, at Detroit

DIETRICH CONVERTIBLE SEDAN

he **LINCOLN**

HOWEVER MUCH events of the past few years may have restrained the purchase of fine things, desire for them has been constant. People who, momentarily, feared that they could not afford the best are discovering now that its possession can give confidence, can build morale. The rewards of owning and driving a Lincoln are real. . . . The new Lincoln is not a fine engine—alone; or a luxurious body—alone; or any other single excellence, but a fusion of them all. Yet certain individual attainments in design and engineering deserve special consideration. The V-12 cylinder engine, 150 horsepower, Lincoln engineers judge superior to any they have thus far designed. Its aluminum cylinder heads result in faster acceleration, more nearly perfect fuel consumption. The new clear-vision ventilation system maintains desired conditions, without drafts. Two wheelbases—standard and custom-built body types. From $3200, at Detroit.

Now You can Own a Lincoln

MANY have long thought of the Lincoln as the finest car they could buy. Perhaps you are one of these. You may now own a Lincoln for a price as low as $2900 at Detroit.

Very likely you already know something about the way all Lincolns are built. They are made unhurriedly with the most minute attention to detail. Advanced engineering, precision manufacture to a fraction of a hair's breadth, scrupulous testing of all materials and parts — such methods produce every finished Lincoln motor car as nearly perfect as it can be made.

This is Lincoln's single aim. And, as always in the past, living up to it is made possible by the support of the entire F organization. The 8 cylinder Lincoln is built to exactly the sa high standards of mechanical excellence as the 12 cylinder I coln. With a wheelbase of 136 inches, its beauty is typica Lincoln. Its engine is the V-type which has built Lincoln's p ent reputation for smooth, powerful performance.

The 8 cylinder Lincoln today is bringing the joys and sa faction of Lincoln motoring to more people than ever befo

THE **LINCOLN**

THE LINCOLN EIGHT, FULLY EQUIPPED, IS PRICED FROM $2900 AT DETRO

THE LINCOLN
12

Lincoln has always aimed to make available to the public a motor car as nearly perfect as it is possible to produce. . . . In this age of mechanical progress, a natural evolution of this policy is the Lincoln V-12. . . . Its background is the traditional Lincoln background . . . expert engineering, painstaking testing, unhurried man-ufacture, world-famous precision methods, and in every activity, the support of the entire Ford organization. Prices of the Lincoln V-12 range from $4300 at Detroit.

Engine of 12 cylinders cast in two blocks of six and set at a V angle of 65 degrees to give out-of-step firing and insure smooth operation. Three-point suspension on rubber. Brake horse-power, 150. Bore and stroke—3¼ x 4½. Dual down-draft carburetor with special intake silencer and air cleaner. Exhaust pipe carried forward of and below engine to keep heat from front compart-ment. Silent camshaft drive chain with automatic adjustment requiring no attention. Soft-acting double-disc clutch. Free-wheel-ing unit controlled from dash operative in all forward speeds.

Transmission equipped with a special synchronizing unit to facilitate gear shifting. Helical second-speed gears insure quiet operation. Wheelbase, 145 inches. Tread, 60 inches. Brakes equipped with vacuum booster to augment foot pedal pressure. Thermostatically controlled radiator shutters and hood venti-lators. Springs semi-elliptic—rear, 62 inches; front, 42 inches. Welded steel-spoke, one-piece demountable wheels, diameter, 18 inches, with 7½-inch tires. Steering of worm and roller type. Twenty-three custom and standard body types are offered.

MARMON

With its origin in the early 1900s, the Marmon was one of the few remaining Indiana-built makes available nearly thirty years later. It was built by the Marmon Motor Car Company of Indianapolis.

Much of Marmon's 1930 magazine advertising was unique in color and style: it had a startling "neon-lit" appearance. The cars and figures were illustrated in black, and all fine details were outlined in red, orange, yellow, blue or green.

For four years Marmon had built nothing but straight-eights, so the 1930 line consisted of three such Marmon models and one lower-cost Marmon-Roosevelt eight.

The 1930 Marmons were larger, longer and roomier than their predecessors. The new Model "8-79" was a full ten inches longer than the 1929 "78" it had replaced.

The radiator shutters on "8-69" and "8-79" models, as well as on the "Big Eight," were new for 1930. The three models had, respectively, 84, 107, and 125 horsepower, though in mid-season the "Big Eight" appeared with 145 horsepower, making it one of the mightiest machines of the year.

Marmon featured the double dome high compression combustion chamber (5.5 to 1) on the three straight-eights. Marmons and Roosevelts had long,

MARMON
SIXTEEN

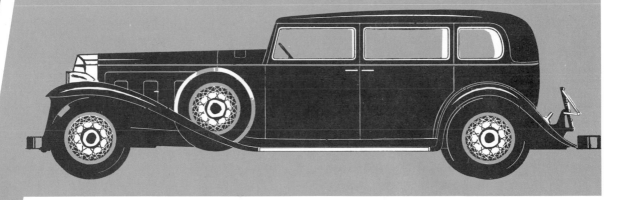

IN DESIGN AND ENGINEERING, THE WORLD'S MOST ADVANCED MOTOR CAR

The Marmon Sixteen looks like no other car. It borrows little from the past. It will lend much to the future. It is the one example of unhampered co-ordination of effort by artist and engineer. Its 200-horsepower, all-aluminum engine is viewed by the technical world as an accomplishment of prime importance by Howard C. Marmon. A mere sight of it promises more than any other car has ever promised. Now on display in leading cities. Prices under $5000. Marmon Motor Car Company.

horizontal hood louvres, though the "Big Eight" had four ventilating doors on each side. The front body pillars tilted forward above the windshields, but none of the 1930 Marmon products had an outside sun visor.

As a styling note, all four-door sedans had a single reveal moulding extending around all side windows.

Marmon displayed new models for 1931. There was the "88," with 125-horsepower engine and either 130 or 136-inch wheelbase. A lower-priced Model "70," a light eight in the $1000 field, replaced the 1929 and 1930 Roosevelt cars. But Marmon's greatest news for 1931 was the introduction of the 200-horsepower, 16-cylinder model, a mighty classic engineered by Howard C. Marmon and designed by Walter Dorwin Teague. This huge car, on a 145-inch wheelbase, spelled out high class and power from the horizontal shutters of its V-shaped radiator to the elegant trunk sloping down at the rear (on some models). The Marmon V-16 was priced under $5000, and its advertisements truly stated that it "looks and performs like no other car." The modern, sweep-hand speedometer registered up to 120 miles per hour, and all gauges were mounted high in the center of the dash for easy visibility.

The Marmon Sixteen had an engine built mostly of aluminum alloy, and had a high (3.69 to 1) gear ratio. Therefore, any of the 850 V-16 Marmons built would exceed 100 miles per hour with ease. One stock model was clocked at 111, and another, a roadster, was reported to have attained 130 miles per hour in a Florida run! Even the fabulous Duesenberg couldn't top that.

The 2½-ton Marmon Sixteen had a piston displacement of 490.8 cubic inches, more than that of the Duesenberg, but one must remember that the Marmon had twice as many cylinders. The compression ratio was a high 6 to 1, that year.

Needless to say, 16-cylinder cars were shameless gas consumers; the big Marmon had a 29-gallon fuel tank!

The Marmon Sixteen was continued, with few changes, for 1932. Minor refinements appeared, such as chrome-plated radiator shutters and a radiator ornament, parking lights on front fenders, leather-edged upholstery, improved arm rests with built-in ashtrays and vanity cases, and a new assist cord that slid along a bar above the quarter window.

The new Marmon Eight was restyled to bear a closer resemblance to the Sixteen (though the Eight had a different grille), also trumpet horns in front. The speedometer registered engine RPM also, and a pleasing new instrument panel featured five gauges set in a section directly in front of the driver, with a symmetrical glove compartment at the right. The recessed center section of the dash contained the ignition lock and various controls.

Model 8-125 had 125 horsepower and a 125-inch wheelbase. Gear ratio was 4.08 to 1, tire size was 6.00 x 18″, and body-types consisted of a 5-passenger sedan at $1375, a rumble-seat coupe, and convertible coupe with rumble-seat and "disappearing top." De luxe models had six wire wheels, and standard Marmons had only one spare, at rear. Choice of upholstery was whipcord or mohair edged with leather. The horn button could be pulled out for starting the car, and turned to control the lights.

Weight of the five-passenger 8-125 sedan was 3500 pounds. The Marmon Sixteen sedan weighed 5300, so at a price of $5700, f.o.b., it sold for slightly above a dollar a pound. A classic automobile for less than the present pound-price of ordinary meat!

For 1933, only the 16-cylinder Marmon was offered. Prices on this model had been cut as much as $925, and the Sixteen was now available for $4825 and up.

Early in 1933, Marmon completed an experimental two-door sedan (designed by Teague) that was powered by a new V-12 engine. This engine was created simply by cutting four cylinders from the V-16, and the unusual car featured a remarkable 8½-inch "tubular backbone" (instead of a conventional chassis frame), also, de Dion suspension at the rear with multiple transverse springs and inboard brakes. Remarkable, too, was the styling of the car, which had pontoon fenders with built-in headlights similar to Pierce-Arrow's. The 1933 body was as streamlined at the rear as any 1936 model, though the rectangular and rather stark-looking windshield left something to be desired. Unfortunately, the over-all design of the car was not unified; it looked like the hybrid custom job it was, and the Marmon V-12 was never put into regular production.

Only the V-16 remained, and it continued, unchanged, into 1934, during which year Marmon left the automobile business to build such vehicles as Marmon-Herrington electric busses.

M A R M O N

Always one of the great creators of motor car fashions and engineering advances, Marmon

for 1930 cites these great factors as its most important contributions: All Marmons are

Straight-Eights, each with an even greater abundance of power ✦ ✦ ✦ All Marmons are

extra spacious and luxur ious inside ✦ ✦ ✦ All Marmons reflect fully the

Marmon tradition of smart ness and good taste ✦ ✦ ✦ This time-honored

motor car is now avail able to practically all families ✦ ✦ ✦ Four great

Straight-Eights in four

great price fields: The Big Eight; the "Eight-79";

the "Eight-69"; and the Marmon-Roosevelt. (illustrated—the Marmon Big Eight.)

MARQUETTE

Available in six body styles—2-door sedan, 4-door sedan, business coupe, rumble seat coupe, roadster, touring car—the 1930 Marquette was a brand-new make introduced by General Motors on June 1, 1929. The Marquette was produced and sold by General Motors Buick Division, at first for $990 and up. The price was later reduced to a range of $965 to $1035. The Marquette was a light six, and its L-head engine had a piston displacement of 212.8 cubic inches.

The Marquette developed 67½ horsepower at 3000 RPM, and had a 114-inch wheelbase. Gear ratio was 4.54 to 1. Tire size was 5.25 x 18″. The Marquette was conceived to compete with Chrysler's popular new De Soto. Hood louvres were vertical, in one long group. Headlights were solidly attached, being mounted to the tie bar as well as to vertical stanchions. Parking lights were mounted on the cowl band.

Despite its resemblance to the De Soto, the Marquette was actually more in keeping with General Motors' own 1930 Oldsmobile in general specifications, as well as in body design and price. Marquette's engine had a smaller bore and longer stroke than the Oldsmobile L-head six.

The Marquette had mechanical brakes with 12-inch drums, and a positive-feed fuel pump. Upholstery was "waterproof and dustproof," and the front seat was adjustable by turning a handle which actuated a long, regulating screw underneath. The Marquette was one of the first cars to appear with General Motors' new windshield tilted 7 degrees to prevent night glare.

The little car would go from 10 to 60 miles an hour in 31 seconds, and reach a top speed of 68 to 70. It was well-built for its size, and most Marquettes lasted for many years. Strangely, since the Marquette was "built by Buick", it did not have overhead valves like its parent car.

Though it was obviously good, it was too similar to the Oldsmobile and the Marquette was not continued after the 1930 season. Oldsmobile dealers were more than a bit miffed that the Buick dealers in their localities were allowed to offer a car so similar to their own. However, Oldsmobile offered its own companion car also, in 1929 and 1930; that car was called the "Viking".

NASH

Nash cars for 1930 were known as the "400" series, and were available in three basic models.

The "Single-Six," had a 6-cylinder, L-head engine of 60 horsepower (at 2800 RPM) and 201.3 cubic inches, with 114-inch wheelbase. The sedan cost $985, weighed 2850, and had a 4.70 gear ratio.

The "Twin-Ignition Six," had overhead valves, 74½ horsepower (at 2800 RPM) and 241.5 cubic inch displacement. The wheelbase was 118 inches, and the sedan cost $1385. It weighed 3535 and had a higher 4.50 gear ratio.

At the top of the line, the new "Twin-Ignition Eight," had overhead valves. Its 298.6 cubic-inch, straight-8 engine developed 100 horsepower at 3200 RPM, and the $1695 sedan had a 124-inch wheelbase, and a 4.50 gear ratio, and weighed an even two tons.

"Twin ignition" was a feature of the larger Nashes, the idea being that greater engine efficiency could be achieved with two spark plugs for each cylinder.

Other Nash features, in addition to new body lines for 1930, included new "narrow-rim" radiators with built-in automatic shutters, 7 main bearings (9 in the Eight), self-energizing, cable-actuated mechanical brakes, new double-action Lovejoy hydraulic shock absorbers, Bijur centralized chassis lubrication, steel-covered springs with "lifetime" coating of grease and starter control on a "moderne" instrument panel (later replaced by clutch-pedal starter control). The Nash had an adjustable seat, and "the world's easiest steering." Also, Duplate shatter proof glass was standard in the Eight, optional in Sixes.

Nash built 54,605 cars in 1930, and entered 1931 in twelfth place.

In 1931, Nash production fell to 38,616 units, close to its total figure in 1920. However, Nash Motors earned nearly five million dollars in its 1931 fiscal year. Located at Kenosha, Wisconsin, with a branch factory in Milwaukee, Nash was about to become the only surviving Wisconsin automaker, as Kissel ceased production.

Nash bodies in 1931 no longer had their distinctive combination window-moulding and belt line. Three new eights were featured for the new year (the models "870," "880," and "890"), ranging from $945 to $2025.

In 1931, the "Ambassador" model name was given to an $1825 de luxe sedan. Another attractive, new model featured sofa-like "Zenobia" floral-pattern upholstery on the divided rear seat.

The only six available in the early 1931 line was the "660" Nash, on the 114¼" wheelbase, with 65 horsepower at 3200 RPM. This model was priced at $795 (coupe or 2-door sedan), and was lower-priced than any Nash six previously built. The slogan of the 1931 Nash was, "A New Deal for Today's Dollar"; interesting, when one realizes that this was two years before the beginning of F.D.R.'s "New Deal" administration.

The better eights carried a smart stone guard in front of the radiator, but, on June 28, a new series was introduced with a V-shaped grille, front fender parking lights, and "synchro-safety shift" transmission with silent second gear. New, soundproofed bodies were also introduced. These late '31 models were carried into the early weeks of the following year as "first series" 1932s.

On February 27, 1932, came the all-new "second series" Nash, with modern "slip-stream" styling that featured a sloping "beaver-tail" lower back panel for reduced rear-end wind drag. New visorless windshields appeared with curved top panels. Vent doors were used on the sides of the hood.

An X-dual chassis frame and ride-control, adjustable shock absorbers were also a part of the new models. The three largest eights had underslung worm drive.

With five models, the second series included the "Big Six," "Standard Eight," "Special Eight," "Advanced Eight," and the "Ambassador Eight" which boasted a 142-inch wheelbase! This Ambassador was one of the longest cars ever built by Nash.

The 1932 Nash's attractive instrument panel was somewhat reminiscent of

NASH

STEPS OUT AHEAD

WITH 5 NEW SERIES

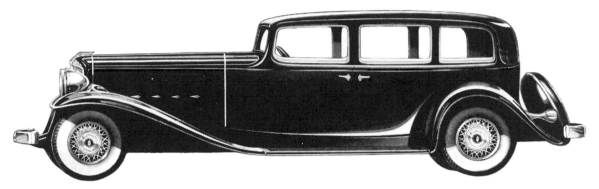

This Year's Most Interesting New Car

THE 5 new series of Nash models introduce important basic advancements in both body design and chassis.

Both new style and a practical purpose are achieved by the Slip-Stream body, V-radiator, sloping windshield, and Beavertail back, for frontal air resistance is reduced and the usual vacuum "hold-back" is minimized, resulting in higher top speed.

The three upper series introduce a Silent, Underslung Worm Drive which enables Nash to secure much lower over-all height without decreasing head room or road clearance.

All models have the new super-rigid X-Dual frame; dash adjusted, full range Ride Control; greater horsepower; longer wheelbases; wider bodies and seats; Synchro-Shift transmission with silent second; Selective free wheeling; two glove compartments, chromium trimmed, in instrument panel; and adjustable driving seat for all Coupes and regular Sedans; as well as many more outstanding features.

You are invited to view these new cars at your Nash Dealer's and to drive them, for it is our sincere conviction you will prefer their performance to any you have ever known.

BIG SIX	STANDARD EIGHT	SPECIAL EIGHT	ADVANCED EIGHT	AMBASSADOR EIGHT
116-inch Wheelbase	*121-inch Wheelbase*	*128-inch Wheelbase*	*133-inch Wheelbase*	*142-inch Wheelbase*
$777 *to* $935	$965 *to* $1095	$1270 *to* $1395	$1595 *to* $1785	$1855 *to* $2055

——— ALL PRICES F. O. B. FACTORY ———

EVERYTHING ABOUT THIS CAR SUGGESTS A HIGHER PRICE

● Nash builds one of the finest of today's motor cars — the 125 horsepower Nash Ambassador Eight. ¶ Compared to others which sell for $500 more, and higher, the Ambassador will make you ask "*$500 more for what*". ¶ It is one of the smartest-appearing and performing cars on the road — with long, low, flowing Slipstream lines, Slipstream fenders, V-radiator, Beavertail back, Twin-Ignition motor and Silent-Underslung-Worm-Drive. *You ride in luxury!*

¶ Illustrated here is the Ambassador Eight Brougham. 142 inch wheelbase. $1820 f. o. b. factory. ¶ Nash also builds cars of corresponding quality and value in four other price fields. *Do you know that today you can buy a big, quality-built, 4-door, 5-passenger Nash Sedan for as little as $695 f. o. b. factory, $130 under 1932?* ¶ Your Nash dealer now has these 1933 Nash cars ready to show you, and ready to demonstrate their marked superiority on the road.

NASH

BIG SIX	STANDARD EIGHT	SPECIAL EIGHT	ADVANCED EIGHT	AMBASSADOR EIGHT
116-inch Wheelbase	*116-inch Wheelbase*	*121-inch Wheelbase*	*128-inch Wheelbase*	*133 and 142-inch Wheelbases*
*$695 to $745	*$830 to $900	$965 to $1095	$1255 to $1575	$1545 to $2055
4-Door Sedan	4-Door Sedan	Six Body Styles	Six Body Styles	Nine Body Styles
Four Body Styles	Five Body Styles			

All Prices Quoted f. o. b. Factory—Special Equipment Extra the 1928–29 Chrysler Imperial 80 designs, except that, in the Nash, each gauge was framed separately, then mounted in the long panel. There was a glove compartment at each end of the dash.

Freewheeling was also a feature, as were aluminum-alloy Bohnalite pistons and connecting rods.

Prices of these good looking cars ranged from $777 for the least expensive "Big Six" (on 116-inch wheelbase) to $2055, and up, for the best "Ambassador Eights."

Modern Goodyear "Airwheel" tires were optional on later 1932 models. Most cars were using 18-inch wheels in 1932, but smaller 16 and even 15-inch wheels were being offered as "extras" by a few manufacturers and dealers. They were seen as a great improvement by a few visionaries who remembered the great improvement of 1924, the balloon tire.

Only 17,696 cars were built by Nash in '32. Yet the company reported a profit of $1,029,522 that year, more than *six times* the profit reported by General Motors! Most autobuilders were deeply "in the red" then.

The 1933 Nash has always been scarce. Only 14,973 were produced. Styling wasn't changed much from 1932, yet the 1933 Nash looked more behind-the-times, in comparison with other cars. Dual mufflers were featured on all models.

Horsepower of the "Big Six," which now had a ⅛" larger bore, was boosted from 70 to 75. The new "Standard Eight" shared the same 116-inch-wheelbase chassis as the "Six," and sold for $830 to $900, f.o.b. The "Big Six" could be had at the factory for as little as $695.

"Special" and "Advanced Eights" had, respectively, 121 and 128-inch wheelbases. Top car was still the 125-horsepower "Ambassador Eight," selling for $1545 to $2055 and available in nine body styles. Wheelbases offered 133 or 142 inches; shorter than in 1932.

Dash-regulated ride-control was offered for the second year, on "Special," "Advanced" and "Ambassador Eights."

The instrument board on 1933 models was unusual in that a large, oval speedometer dominated the center, flanked by two, small, circular gauges on either side. The entire set was placed in a raised, tapering panel-within-a-panel. The large lever for swinging out the windshield was located not far above the speedometer.

In 1934, Nash put its 217.8 cubic-inch, 75-horsepower L-head, six engine in the new $695 Lafayette car, and put a new 88-horsepower valve-in-head engine of 234.8 cubic inches in the Nash "Big Six." Among the eights, only the 100-horsepower "Advanced" and 125-horsepower "Ambassador" models remained.

Production was up in 1934, with a greater choice of low-priced sixes. Nash built 28,644 cars during the year. Also in 1934, the company built its millionth car, and Charles W. Nash posed proudly with it for a publicity photo.

The 1934 Nashes looked much larger than before, with broad new grilles strongly resembling General Motors' Buick. Hoods were unusually long, with horizontal vent doors along the sides. The new fenders were broad and semi-skirted, with decorative ridges stamped in. Detachable, full-cover rear fender skirts, bearing the Nash emblem, were also available.

The new models were large, but were pictured in advertisements as being fantastically *huge,* literally dwarfing their owners and drivers. One illustration pictured a young girl talking to her father as he drove a new Nash. She asked, *"Daddy, are we richer than we used to be?"* Ahead of them stretched a hood that looked nearly as long as the highway itself! Yet such gross exaggerations (obvious as they may have appeared), were not uncommon, especially in the early and mid-'30s when streamlining was coming into vogue. It would appear that some manufacturers did not want to be outdone when it came to picturing their cars as rolling palaces! Size was exaggerated, and often the curves and slants of the body lines were distorted from reality in a hand-drawn illustration so that a car could look completely different, nearly unrecognizable! Another trick of the illustrators, in some of these ads, was to omit the borders around the roof insert so the car would appear to have an all-steel top.

Individual front wheel suspension was optional on all '34 Nash models. Each model had "equal-action," cable-controlled Bendix mechanical brakes.

Praised in Nash advertisements, that year, were the X-dual frame, thermostatically controlled shock absorbers, enclosed self-lubricating springs, "dual-construction" soundproofed body, and "easy-action" worm and roller steering.

During 1934, all Nash models had overhead valves and twin ignition; the only exception was the low-cost, new Lafayette.

"RIGHT with the WORLD!"

Individually-Sprung Front Wheels Optional at Slight Extra Cost

★ Nash is certainly on the right side of public opinion!

It's apparent in the way the 1934 Nash is clicking. The public clearly likes the style of its appearance, *and* the appearance of its style. The Nash speedstream design achieves refreshing smartness without a semblance of straining for effect.

Smart outside, rich inside. Everybody who steps into a 1934 Nash comes at once under the spell of the car's luxury. Likes the appointments. Likes the clear-vision ventilation system. Likes the way a touch on the clutch pedal starts the motor. And Nash Twin Ignition valve-in-head performance is something never to be forgotten.

Great automobiles . . . styled right, powered right, built right, priced right. Nash invites and *thrives on* all kinds of comparisons!

1934 TWIN IGNITION VALVE-IN-HEAD NASH

BIG SIX				AMBASSADOR EIGHT		
116″ Wheelbase	•	88 Horsepower	• $775 to $865	133″ Wheelbase	• 125 Horsepower	• $1575 to $1625
ADVANCED EIGHT				**AMBASSADOR EIGHT**		
121″ Wheelbase	•	100 Horsepower	• $1065 to $1145	142″ Wheelbase	• 125 Horsepower	• $1820 to $2055

NRA

New Nash-Built LaFayette, the Fine Car of the Low Price Field, $635 TO $695

(All Prices f. o. b. Factory—Special Equipment Extra—All Prices Subject to Change Without Notice)

NASH

PRESENTS THE "400" SERIES FOR 1930

WIN-IGNITION EIGHT...TWIN-IGNITION SIX...SINGLE SIX

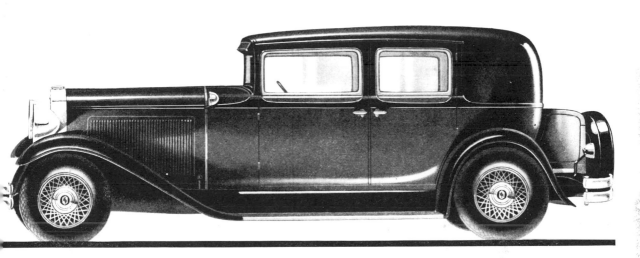

MERICA'S FOREMOST EIGHT . . . TWO INCOMPARABLE SIXES

the 1930 Motor Show, Nash presents the new-
 and greatest products of Nash engineering
nius. There is a new straight eight—a master-
ece of motordom—powered by the sensational,
w Twin-Ignition Eight motor—instantly recog-
ed as the finest instrument of power ever built for
y motor car. There are also two new sixes—the

Twin-Ignition and Single Six, likewise engineered
for leadership in their fields. These new Nash
cars introduce engineering advancements that
unquestionably forecast the future in motor car
design—they provide a new type of performance
that instantly convinces everyone that motoring
has been strikingly, gloriously improved.

─────A PARTIAL LIST OF 1930 NASH "400" FEATURES─────

Body Designs—Long Wheelbases—Radiators with Built-in
matic Shutters—7-Bearing, Hollow Crankpin Crankshafts—
Energizing, Cable-Actuated 4-Wheel Brakes—Fuel Feed Pump
ntralized Chassis Lubrication—Double Action Hydraulic Shock

Absorbers—Adjustable Drivers' Seats—Steel Spring Covers, with
Sealed-in Lifetime Lubrication—World's Easiest Steering—Starter
Control on Instrument Panel—Insulated floor board and dash—AND
THESE ADDITIONAL FEATURES IN THE EIGHT: Straight-Eight, Twin-

Ignition, 16 Spark Plug, High-Compression, Valve-in-Head Motor—
9-Bearing, Integrally Counterweighted, Hollow Crankpin Crankshaft—Aluminum Connecting Rods—Steering Shock Eliminator—All
windows, doors, windshields, Duplate Non-Shatterable Plate Glass.

(1370)

OAKLAND

Founded in 1907, Oakland soon became a member of the General Motors family of cars. In 1926, the Oakland Motor Car Division (of Pontiac, Michigan), launched a new companion car, Pontiac ("The Chief of the Sixes") which soon surpassed the Oakland car in sales. During the first ten months of 1929, for instance, 149,088 Pontiacs but only 29,352 Oaklands were sold, the two cars taking sixth and twentieth places on the market that year.

Despite the sales charts of 1929, the Oakland "All-American Six" was a durable, well-built automobile, actually superior to the smaller Pontiac that was outselling it.

However, in 1930 the Oakland people made a serious error in judgment, for they replaced the dependable 6-cylinder Oakland engine with a V-8 that was a "lemon." The unreliability of the new Oakland V-8 was soon known throughout the country, and, by 1932, the Oakland had been put out of the running in favor of Pontiac.

What was the 1930 Oakland like? Available in seven body types (for $1025 and up), the 1930 Oakland with the new 251-cubic-inch V-8 engine developed 85 horsepower and had unusual horizontal valves. The 1930 Oakland weighed less than the '29 model, and had one horsepower for every 37 pounds of weight, a favorable ratio for those days. Its top speed was over 70,

MAKING
NEW FRIENDS
AND KEEPING
THE OLD

An Earnest Purpose, Earnestly Pursued

To make every car so sound and good that it will inevitably make a friend. . . . Such is the guiding spirit of the entire Oakland-Pontiac organization. . . . It is the spirit of the executives, of the engineers at their drawing boards, of Oakland-Pontiac sales and service representatives. . . . It is not a studied, artificial atmosphere, but the policy of men who sincerely prefer to serve well—who have a model plant and

unlimited resources to aid them —who believe in endowing their products with that extra goodness and reliability which are the real key to making new friends and keeping the old. . . . You find pleasing evidence at your local dealer's of how fully Oakland and Pontiac cars reflect this spirit. Your dealer offers these fine automobiles in Fisher body types which embody the same ideals of quality and value as the Oakland and Pontiac chassis mechanisms.

OAKLAND 8 PONTIAC 6

with Bodies by Fisher

PRODUCTS OF GENERAL MOTORS

and it would accelerate from 5 to 35 m.p.h. in 10.4 seconds. The standard gear ratio was 4.42, but 3.9 or 5.2 differentials were also available. Introduced the year before, Oakland's self-energizing internal-expanding mechanical brakes were again offered, with 12-inch drums.

Though the wheelbase was 117 inches as before, the Oakland styling for 1930 was new, with longer, lower Fisher bodies and vertical-ventilating windshields slightly tilted to prevent glare.

Gone was the hazardous, wooden-rimmed steering wheel of the 1929 model, and replacing it was a black, three-spoke steel core wheel covered with hard rubber. Another safety feature was the new running light mounted on each front fender; it was not only a parking light, but, also, a "safety" light. It remained on whenever the headlights were set to low beam. This was for city driving, so that the car could be seen from the side at a darkened intersection.

The radiator design of the 1930 Oakland was new, with a square look to the shell and a slightly "veed" split grille which concealed the cross-flow radiator core. Hood louvres were vertical and, unlike the '29 model, all in one group.

A vibrator horn was mounted on the tie-bar near the left headlamp and either wire or wood wheels were supplied, buyer's choice.

The Oakland V-8 engine, though it was admired by few, deserves further description. It *did* have several interesting features.

The Oakland engine was different from the V-8 used in General Motors' Viking car of 1929–30, and it was also unlike the V-8s used by Cadillac or La Salle. The compression ratio of the 1930 Oakland engine was 5 to 1, and bore and stroke, $3\frac{7}{16}$ by $3\frac{3}{8}$ inches. The two 4-cylinder blocks were 90 degrees apart and cast as one unit with the crankcase, unlike many earlier V-8s. The horizontal valves were easy to reach, and the valve springs were partially encased to prevent chatter. Valves were actuated by rocker arms working from a central, chain-driven camshaft. The distributor was situated at the rear of the valve alley, and was driven from the camshaft by a vertical connecting shaft that also drove the oil pump. The generator was located just behind the fan, and, like the water-pump, was driven by the fan belt. A Marvel downdraft carburetor was used, and the four-port intake manifold provided an equal path downhill to each cylinder. For smooth performance, the engine was attached to flexible mounts.

Most noticeable change on the Oakland for 1931 was the new stone guard grille, with chrome-plated mesh. Wire wheels were now standard equipment, with 5.50 x 18″ tires, and one-piece bumpers were used.

Below the surface there were many improvements. Most notably, Oakland now had a new synchro-mesh transmission with "silent second," larger "Steeldraulic" brakes with 13-inch drums, improved rear axles, and a gear ratio of 4.55 (lower than before, the new standard gear ratio was only an improvement so far as quick "pick-up" was concerned.) The chassis frames were strengthened, and the 1931 Oakland's hood was now closed by one latch handle on each side, at lower center.

Particularly interesting was the jaunty little convertible coupe, frequently painted in yellow and black, with folding landau top and folding windshield, as well as side-mounted spare wheels.

The slogan for the 1931 Oakland and Pontiac cars was *"Making New Friends And Keeping The Old."* But after 1931, the Oakland was unceremoniously dropped for good. Only 12,103 Oaklands had been sold in '31.

Remaining Oakland cars are few and far between. Of all models, the 1929 "All-American Six" appears most often.

OLDSMOBILE

The Oldsmobile was in its thirty-second year when the 1930 model was produced in Lansing, by the Olds Motor Works Division of General Motors. At that time Oldsmobile was among the oldest names still on the market (and still is), having outlasted many newer makes.

In general appearance, the 1930 Oldsmobile was not much different in design from the 1929 model, though the 1930 version had a new instrument panel with five, small, black, circular gauges arranged separately in an arc on an arched, black panel. With the exception of the Viking car, all-black dashboards were in vogue at General Motors in 1930.

Oldsmobile bodies were slightly larger than before, and all 1930 General Motors products had windshields at the new seven-degree slant. Bodies were strengthened, at many spots, by additional metal bracing and the use of bolts in places where screws and glue formerly sufficed. Fisher bodies were still of composite wood-frame construction, however, and remained so for a few more years.

New, continuous mouldings along the sides of the hood and cowl replaced the separate-cowl "saddle" design of '29 Oldsmobiles. Window reveals were often painted in a lighter tone than the rest of the body, and were joined on each side of the car as one, long, recessed panel.

ISHER has created bodies for the new Oldsmobile Six which are smartly styled and brightly ished in the sunny hues of spring, and which combine a wealth of comfort and a wide utility.

hese bodies by Fisher are ready for the swift anges from sun to shower—ready with carefully gineered, easily operated window regulators and e Fisher vision-ventilating windshield. They are ugly insulated for the chilly day—instantly made ol and airy for the warmest weather.

rthermore, Fisher wood-and-steel type construcn provides Oldsmobile with bodies of greater strength plus resilience—eliminates squeaks and rattles and assures comfort and good-looks through many seasons.

Be sure to examine carefully the new Oldsmobiles and compare their greater value. For in Oldsmobile's price field, the new Oldsmobile Six alone will give you these important Fisher superiorities, because Oldsmobile is one of the General Motors cars—the only cars with Body by Fisher.

BODY by FISHER

LOOK TO THE BODY!

FISHER BODY CORPORATION · DETROIT, MICHIGAN
Division of General Motors

The 1930 Oldsmobile engine, as before, was an L-head six. The cylinder head was designed so that the spark plugs were placed more to the center. Though the horsepower was raised to 62 at 3000 RPM, the compression ratio remained 5.20 to 1. Gear ratio was lowered to 4.54, which meant that an Oldsmobile owner could not expect his new car to exceed 65 on the open road.

De luxe models had wire wheels, side-mounts, and a luggage rack at the rear. Oldsmobile prices began at $875 for the coach, and five wire wheels, if preferred, were $55 extra.

Oldsmobile sales reached 45,671 by November, 1930.

Oldsmobile appeared with many changes for 1931, including a new radiator design and double tie-bar, as well as a one-piece bumper.

Among new mechanical features, the most important was the synchro-mesh transmission with quiet second gear. This new transmission was similar (but not identical) to that used in the 1931 Oakland. Horsepower was increased to 65 at 3350 RPM and a new downdraft carburetor (Stromberg DXR-2) with intake silencer-air cleaner was added.

There were many other minor mechanical improvements, such as the automatic part-opening of the throttle when the starter pedal was depressed.

Car bodies were insulated for driver comfort, and the chassis frame was deeper and sturdier than before. Tire size, again, was 5.25 x 18 inches.

The 1931 Oldsmobile, tested at the General Motors Proving Grounds, accelerated from 5 to 60 miles per hour in 30.8 seconds. Although not much by later standards, this was an improvement over the 37.1 seconds it took for the 1930 model to accomplish the same thing.

Price of the 1931 4-door sedan was $70 lower, or $925.

In 1932, Oldsmobile offered new styling again, with visorless, rounded-edged Fisher bodies typical of General Motors' new output. Ventilating doors (5) were on each side of the hood, which was three inches longer.

The 6-cylinder L-head engine was enlarged to 213.3 cubic inches, giving 71 horsepower at 3200 RPM. In addition, there was a straight-eight L-head engine that developed "82 at 3200." Early in 1932, the horsepower on the two engines was increased to 74 and 87.

Wheelbase of the "Six" or "Eight" was 116½", and tire size was 6.00 x 17.

The list of other features for 1932 was headed by the new freewheeling unit with dashboard control, double-action Delco-Remy ride control hydraulic shock absorbers, an automatic choke, and oil temperature regulator.

The instrument panel was attractively done in silver-aluminum with horizontal ribbing, while the four, inset, black-faced dials were symmetrically arranged; two large gauges near the center, flanked by a small ammeter at left and gas gauge at right, with the Oldsmobile crest at the upper center and ignition keyhole at lower center. Four hand-pull controls were located in the recessed panel below the instruments.

As a head-on styling touch, a chrome strip ran back from the center of each tip of the front fender crowns, and met a streamlined auxiliary lamp. These safety lamps had curved glass so they could be seen from the sides as well as from the front. As on earlier Oaklands, these lamps went on with the low beam of the headlamps, and also could be used as parking lights.

The 1932 Oldsmobile was one of the early cars to have dual taillights. The red Stinsonite lenses were so designed that they could serve as reflectors should a bulb fail.

A very interesting little gimmick was the new "decarbonizer," which consisted of a container of solvent on the firewall, connected by a tube to the intake manifold. As the engine was shut off, the driver could press a button on the dash causing a spray of solvent to be sent from the container into the manifold and upper cylinders. After the engine stood for three hours, it could be started and all the loosened carbon would be blown out of the exhaust.

Prices of the Oldsmobile "Six" began at $875, with the "Eight" beginning at $975, f.o.b. Lansing. Only 22,657 units were sold during the first ten months of the year, a decline of 48.8%. The Depression was taking a heavy toll in sales.

The fabulous new "Century of Progress" Exposition opened in Chicago in 1933, and in one magazine advertisement two new Oldsmobiles were pictured in front of the new fair's Science Hall. The Chicago Fair figured prominently as a backdrop for many advertisements during 1933–34.

The Fisher bodies of the new Oldsmobiles for 1933 were greatly modernized. They had become lower, and considerably expanded. New, sloping V-grilles were featured, the Oldsmobile "Eight" having grille members that flared up and out from the center, the "Six grille," many vertical members crossed by eight horizontals. Hoods were broader and larger, with three horizontal "teardrop" louvres on each side. The massive new fenders were well-skirted, a major change from before. The front fenders blended nicely into a broad lower panel which contained the running board.

Dashboards were finished in imitation wood grain, with instruments in two, large, black-faced circles. A glove compartment was on the right side of the convex panel.

You simply don't know what you're missin[g]
till you try them out on the road!

This vivid demonstration of Fisher No Draft Ventilation and how [it] operates may be seen at the Automobile Shows. The arrows at front [and] rear windows show how fresh air is drawn in, how used air is drawn [out,] entirely without chilling drafts on anyone in the car

As THIS magazine appears, eager throngs are getting their first thrilling glimpse of the motor car industry's brilliant new offerings at the New York Automobile Show.

Doubtless you will be one of the fortunate people to see the new cars and the new styles at one of the many automobile shows throughout the country this season.

Of course you will inspect the strong, safe, new Bodies by Fisher, and you will find them more generously spacious, more luxuriously comfortable, more beautifully appointed than even they have been before.

But you simply don't know what you're missing till you try them out on the road! Only then will you appreciate fully their spaciousness and comfort — *and in no other way can you understand [the] real importance of Fisher No Draft Ventilation.*

It is hard to believe that a closed car could be so free fr[om] stuffiness — that anyone in the car can smoke witho[ut] disturbing others — that the inside of windows a[nd] windshields could be so unclouded in cold, stormy weath[er] — that you could enjoy such fresh, pure air without dra[fts.]

But it's true, as your first ride in any General Motors car w[ill] prove to you. For your health, your safety, your comfort, a[nd] for your family's sake, you will surely want Fisher No Dr[aft] Ventilation on your new car, and that mea[ns] you will want a Body by Fisher, which originat[ed,] pioneered and perfected this advantage.

BODY BY FISHER on GENERAL MOTORS CARS ONLY: CHEVROLET   PONTIAC · OLDSMOBILE · BUICK · LA SALLE · CADIL[LAC]

Madam,

your car awaits without

Echo of an old jest though it is, the title of this advertisement explains why so many women value Body by Fisher, and will have nothing less. Madam's car awaits WITHOUT a host of little flaws and faults that lessen the joy and ease of travel. No chilling drafts, for example, blow through the car on crisp autumn and winter days— thanks to Fisher-pioneered and perfected No Draft Ventilation. Nor is it necessary that the driver's elbow perch on the window-sill— deeply tufted arm rests are provided, front and rear. Even the keyholes in Body by Fisher automatically protect the locks from rust. Details, perhaps, but added to numberless other provisions for your safety and comfort, they point to any car with Body by Fisher as a car exacting folk will wish to have.

Body by Fisher

on GENERAL MOTORS CARS ONLY: CHEVROLET · OLDSMOBILE · PONTIAC · BUICK · LA SALLE · CADILLAC

No-draft ventilating wings were standard equipment. And there were many new, unseen features like the optional Bendix automatic vacuum clutch. Hand-operated radiator shutters were discarded, for a thermostatic manifold heat control. The Stromberg automatic choke was continued.

Under the car, a new double-drop X frame was used, and the new wheels were the 17-inch steel artillery-type, which were easier to clean than either wire or wood-spoked varieties.

Some sedans had a built-on trunk which blended well with body lines, and all models had sloping "beaver tail" panels to conceal the gas tank.

Horsepower had increased to 76, later to 80, on the Six. The "Eight" for 1933 had 90 horsepower. Top speeds of the two models were now 80 and 85; very good, considering that these cars were held back by a comparatively low 4.54 gear ratio. Wheelbases of the "Six" and "Eight" differed in 1933, at 115 and 119 inches, respectively. Treads were wider, to match the broader bodies. Despite the many improvements, prices were reduced $130 to $145, per model.

An advertisement in the March, 1933 issue of FORTUNE magazine declared:

"You may never have thought of Oldsmobile as a style car. For Oldsmobile, in its program of advancement, has preferred first of all to attain utmost brilliance in performance and dependability. This year, however, Oldsmobile and General Motors have called upon every resource to create two cars completely new and modern in line and contour." Good appearance helped to sell automobiles, and Oldsmobile moved up from twelfth to eighth place in 1933, selling 32,612 units for a gain of 43%. The only other cars exceeding this gain in 1933 were Plymouth (up 128½%), Austin Bantam (up 103½%) and Dodge (with a phenomenal 203.7% increase in sales.)

Oldsmobile for 1934 featured Bendix servo-hydraulic brakes, helical transmission gears, and "knee-action" independent front-wheel suspension.

The grille on the 1934 Oldsmobile resembled that of the 1933 "Six," but it was wider. Two long, horizontal torpedo louvres were on each side of the hood for engine ventilation, and the longer headlamps were bullet-shaped. Wheel wells with side-mounted spares were available, but, otherwise, the new Oldsmobile wasn't much different on the outside from its 1933 counterpart.

Interiors, also, were little changed from the previous year. The two, large, dash gauges were ringed with a lighter color for easier reading at night. A large "bubble" horn button (bearing the Olds insignia) gave a modern touch to the steering wheel.

The 8-cylinder engine was unchanged, with ninety horsepower. But the 6 was raised to 84 horsepower with a new compression ratio of 5.7, despite the fact that its bore was reduced by $\frac{1}{16}$ of an inch, to $3\frac{5}{16}''$. Top speeds of the "Eight" and the "Six" were 82 and 77, and at 50 miles per hour these cars could travel 14 and 17 m.p.g. respectively. The "Eight" had a push-button starter on the dash.

Wheelbase of the "Six" was shortened to 114, and the "Eight" remained at 119. The "Six" had 5.50 x 17'' tires which carried 35 pounds of air pressure, but the "Eight" had low-pressure 7.00 x 16s that required only 22 pounds!

Safety glass was standard in the windshield and ventilating wings. The automatic choke was optional on the "Six," which was priced from $640 up. Prices on the 8-cylinder models began at $845.

For many years, the 1934 Oldsmobile has been one of the most infrequently seen of all models. Oldsmobiles from the later thirties survived in greater numbers.

THOUSANDS of boys all over America are completing miniature model Napoleonic coaches in the first year's activity of the Fisher Body Craftsman's Guild. These models they will shortly submit in a nationwide competition for four university scholarships of four years each, 98 trips to Detroit, and 882 other valuable awards.

BODY by FISHER

PRODUCT OF GENERAL MOTORS

The Fisher Body Corporation sponsored this inspiring movement, believing that this exercise of creative talent, this quickening of the hand of youth, are essential steps toward the development of high ideals— that only by training the coming generation can fine craftsmanship be perpetuated and superior coachcraft be assured.

CADILLAC ▸ LA SALLE ▸ BUICK ▸ OAKLAND ▸ OLDSMOBILE ▸ PONTIAC ▸ CHEVROLET

PACKARD

Many readers may have heard the following anecdote, but for the benefit of those who have not, here it is: In 1898, James Ward Packard bought an early Winton automobile in Cleveland. The car was troublesome, and Mr. Packard confronted Alexander Winton with his complaints. Mr. Winton was taken aback, and flatly suggested that if Mr. Packard knew so much about automobiles, he should build his own car. Surprisingly, Mr. Packard did just this, and late the following year the first Packard car was completed. More cars followed, and soon Packard was in the automobile manufacturing business. In 1903 a corporation was formed, and Packard operations were transferred from Warren, Ohio, to Detroit.

Quality and performance was the rule at Packard, and within a few years these cars became favorites of the famous and well-to-do. On Packard Avenue, the main thoroughfare within the busy factory, hung a permanent sign which simply read, "QUALITY FIRST." It was placed there and retained as a reminder to all Packard personnel that the company's principal aim was "the building of quality cars for a clientele of means and discrimination."

By 1930, the Packard car had long been a world favorite that was chosen by many kings and potentates. Three series of '30 Packards were available, all of them with straight-8 engines. The best, the "745" Eight De Luxe, sold f.o.b. for $4585 to $5350, had a big 145½-inch wheelbase, 4.38 gear ratio and 106 horsepower.

Second in line, the "740" Custom Eight, was priced between $3190 and $3885. It had the same engine, gear ratio and 7.00 x 19″ tires as the De Luxe, but a shorter wheelbase of 140½ inches.

Smallest, the Standard Eight, models "726" and "733," had a 90-horsepower engine, 127½ or 134½-inch wheelbase, and 4.38 or 4.69 gear ratio. The price range was $2425 to $2885. The Standard Eight had 20-inch wheels.

There were no Packard sixes in 1930, the 6-cylinder models having been discontinued temporarily after 1928. And the V-12, the famous "Twin Six" Packard, had been off the market since 1922. But both would return, later.

Standard Eights had vertical hood louvres. The larger Packards had ventilating doors, also parking lights on front fenders. All 1930 Packards had Bendix mechanical brakes with huge 16-inch drums. Four-speed transmissions were available, as they were then briefly in vogue on several makes.

Dual-cowl phaetons and powerful sport roadsters were among the most beautiful of 1930 Packards. And another great-looking car was the "745" Eight De Luxe convertible coupe, selling for $4885 at the factory and weighing in at a hefty 4665 pounds. It was available in a variety of colors, one beautiful combination being a light blue body with black fenders and running gear, vermillion wheels, striping and belt-line. Windshield and upper door panels were black, and the top was khaki, with chrome-plated landau irons. This convertible was available with wire wheels and side-mounts, but the characteristic Packard in that era had steel disc wheels.

Also worthy of mention is the "745" convertible sedan with six wire wheels and body by Brewster.

In 1930, nearly twice as many Packards as any other car costing over $2000 were sold overseas. The Packard was extremely popular in Asia. And Packard rose to sixteenth place in 1930, selling 25,930 cars in ten months. True, this was considerably less than the 40,960 Packards sold during the same period in 1929, but all automobile manufacturers suffered a decrease in volume during 1930, with the exception of Cord, which had appeared on the market only a few months previously.

Packard's public slogan had long been, "Ask the Man Who Owns One." Satisfied owners were the car's best salesmen, and it has often been said that the slogan originated back in 1902 when someone requested, of Mr. Packard, a then-unavailable sales catalog.

"For a Discriminating Clientele" was another slogan that dominated Pack-

REST

You leave your office at the end of the day, wearied by a hard day's work.

● Ahead of you wait the responsibilities of the evening. If only there could be a little relaxation sandwiched in between!

● There is—for the man who owns a Packard. He steps from his office into his car, and instantly he is cradled in quiet and comfort. The worries of the day are forgotten in the pleasure of driving a car that almost drives itself. He enjoys a bodily peace, a mental solace. He arrives home refreshed.

● For of all the cars man has ever designed, the most restful, we believe, is the new Packard. There's not a sound from its body, barely a whisper from its motor. The cushions, contoured by experts, *make you* relax. The brakes that stop you so quickly work with such a velvety softness you scarcely know you're stopping. Shock absorbers and spring action are so perfected that ruts and bumps go unnoticed. Instead of riding, you *float!* You *rest!*

● We believe that you, as a business man, deserve the restfulness that a new Packard can bring you. We believe you want and need this car. Why not buy it—now? See the new Packards at your Packard dealer's. Or simply phone him—he will arrange for you to ride home from your office in one of these new cars. Very soon after that, we feel confident, you will be making the homeward trip each evening in your own Packard.

PACKARD

ASK THE MAN WHO OWNS ONE

ard's advertising in 1931. During the early months of that year, Packard's styling was similar to that of the '30 models. Though these early '31 models appeared stodgy with their flat radiators and over-hanging roof visors, the well-known fact that Packard did not indulge in frequent or drastic style changes appealed to many conservative owners. They could enjoy their Packards for many years, without feeling that the cars would soon be hopelessly outdated. A new Packard represented a sizable investment, and that investment should be protected. The traditional shape of the Packard radiator was carried on from one year to the next, much in the same fashion as on the Rolls-Royce.

In mid-1931, Packard produced a new series of "Continental Eights," completely restyled and vastly improved. New bodies were lower, with modernized lines and insulated interiors. Wheelbases were lengthened, engines were improved and "floated" on rubber mounts. Also, there was a new synchromesh, four-speed transmission. "Ride Control," a popular feature which was found on many cars the season following, permitted "instant shock absorber adjustments from the dash."

New series bodies had a sloping windshield, with no visor. Elegant twin trumpet horns appeared in front. A number of Packard enthusiasts consider these models to be "early 1932s." A notable classic was the convertible Victoria for five, with its long hood, low, sloping windshield, and heavy top. It had a definite air of aristocracy.

Packard's most interesting development during 1932 was the introduction of the all-new "Light Eight" model, which was easily distinguished by the broad sweep forward of the lower portion of its V-shaped grille. With finger control freewheeling and silent synchro-mesh transmission, the "Light Eight" was priced $500 less than previous Packards, opening broader markets. This new 110-horsepower model had an ample 128-inch wheelbase. The chassis embodied a double-drop frame and "Angleset" rear axle assembly for a lower center of gravity. Ride control shock absorbers, adjustable from the dash, were offered at no extra cost.

Shatterproof glass was used in the windshield and *all* windows of the "Light Eight." The price of the 4-door sedan in this series was only $1750, f.o.b. The three other "Light Eight" models were priced at $1795. They were the coupe-sedan (Victoria), 2-passenger coupe with rumble seat, and coupe-roadster (convertible coupe) with rumble seat. As in the case of more expensive Packards, each body was fully insulated.

Along with the "Light Eight," Packard uncovered another new car at the 1932 National Automobile Show, the new "Twin-Six" (V-12) model. This

World Supremacy

A new regime in Madrid has not lessened Spanish appreciation of the luxury and distinction of Packard transportation. Packard cars in Spain outnumber those of every other fine American make. Among families of rank and prominence there, as throughout all the world, Packard is the favored fine car. Packard's world supremacy has long been an established and accepted fact.

e new Packard Light Eight is a strikingly
dsome car. In appearance it belongs un-
stakably to the distinguished Packard fam-
And, in addition, it is smartly new in its
thful grace of line and proportion—as is
ll illustrated by the popular Convertible
upe below. ¶ When you first inspect the
kard Light Eight, you will be surprised at
size and roominess. It is a big and sub-
ntial car, with wheelbase of 128 inches. It is

"light" only in comparison with other, larger
cars of the Packard line—the Standard Eight,
Eight DeLuxe and the new Twin Six. ¶ Richly appointed and upholstered, truly advanced
in all mechanical features, the Packard Light
Eight now offers the luxury of *fine car* transportation to motorists who have been accustomed to paying from $1500 to $2000 for their
cars. For here is an eight—"Packard" in person-
ality, prestige and performance—factory-priced

at the astonishing range of $1750 to $1795.
¶ Before buying *any* car be sure to *see* and *drive*
the Packard Light Eight. You will thrill to its
velvety, 110 horsepower motor, its Silent Synchro-mesh Transmission, *quiet in all three speeds,*
its simple, *safe* Finger Control Free-Wheeling.
Why not take your old car to your Packard
dealer today? He will allow you all that it is
worth—and, if you wish to buy out of income,
you will find the payments surprisingly small.

PACKARD *Ask the man who owns one*

was the first time in ten years that a 12-cylinder Packard had been available. The popular Clark Gable bought a new "Twin-Six" convertible, and, while many others admired the new twelve, because of the general national and worldwide financial conditions, there weren't many buyers.

The most modern of the new V-12 Packards was a coupe which had an extremely slanted V-windshield—something other Packards didn't offer for another six years! The side doors of this coupe matched the slant of the front pillars, and were hinged at the rear.

Many of the 1932 Packards were available with wire wheels instead of the usual disc type.

In addition to the "Light Eight" and "Twin Six" models, Packard offered thirteen body-types of the Standard Eight, also twelve Eight De Luxe models for 1932, the latter having 135 horsepower. Sedans listed from a base price of $2485, up to $4150, f.o.b., in these two series alone.

On the new models for 1933, Packard's most noticeable change was the new, semi-skirted fender. Models came in three basic series; the 120-horsepower "Eight," the 145-horsepower "Super Eight," and the 160-horsepower "Twelve" with 445½ cubic inches of piston displacement.

There were new power brakes, the pressure of which could be adjusted by the turn of a lever on the dash, so that, "the feather touch of a woman's foot stops the car as quickly and easily as the heavy tread of a man."

An automatic choke was included, as well as new ventilation-control windows. For the utmost in comfort, seat cushions in the 1933 Packards were contoured by "one of the world's most famous orthopedic surgeons." The ride control was adjustable three ways.

The 1933 Packards were advertised as more economical, quiet and powerful than their 1932 predecessors. The new models had undergone 600,000 miles of thorough testing during 1932 at the Packard Proving Grounds. The new lubricating system on the 1933s, Packard claimed, would double the life of engine parts.

Packard Eights were priced from $2150. The "Super Eights," first of a famous line, were priced from $2750. And the prices of the fine "Twelves" began at $3720. All the 1933 Packards had 17-inch wheels, and wheelbases ranged from 127 to 147 inches.

Packard exteriors for 1934 were similar to '33 models, but there were numerous minor improvements in the design of the running boards, radiator ornament, fenders, and new combination tail stop-and-backing light.

Inside, the 1934 instrument panel was gratifying in design, with a cluster of six circular gauges surrounding a panel (shaped like the famous Packard radiator) that accommodated the radio controls. All Packards, needless to say, were fully wired for radio installation by 1934, and many Packard owners ordered this desirable accessory.

A large-capacity, "Dyneto" air-cooled generator was added, as well as several other, unseen, mechanical improvements.

Packard sales were low in 1934, and the company decided it would be wise to advertise "Who's Who" books that listed the names of Packard owners in many communities. Packard dealers distributed these books on request, and prospects were urged to contact any of their friends or acquaintances listed and get a firsthand endorsement of Packard's merits. This was certainly in keeping with the "Ask the Man Who Owns One" slogan. Packard dealers, moreóver, were willing to deliver their cars to any home for a demonstration and, before long, the "weekend demonstration" became a courtesy offered by any Packard dealer; a reputable prospect could give the new car a three-day trial, if he so desired.

Packard's wisest move, however, was not the weekend demonstration. Instead, it was the decision to introduce the new "120" series in 1935, for the "120" offered real Packard quality and design for prices of only $995 and up, and Packard's sales climbed once again until a high point was reached in 1937. If Packard had clung to the upper-crust market, exclusively, it would have gone the way of Pierce-Arrow and could have died with the thirties.

FOR A DISCRIMINATING CLIENTELE

The fragrance of perfumes and incense was the very breath of life to the monarchs and nobles of ancient Assyria. Assurbanipal fostered the distilling of rare flowers and highly rewarded those whose art produced a new and lovely odor. Thus throughout all history advancement in every art has been achieved through the appreciation and patronage of the great and the discriminating

To own a Packard is to enjoy *luxurious* transportation. Yet a Packard is not a luxury. Packard ownership is not necessarily the hall-mark of great wealth—it *does* indicate sound judgment. For Packard ownership need *cost* no more than motoring in any other car of like size and power, whatever its price.

There is but one really important cost in motoring. It is depreciation—the natural loss in value suffered through years of use. Owners of the Packard Standard Eight find that they can keep it far longer than was their habit with cars of lower

price and less distinction—thus, that depreciation cost is no greater. Operating costs are virtually the same—and need not be considered.

Packard cars—Standard Eights, DeLuxe Eights and Individual Custom creations—*are* owned by the

wealthy, it is true. This is because Packard cars are good investments. Wealth generally reflects the type of judgment which selects a Packard —knowing that the best is always the least expensive in the long run.

Why not apply the same reasoning to your own motoring? The prestige of Packard ownership is a definite asset. And if you *are* paying for Packard luxury and distinction— then why not *have* a Packard?

ASK THE MAN WHO OWNS ONE

PACKARD

PEERLESS

"Alexis De Sakhnoffsky, a young Russian artisan, already prominent in designing circles abroad, was commissioned to design the new Peerless cars," said a 1930 advertisement. "The three new cars are his conceptions and abound in innovations in appearance, interior arrangements and fitments." As we read earlier, De Sakhnoffsky was also the styling designer of the De Vaux car.

In its thirtieth year, the Peerless Motor Car Corporation was located in Cleveland. Never a volume producer, Peerless, by 1930, had a long-established reputation for quality, good taste, and lack of ostentation. Peerless cars never were glamorous (at least, not until near the end of production) but their slogan was, "All that the Name Implies."

Four models were offered for 1930, three of them straight-eights (V-8 models had been built a few years previously.) Top of the line was the 120-horsepower "Custom Eight," with a 130-inch wheelbase and pleasing lines. The de luxe sedans were fitted with six wire wheels, and the side doors were distinctively bowed along the bottom edges, unlike those of any other car. Sedan prices started at $2845. (f.o.b., Cleveland). The "Custom Eight" had a displacement of 322 cubic inches. Compression ratio was 5 to 1. Fuel feed was by AC pump, and an air cleaner and Purolator oil filter were standard equipment. The gear ratio was 4.45 to 1 on the "Custom Eight," as well as on the "Master Eight," and both series had four-speed transmissions.

The "Master Eight" sedan sold for $2045., f.o.b. "Master Eights" had a 125-inch wheelbase and developed 100 horsepower. The sedans did not have the bowed side doors characteristic of the larger models, nor did the "Master Eight" have the "Custom Eight's" four ventilating doors along each side of the hood. Instead, the "Master" and "Standard Eight" had six, alternating groups of vertical louvres on each side of the hood, all grouped within one raised panel. Parking lamps were mounted on the fenders on each of the Eights, and each model had vertical radiator shutters and two-piece bumpers.

The "Standard Eight" had 85 horsepower and a 118-inch wheelbase. It did not have the shield on the headlamp tie-bar as found on the larger models. The sedan was listed as $1545.

Both Peerless and Continental-built engines had been used during the late '20s. The new Eights for 1930 were described as having Peerless engines; nevertheless, the engine in the "Master Eight" was similar to the 114-horsepower Continental used in the largest 1929 Peerless "125" series, causing one to speculate on whether the "Peerless" engine was actually the old Continental "12-K" block with new trimmings.

There was yet another Peerless for 1930. The 6-cylinder "61-A" was a continuation of the 1929 "61" model, which had 62 horsepower, a Continental engine, and a sedan price of $1165.

The 1930 Peerless cars were a credit to stylist De Sakhnoffsky, whose designs had won the Grand Prize at the all-European Concours d'Elegance for four consecutive years. Despite the fact that Peerless had sold only 7483 cars during the first ten months of 1929, a financial statement released November 30 of that year (shortly after the stock market crash) claimed that Peerless owned twenty-two acres of factories and proving grounds, that none of the properties was mortgaged, and that there was "no bonded indebtedness and no preferred stock."

After selling only 3642 cars between January and November of 1930, Peerless had slipped to thirtieth place in sales, and many of the company's optimistic plans had to be revised. Other Cleveland manufacturers were going "into the hole." Chandler had already sold out to Hupmobile, and Jordan was about to quit. Several additional Cleveland automakers had given up the ghost during the previous, few years.

By 1931, both the "Master" and "Custom" Peerless Eights shared the same 120-horsepower engine. The "Standard Eight" still had 85 horsepower. 1931 sedan prices (f.o.b.) for the three models were $2795, $1995 and $1495.

Each model was priced slightly below its 1930 counterpart. The 6-cylinder series had been discontinued during 1930.

For 1932, only the "Master" and "Custom" Eights were announced, and mechanical specifications were similar to the preceding models. Peerless executives made a last-ditch effort to produce an all-new car.

The new car was a 16-cylinder Peerless! With a body by Murphy, the new sixteen had highly advanced lines; in fact, all who saw it considered it a real knockout! Side doors curved into the roof panels, the visorless windshield was unusually high and had dual wipers attached at the *lower edge* as on much later cars. Headlights had no tie bar, and the bold new radiator had a concealed water filler as well as a V-grille. Aluminum fenders had natural, polished beadings that offered a striking contrast to the dark paint.

Running boards on the Peerless "Sixteen" were inlaid with brightwork strips and, like the later series 1932 Nash, the rear of the new Peerless featured beaver-tail shrouding over gas tank and other vitals.

A tachometer was included on the instrument panel, and all gauges were mounted behind a single pane of glass. The upholstery was of the finest broadcloth.

But, Peerless had been losing too much money, and the company dropped out of the automobile business in 1932. The only finished sample of the all-new 16-cylinder model was later acquired and exhibited by the Thompson Products Museum of Cleveland.

Although the last Stearns-Knight car had been built in 1930, the Stearns-Knight Corporation continued to operate in Cleveland for a few more years. It supplied parts for Peerless cars after they were discontinued, in addition to parts for the Stearns-Knight, Chandler, and Cleveland automobiles.

PIERCE-ARROW

During the early 1930s, Franklin and Pierce-Arrow were the two most notable automakers remaining in business within the state of New York. True, the Cunningham car was built in Rochester, but it was a marque of extremely limited production, on an esoteric plane with the rare Brewster car built on Long Island. Neither the Cunningham nor the Brewster enjoyed wide distributorship; they were actually unknown to a great many prospective buyers in the early thirties, because they were seldom advertised or exhibited at shows.

The Pierce-Arrow was built in Buffalo, by the Pierce-Arrow Motor Car Company (founded 1901) though its later destiny was controlled by South Bend's Studebaker Corporation. Studebaker had purchased Pierce-Arrow in 1928, perhaps taking a cue from Henry Ford's earlier purchase of the Lincoln Motor Company.

After Studebaker acquired Pierce-Arrow, styling improved rapidly. Earlier Pierce-Arrows were of the finest quality, but they looked like arks. There even had been a Pierce-Arrow *truck*. But the '29 models were much better-looking than the earlier cars, and Pierce styling continued to improve after that.

There were three series of Pierce-Arrows in 1930, all with straight-eight, L-head engines. The following types were available:

C SERIES (132-inch wheelbase, 115 horsepower)

Club Brougham	$2595
Coupe	2750
Sedan	2750

B SERIES (134-inch wheelbase, 125 horsepower)

Roadster	$2975
Touring	2975
Sport Phaeton	3275
Convertible Coupe	3250

(139-inch wheelbase on the following B series)

Sedan	$3275
Victoria Coupe	3350
7-Passenger Sedan	3475
Club Sedan	3550
7-Passenger Enclosed-Drive Limousine	3675

A SERIES (144-inch wheelbase, 132 horsepower)

7-Passenger Touring Car	$3975
Convertible Coupe	3975
7-Passenger Sedan	4275
7-Passenger Enclosed Drive Limousine	4475
Town Car	6250

All models had 7.00 x 18 tires except the "C" series, which had 6.50 x 19s. Sales of '30 models totalled 6177 in ten months, a decline of 1341 from the comparable 1929 figure.

Pierce-Arrow, in 1931, offered beautiful models which could have been sold on looks alone. Yet many advertisements for the Pierce-Arrows pictured *early* models; as well as the new, and gave testimonials to the durability of Pierce-Arrows still in use, such as Joseph E. Widener's 1920 landau, the Honorable Horace White's 1917 touring car, Adolph Busch III's 1923 coupe, and the fourteen-year-old, semi-enclosed limousine being driven daily for Mr. Lucius J. Otis of Chicago.

Prices on 1931 models were as much as $810 lower than before, with Group B models starting at $2685, and Group A at $3650. Salon models were priced upward from $4275, and custom models by Le Baron cost up to $10,000!

Freewheeling was the outstanding feature for 1931, though the radiator shell was deepened, doors were wider and body panels were lower, with bottoms of doors flush with the body sills. Running board aprons were narrower and fenders were redesigned. Of course, the characteristic headlights in the fenders continued to be a Pierce-Arrow trademark.

One of the loveliest of all the '31 models was the four-passenger Group A Sport Phaeton, with dual cowls and windshields, side-mounts, a large trunk at the rear, and a striking, two-tone color scheme in beige and black. There were twenty-eight other fine models available from the Buffalo factory, as well as the various custom models which were usually tailored to the buyer's whims. Sales of 1931 Pierce-Arrows reached 4056 by November.

The 132-horsepower eight was not offered by Pierce-Arrow for 1932, but the 125-horsepower model was continued, with choice of 137 or 142-inch wheelbase, for $2850 and up.

Two all-new 12-cylinder models were introduced, with 140 and 150-horsepower engines, and were priced from only $3650. Wheelbases on the V-12 models ranged from 137 to 147 inches. Pierce-Arrow continued to illustrate its early models in some advertisements. A 1908 Pierce-Arrow originally costing $7100 was compared with the latest Model 53 V-12 Club Sedan costing only $3650. The difference in value was obvious!

In addition to the extra running (or parking) lights which had been offered in 1931, the 1932 Pierce-Arrows also had dual, shell-type horns mounted to the tie-bar between the fenders. One-piece bumpers, found on previous custom models, were now standard.

Improved freewheeling was continued on '32 models, usable in all forward speeds, with silent synchro-mesh transmission and silent helical intermediate gears. No starter pedal was necessary on the new Pierce models, which featured stall-proof automatic starting. Dash-adjusted ride control was offered, as in many other 1932 cars, and safety glass throughout was included at no extra cost. Furthermore, every new Pierce-Arrow contained a built-in electric clock.

"Cushioned Power" consisted of eight rubber supports on which the engine was mounted. And bodies were "super-insulated" with felt-lined floors, doors and panels. The "double dash" was also lined with felt and composition insulating material, and the body itself was mounted on cork. A double muffler was used for added quietness, and Pierce-Arrow claimed that their engines were quieter than the V-12s offered by Lincoln, Cadillac, Auburn or Packard.

Late in 1932, in a gruelling test of speed and endurance, a stock Pierce-Arrow "Twelve" was driven around the desert near Salt Lake City, Utah, for twenty-four continuous hours, at an *average speed of 112.9 miles per hour!* This car covered a distance of 2710 miles in the twenty-four hours, which in

THE NEW
PIERCE-ARROW
TWELVES

Model 53 Club Sedan ... $3650 at Buffalo (Special Equipment Extra)

Another Page in
Fine Car History

IN the first few moments of demonstration, any model of the New Twelve line registers as a brilliant example of engineering discovery and creation.

No other fine cars are like or even comparable . . . none has so completely harnessed and controlled the amazing power of twelve cylinders . . . or made this power so obedient to every wish and whim of silent, luxurious motoring.

The New Twelves are endowed, as well, with the enviable social preferment that is ever Pierce-Arrow's own.

In brief, Pierce-Arrow gives timely and characteristic expression to the twelve-cylinder type of fine car . . . offers economic warrant for its present purchase . . . and again supremely justifies the faith of two generations of well-bred Americans.

THE NEW TWELVES ARE IN TWO GROUPS:
142″ to 147″ wheelbase . . . 150 horsepower . . . $3995 to $4500
137″ to 142″ wheelbase . . . 140 horsepower . . . $3295 to $4050

THE NEW EIGHTS ARE PRICED FROM $2495
137″ to 142″ wheelbase . . . 125 horsepower

All prices f.o.b. Buffalo

THE lower picture, first published by Pierce-Arrow in 1908, portrays a car which sold for $7100—the very finest automobile of that day . . . The illustration above shows one of today's new Pierce-Arrow Twelves—the greatest fine car value of the present searching and sophisticated hour.

THE NEW TWELVES are priced, at Buffalo, from

$3295

itself would have been remarkable. But the car that passed this test had already travelled some 35,000 hard miles *beforehand!*

Despite the obvious ruggedness of the Pierce-Arrow, it was in twenty-sixth place in sales for 1932 and 1933. In 1932, only 2470 cars were sold during the first ten months, and in 1933, the figure for the comparable period dropped to only 1776.

For the 1933 season, Pierce-Arrow offered a 135-horsepower "Eight" with 366-cubic-inch displacement, or a 160-horsepower "Twelve" with 429 cubic inches. A 175-horsepower "Custom Twelve" was also available.

Prices for 1933 were lower, beginning at $2385, f.o.b. for the 8-cylinder "836" series Club Brougham with trunk. The minimum price of the V-12 "1236" Club Brougham was $2785 and, model-for-model, the cars with V-12 engines sold for $400 more than those with straight-eights. Though most Pierce-Arrow buyers were still able to pay cash, "payment-from-income" financing was available upon request, discreetly offered to the new buy-now, pay-later customer.

Stewart-Warner automatic power mechanical brakes were added for 1933, and the ordinary brake pedal gave way to an elongated treadle which matched the accelerator foot control just to the right of it. The sight of this unusual setup was strange to most who visited the showrooms that year.

As usual, there were many fine models in the Pierce-Arrow line, but the best of all was the ultra-streamlined *"Silver Arrow."* Five of these remarkable cars were built for the Chicago Century of Progress Exhibition, and at least three exist today in collections. The "Silver Arrow" had many styling characteristics seen in the following year's Chrysler and De Soto "Airflows." But the "Silver Arrow" had a more extreme slant to the back end, and two high, narrow slits that resembed gun-slots in a fortress more than the rear windows that they were supposed to be. The front end, though bearing characteristic Pierce-Arrow styling features, was semi-streamlined. The angle of the grille was still a bit steep to cleave through the windstream like an "Airflow." Though the first few "Silver Arrows" were experimental in purpose, they received so much admiration that a "Silver Arrow" was offered, with modifications, for 1934.

In 1934, Pierce-Arrow enlarged its straight-eight engine to 385 cubic inches, giving it 140 horsepower. One 462-cubic-inch "Twelve" was offered, with 175 horsepower. The smaller V-12 engine was discontinued. Both of Pierce-Arrow's 1934 engines developed their peak horsepower at 3400 RPM.

The "Silver Arrow" model was available with an 8-cylinder engine, and the 1934 version had an enlarged rear window. Except for the sloping rear deck-roofline, the new "Silver Arrow" was not so different from other '34 Pierce-Arrows. Fender and hood designs were similar to other models. A semi-streamlined club sedan was also available, on either "840" or "1240" chassis.

Hoods of 1934 Pierce-Arrows featured horizontal vent doors. The traditional archer radiator figure was retained. Two grille designs were used that year, the most attractive having all-vertical members.

Instrument panels were located in the center of the dash, with a glove compartment at either side. Pierce-Arrow outdid itself with clocks, offering a second clock for the rear compartments of sedans and limousines.

Adjustable ventilating panes were featured in side windows. Pierce-Arrow, by 1934, was considered by many to be the most completely insulated of all cars. It had heavy linings of "all-fibre Kapok," a material derived from the Ceiba tree in Java. For added noise-elimination, Pierce-Arrow included a third muffler in its exhaust system. The engine, gear and drive shaft noise characteristic of a car of the early '30s simply did not exist.

As the 1930s continued, Pierce Arrow's star sank lower in a darkening sky. After the "Silver Arrow," nothing very exciting in design left the Buffalo shops. The 1935 to 1938 Pierce-Arrows looked expensive but, like the big Lincolns of the same era, they seemed too conservative in appearance to be of much interest to buyers. During its last few years, most of Pierce-Arrow's products were sedate sedans and limousines, usually painted light blue, dark blue, or black.

In the mid-thirties, Pierce-Arrow entered a second field—building all-steel travel trailers. In the September, 1936 issue of *Trailer Travel* magazine, the Trailer Division of Pierce-Arrow Motor Corporation ran a full-page ad featuring the Pierce-Arrow "Travelodge." Priced from $595 to $1145, these trailers were of modest size, but moved far ahead of their time in construction. They had the dual advantage of welded steel framework and an all-aluminum exterior. This unit was far superior to most other early trailers, which were usually built of plywood, canvas or masonite, on a wooden frame. Pierce-Arrow trailers even featured independent wheel suspension and (at a slight, additional cost) hydraulic brakes and Houdaille shock absorbers. They were a dream to tow.

Despite the high quality of Pierce-Arrow's products, the company went further into the red in the mid-'30s, and Studebaker regretfully decided it could no longer support this venture. The last Pierce-Arrow automobile was the 1938 model.

Because Pierce-Arrow never built a "cheap" car, any remaining specimen would be either a valuable classic or antique automobile, today.

PLYMOUTH

The Chrysler Corporation introduced its first low-priced Plymouth cars in the summer of 1928, with production beginning in June. During the latter months of 1928, the nameplates on these cars read "CHRYSLER-PLYMOUTH," but by the year's end the 1929 models were simply tagged PLYMOUTH, and 58,000 units already had been sold. The 4-cylinder, 45-horsepower Plymouth continued, with few noticeable changes, through 1929 and into the early months of 1930. Mechanically, the '29 and early '30 Plymouth was a continuation of the 1928 Chrysler "58," which had been discontinued as the first Chrysler-Plymouths appeared.

In styling, the early Plymouths were virtually identical to the 1929 Chrysler "65" light 6-cylinder models. The bodies of the two cars looked alike, as did the hoods and the narrow profile radiator design. The only obvious difference (without looking at the engine or dashboard) was that the earliest Plymouths did not have cowl lamps. Also, they had 20-inch wheels, while the Chryslers had eighteens.

The early 1930 Plymouth was advertised as the "full-size" car. It was roomier than competitive low-priced automobiles and, with the new midget cars coming on the market, Chrysler though it wise to indicate that their new price-leader was not among these.

seen 'All Three' — what's the Verdict?"

"Plymouth . . . it's got all the Features our Salesmen need!"

Only in Plymouth — *(and certain higher-priced cars)* can you get all these Vital Features!

PURCHASING AGENTS get paid for being RIGHT! They can't buy on sentiment or habit. "Look at All Three" is language they understand!

And doesn't it make real sense to discard the old ways of buying cars . . . to pick your automobile on actual comparative facts instead!

Why should you be willing to pay *more* for *any* car that gives you *much less* than Plymouth offers? Consider the following facts carefully. For they are

typical of what you find when you "Look at All Three!"

Safety-Steel Bodies . . . steel reinforced with steel . . . that's *one* big, vital safety factor. Hydraulic Brakes . . . never need equalizing . . . stop more surely, more quickly . . . and naturally the brake lining lasts very much longer. That's the other vital safety factor.

Yet Plymouth *alone*, in the lowest-price field, gives you *both* of these features indispensable to safe driving.

And at Plymouth's low price you get the strongest and

simplest type of Individual Wheel Springing for less than any other car offering anything similar.

These—and many other Plymouth features, such as patented Floating Power engine mountings, valve seat inserts that, owners report, make grinding needless under 30,000 miles, Duplate Safety Plate Glass throughout for a few dollars extra (only $10 on the De Luxe Sedan) such features as these have made Plymouth America's most "up-and-coming" low-priced car.

Ask any Dodge, De Soto or Chrysler dealer to give you a demonstration and all the facts about Plymouth.

• • •

LOOK AT THESE PRICES! Plymouth prices start at $495; De Luxe Plymouth Six models at $575 f. o. b. factory, Detroit, Michigan. Prices are subject to change without notice.

IT'S THE
BEST ENGINEERED
LOW-PRICED CAR!

PLYMOUTH SIX $495 AND UP F.O.B. FACTORY DETROIT

In March, 1930, the Plymouth Business Coupe was available for only $655, f.o.b. Detroit. Other models: Rumble Seat Roadster, $675; 2-Door Sedan, $675; Touring Car, Rumble Seat Coupe, or 4-Door Sedan, each $695; and the De Luxe Sedan, $745. Nineteen-inch wooden wheels were standard, with wire wheels available at extra cost.

Chrysler never built a Plymouth car that did not have hydraulic brakes. This feature was a distinct advantage over Ford and Chevrolet and other low-priced cars with mechanical brakes.

Every Plymouth engine was put to a two-hour block test and a careful dynamometer test, which "weeded out" any faulty units. In March, 1930, Plymouth cars became available through any dealership that sold Chryslers, Dodges, or De Sotos. That opened more than 10,000 sales outlets.

In April, 1930, Plymouth made dramatic styling changes, as the "New Finer" models appeared. The greatly improved Plymouth had 48 horsepower and an all-new safety-steel body with a welded steel frame. The new body, on closed models, had the smart cadet visor and "military front," which meant that the front section above the visor was of steel and curved forward near the top. Also, on "New Finer" models, the side portion of the roof just above the doors was of steel rather than of fabric over wood, as before.

The radiator design on the "New Finer" Plymouth was also new. The narrow profile motif was dropped, and the deeper radiator shell bore a faint resemblance to that of a Chevrolet. The new horn was a disc-shaped vibrator-type, suspended from the middle of the headlight tie-bar.

Rear windows on the first of the closed "New Finer" models were rectangular, as before. But, after a short time, they were changed to an oval design, as previously seen on General Motors' '29 Oaklands and Pontiacs.

Inside the car, the dash had been redesigned; gauges were set directly into the dashboard, instead of on a separate panel. An electric gas gauge was now included, early Plymouths having nothing but a mechanical gauge in the rear, atop the tank. A black, hard rubber steering wheel had since replaced the old wood-rimmed type seen on the '29 Plymouths. The engine, still a "four," featured a mechanical water pump and fuel pump rather than the simple thermo-syphon water system and vacuum-tank fuel feed of the older units. During the run of the "New Finer" models, horsepower was increased to 50.

On order, Plymouth closed cars were factory-wired for immediate installation of a radio. And despite the many improvements, "New Finer" Plymouth prices began at only $535 for the new 2-passenger Business Roadster (minus a rumble seat) and $565, for Business Coupe. A new model at the top of the line was the $695 Convertible Coupe. With its glass side windows rolling up from the doors, it was far more comfortable than a side-curtained roadster in chilly weather.

Plymouth sales, contrary to the Depression trend, rose during the early '30s. Buyers recognized the Plymouth as a great value with many excellent features. Sales reached 63,000 in 1930, and 94,000 the following year. The figure continued to rise until 499,000 were sold in 1936 alone!

The early 1931 Plymouth model was the same "New Finer" offered during the latter part of 1930. Wood wheels were still standard equipment, but more and more buyers were paying extra for wire wheels. The 4-cylinder "Silver Dome" engine delivered 20 miles per gallon at highway speeds below 50, and the top speed was 60–62 m.p.h. with the standard 4.3 gear ratio. During the first part of the year, prices remained the same as in 1930.

Though there was no panel surrounding the gauges on "New Finer" dashboards, some models were offered with a contrasting paint scheme and striping on the dash, which simulated such a panel. Wire wheels soon became optional at no extra cost. In June, 1931, an all-new model made its appearance.

The new, late '31 Plymouth was known as the "PA" model. It was considerably restyled, with a new rounded radiator shell and built-in grille, as well as one-piece bumpers, new wire wheels (still 19-inch diameter) and many refinements in trim and detail. Bodies were somewhat similar to the previous "New Finer" models, but mouldings and windows were slightly changed. Also, the new windshields could be swung out for ventilation instead of cranked up just a few inches as before.

The most notable improvement in the "PA," however, was the sensational "Floating Power" feature. This consisted of live rubber engine mounts plus a very flexible cantilever spring which supported the engine at the rear. The engine was extremely flexible in its cradle, and the new mounting design virtually eliminated vibration, giving the 56-horsepower 4-cylinder engine "the smoothness of an eight."

In addition to the exciting, new "Floating Power," the Plymouth "PA" also offered freewheeling and a new easy-shift transmission, making the car a real pleasure to drive. It could reach 40 miles per hour from a dead stop in less than ten seconds, and could reach a top speed of 70. Automatic vacuum spark advance was standard equipment, and the new double-drop frame gave an overall lower silhouette to the car. A distinguishing feature was the new winged goddess figure on the radiator cap.

Even with its many improvements, the "PA" Plymouth was priced the same as the "New Finer" it replaced. The standard roadster was still available at $535. The new, top price was $645 for either 4-door sedan or convertible coupe. Every Plymouth, at this time, was guaranteed in writing for 90 days or 4000 miles; this guarantee included the full cost of any parts or labor.

Shatterproof plate glass was offered at a small extra cost, and every closed car was wired for Transitone radio which became a Philco product in 1931.

As many as 105,096 "PA" models were built in the following groups and quantities:

Phaeton	528
Business Roadster	200
Sport Roadster (with rumble seat)	2680
Business Coupe	12,079
Sport Coupe (with rumble seat)	9696
Cabriolet (cvt. cp. w. r/s)	2783
2-Door Sedan	23,038
4-Door Sedan	49,465
Deluxe 4-door Sedan	4384
Taxi Cab (specially equipped)	112
Chassis only	131

The new "PB" models appeared in February, 1932. After that "PA" sedans were continued for a few more months, minus a few appointments, as low-cost "thrift" models. The 2-door sedan and 4-door sedan were reduced to $495 and $575, respectively. These last "PAs" are rare, for most buyers chose to pay more and get the new features of the "PB."

There were ten new models of the 1932 "PB" series which offered all-new bodies. The windshield was slanted and, on closed models, the old-fashioned metal sun visor was eliminated from the outside and replaced with a movable inside visor. Rear windows were broad and rectangular. The hood was longer, and swept back to the windshield posts. This feature made it impossible to raise the hood with the swinging windshield open.

The grille was placed at a slight slant, and front doors now swung open at the front. Wheelbase was lengthened three inches to 112⅜", and new 18-inch wheels (wire unless otherwise specified) were adopted.

Mechanically, many changes were in evidence. The new engine was still a four, but it developed 65 horsepower at 3400 RPM because of a new downdraft carburetor and improved manifold. New "centrifuse" brake drums (with cast iron fused to outer rims of steel) helped to dispel heat and prevent "brake fade." The 1932 "PB" Plymouth was one of the most powerful, smoothest-running 4-cylinder cars ever built in this country. And it was the last 4-cylinder model that Plymouth or the Chrysler Corporation offered to the public.

Big news from Plymouth in 1933 was the 6-cylinder (L-head) engine. The

"THE _Real Fun_ STARTS WHEN YOU DRIVE A CAR THAT'S SAFE!"

"Plymouth alone has everything for happy driving...with safety"

"WHEN WE STEP OUT in our Plymouth, there's nothing to think about but having a good time. Even the kids enjoy it without tiring. And we know they're perfectly safe."

This family might be yours. They wanted the most for their money. So they looked at "All Three" and found what they wanted.

We urge you to do the same ... to convince yourself that Plymouth alone, in the low-price field, has all four of the vital features you need.

It gives you both _safety_ and _comfort_. For it has self-equalized Hydraulic Brakes . . . a Safety-Steel Body . . . Floating Power engine mountings . . . Individual Wheel Springing.

You'll find but one of these features in any of the other lowest-priced cars. Only Plymouth has them _all_. Any Dodge, De Soto or Chrysler dealer will demonstrate its _extra_ value.

• • •

PICTURED ABOVE—the De Luxe Plymouth Sedan. Plymouth prices begin at $530 at the factory, Detroit, subject to change without notice. Duplate Safety Plate Glass _throughout_ for low extra charge.

THE NEW PLYMOUTH   THE BEST ENGINEERED CAR IN THE LOW-PRICE FIELD

new unit in the '33 "PC" and "PD" models developed 70 horsepower and had a displacement of 189.8 cubic inches. It was used only one year. The 1934-through-1941 engines were 201.3 cubic inches, due to an increased stroke (4⅜".)

Body lengths varied on the '33 Plymouths. The first "PC" models had a comparatively short 107-inch wheelbase, 17-inch wheels, and were easily identified by the heavy chrome "radiator shell" around the grille. In March, 1933, the "PD" models appeared, with 107¾" wheelbase on "Standard" models and 113½" on the "De Luxe."

Despite the new 6-cylinder engine, completely restyled (and smaller) bodies and many mechanical improvements, prices were cut again in 1933. The price of the utilitarian Business Coupe was only $495. Coupe bodies on 1933–34 Plymouths were unusually sporty in appearance, owing to the small, low-roofed cab and the high hood and deck.

"Look at all three" was a well-advertised Plymouth slogan during 1933. It, of course, referred to Plymouth's favorable comparison with its two major rivals, Chevrolet and Ford. A total of 7,355 De Soto, Dodge and Chrysler dealers were still in business in 1933, and they all handled the Plymouth which had become their "bread-and-butter" car.

Later in 1933, while the "PD" models were in production, Plymouth's minimum f.o.b. price dropped to only $445. This was the lowest in Plymouth's history, before or since! In 1933, Plymouth sold 249,667 units, well over *double* the 111,926 sold in 1932.

For 1934, Plymouth featured new semi-skirted fenders, and a longer hood which bore, along the sides, a combination of two ventilating doors and sixteen louvres on de luxe models. Gone was the winged goddess with mermaid body and flowing hair. In her place, as a mascot, was a disc-shaped ornament bearing the encircled and stylized figure of a sailing vessel.

De Luxe models had a new wheelbase of 114 inches, and all models had the new 201.3 cubic-inch six which developed 77 horsepower with the 5.8 compression cast-iron cylinder head or 82 horsepower with the optional 6.5 compression aluminum head.

Independent front wheel suspension with coil springs now provided an easy ride on rough roads. Added comfort on "De Luxe" Plymouths was insured by the "butterfly" ventilating windows which could be swung shut and lowered into the front doors, if desired. These disappearing vent windows were a Chrysler Corporation feature only in '34.

"De Luxe" models had several added features; a foot dimmer control for headlights, a voltage regulator, a vibration dampener, also, better brake drums and deeper frames. A vacuum-controlled clutch was still used.

In the first six months of 1934, Plymouth shipped 235,215 cars, according to an advertisement in the August 18 issue of *Saturday Evening Post,* "Let's Look at the Record." The advertisement stated that, in the closing months of 1928, only one out of fifty cars sold had been a Plymouth, yet by 1933 the ratio had changed to one in every five! Floating power and hydraulic brakes were still Plymouth's major selling points.

Plymouth continued to use an L-head engine, and 6-cylinder models were built, exclusively, until the first Plymouth V-8 appeared (with overhead valves) for 1955.

America wanted a Low-priced Car.
without that "Low-priced Look"

IT'S A SIX
AT **$90 LESS**

No Wonder they're saying "Plymouth is headed for First Place"

WE'D all like a car that costs little to buy and little to run ... but we don't like it to *look* that way.

So Plymouth designers took heed of human nature ... and took advantage of today's low cost of materials!

The result of their efforts is the new Plymouth Six—a low-priced car without that "low-priced look."

Already people are calling it "America's next Number One Car." It is selling far faster than Plymouth sold a year ago. Many people say it's headed for *first place*.

This would not be the case if its *engineering* didn't match its style. For few people buy a car on looks alone.

The new Plymouth is a Six ... with a powerful 70-horsepower engine ... a Six with Floating Power engine mountings, which make it *completely vibrationless!*

It is a roomy, full-sized car in which the whole family can ride in comfort. It is *safer* than other low-priced automobiles ... for it gives you the protection of hydraulic brakes, a safety-steel body, and a safety-glass windshield!

It is remarkably "easy" on gasoline, tires and upkeep. Engineers have c its engine "the most efficient ever b

So look at the New Plymouth ..." at All Three" low-priced cars .. may the best car win!

LOOK AT THESE NEW LOW PR
4-door Sedan $545, Convertible Coupe Rumble Seat Coupe $525, Business Coupe $4 prices f.o.b. factory. Convenient terms. Low ered prices. *On all models*—Floating Power mountings, hydraulic brakes, free-wheeling, glass windshields. Closed cars wired for P Transitone radio. Automatic clutch optional

PLYMOUTH SIX

SOLD BY 7,232 DESOTO, DODGE AND
CHRYSLER DEALERS EVERYWHERE

THE SMOOTHNESS OF AN EIGHT · THE ECONOMY OF A FOUR

NEW PLYMOUTH
FLOATING POWER
and FREE WHEELING

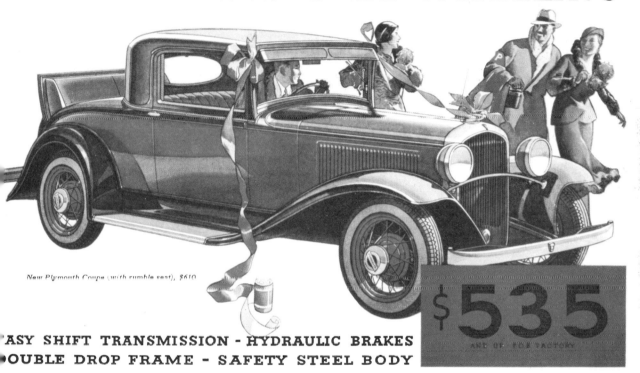

New Plymouth Coupe (with rumble seat), $610

$535

AND UP, F.O.B. FACTORY

EASY SHIFT TRANSMISSION - HYDRAULIC BRAKES
DOUBLE DROP FRAME - SAFETY STEEL BODY

Give Yourself the Vibrationless Ride

THE motoring public wanted something new, and they got it in the New Plymouth with Floating Power and Free Wheeling. Floating Power brought the vibrationless ride for the first time to the lowest-priced field—the Smoothness of an Eight, the Economy of a Four.

This new engineering discovery makes it possible for the New Plymouth to perform as no lowest-priced car, regardless of cylinders, performed before.

The result is a tidal wave of enthusiasm that has swept the country from coast to coast. Everywhere thousands and thousands are talking, driving and buying. Not in years has the motor car industry seen such sensational interest.

So revolutionary is this achievement in the New Plymouth that words alone cannot possibly do it justice.

Floating Power with Free Wheeling, *at no extra cost,* cannot be expressed—it must be "felt."

Floating Power with Free Wheeling and with Easy-Shift Transmission cannot be explained—it must be enjoyed.

Safety-Steel Bodies, Double-Drop frames, hydraulic brakes are but a combination of words, but just drive a New Plymouth.

You get results so amazing that you wouldn't believe them yourself unless you had actually *experienced* them.

So don't buy any car until you have seen and driven the New Plymouth. Be fair to yourself and your pocketbook. Buy the most for your money.

NEW LOW PRICES—Roadster $535, Sport Roadster $595, Sport Phaeton $595, Coupe $565, Coupe (with rumble seat) $610, Convertible Coupe $645, Sedan (2-door) $575, Sedan (4-door, 6-window) $635, f.o.b. factory. Low delivered prices. Convenient time-payments.
   Non-shatterable plate glass is available on all models at small extra cost. All enclosed models wired for Philco-Transitone radio without extra cost.

NEW PLYMOUTH IS SOLD BY DE SOTO, CHRYSLER AND DODGE DEALERS

PONTIAC

The Pontiac "Big Six" of 1930 had 60 horsepower, and, as before, a wheel-base of 110 inches. Priced at $825, f.o.b. for the sedan (the same price as in 1927), Pontiac filled a market for a light 6-cylinder car—just $150 above the Chevrolet range.

Seven models were available, starting at $745. Pontiacs for 1930 had a slightly slanted windshield, and the instrument panel also followed the 1930 General Motors trend; small round, black gauges on a simple, glossy-black dashboard. As in 1929, the rear window was oval-shaped and the general body-styling was not radically changed from the previous year, except for a new belt moulding.

An ignition lock attached to the coil (in the dash) replaced the transmission lock formerly used. Among other mechanical improvements was a gear-drive safety device that would automatically shut off the ignition should the engine's oil pressure fail.

For 1931, Pontiac featured new bodies (by Fisher, as before) and an all-new V-shaped mesh grille of pressed steel over the radiator. Wire wheels were standard equipment. Fender-mounted auxiliary lights were featured, as on the Oakland. Closed Pontiacs were upholstered in either mohair or whipcord; open cars were upholstered in leather. The price of the 1931 sedan was cut to

Smiling in the rain

EVEN when rain pelts against the windows of your car, you'll be dry and comfortable inside if your car has Fisher No Draft Ventilation. You can open one of those smart Ventipanes just a little, and out goes the stuffy air, in comes the pure fresh air, without drafts or any splatter of raindrops. This helps to keep the inside of the windshield clear for folks in the front seat, which certainly makes driving safer. And it keeps little folks in back seats from being chilled by drafts, or getting all hot and squirmy and restless. In fact, it would be hard for anyone to get tired of riding in the smart, strong, safe new Body by Fisher. The seats are wider, deeper—the cushions more luxuriously restful—the whole interior noticeably more spacious. That's one of the first things which will impress you, when you see and examine any of the new General Motors cars.

$745, although the wheelbase was increased to 112 inches. Horsepower was unchanged.

During January to November of 1931, Pontiac sold 68,087 cars; better than the comparable period, 1930, when 64,226 were sold.

Horsepower was increased to 65 in the 200-cubic-inch Pontiac "Six" for 1932. In addition, Pontiac offered a 251-cubic-inch, 85-horsepower V-8 engine with horizontal valves. The latter engine, the one which had been used in the discontinued Oakland car, was offered in Pontiac only during the 1932 model year. No other Pontiac V-8 was available until the 1955 models appeared.

The 1932 Pontiac "Six" had a 114-inch wheelbase, and the V-8 model had a wheelbase of 117. Prices of sedan models (f.o.b.) were $765 and $945.

The '32 had a V-shaped grille, plus a trumpet horn below each headlamp on V-8s and some Sixes. Streamlined fender parking lights remained. There were four ventilating doors on each side of the hood, painted to match the car, and two different radiator mascots were used. One was a stylized bird with raised wing, and the other was the Pontiac Indian head in a circle.

Features for 1932 included synchro-mesh transmission with quiet second, freewheeling, ride control and fabric-covered enclosed springs. Modern, visorless Fisher bodies were used, and there was "rubber cushioning at 47 points."

The instrument board of the '32 Pontiac was unusually attractive. Entirely in black, it was divided into three panels, the center panel containing two large and two small circular gauges which could be illuminated either directly from the outside or indirectly from behind. The large, right-hand dial contained both the water-temperature and oil-pressure gauges, one above the other, and was complemented at the left by a sweep hand speedometer. The smaller gauges, between, were the ammeter and fuel indicator.

This was the final year for the unusual Pontiac 6-cylinder engine which had twin cylinder heads (one for each three cylinders.) Pontiac continued to use its cross-flow radiator.

Wire wheels were standard, with twelve-spoke demountable wood wheels available as optional equipment. Not long before, wood wheels had been standard on most cars and wire wheels were considered a luxury. Now, it was the other way around, though the high-quality wood wheels offered as optional equipment on some cars of the early '30s were much better than the cheap-looking originals. The Pontiac "Six" had 5.25 x 18″ tires, while V-8 models rolled on 6.00 x 17s.

The ill-fated Pontiac V-8 would do 75 miles per hour top speed, with a

Please do not disturb

Believe it or not, this young fellow is going places! And he's going in the most comfortable, safe, healthful way you can imagine—in Body by Fisher. That means he's traveling first-class, in a body notable for rugged strength and durable quiet as well as for luxurious appointments and suave streamline beauty. It means wider, deeper seats, too, and the stretch-out-and-relax kind of room that grown-ups prize so much. It also means Fisher-perfected and owner-approved No Draft Ventilation, enabling enjoyment of crisp autumn and tonic winter air without a draft in a carful. All these are yours in Body by Fisher no matter which General Motors car you may choose.

Body by Fisher

bland gear ratio of 4.22 to 1. No one cared much for this model, yet, in 1932, Ford introduced a V-8 which was a great hit!

Undoubtedly, the most attractive of the '32 Pontiacs was the little convertible coupe with folding windshield and practical, roll-up windows in the side doors. The khaki top was set off nicely by folding, chrome-plated landau irons on either side. The rear window was oval, though closed '32 Pontiacs had rectangular rear windows like other General Motor cars that year.

Pontiac revealed sweeping changes for 1933. Never before in the car's seven-year history had it been so dramatically restyled—and with an all-new engine! The 1933 model had a new 115-inch wheelbase and a 77-horsepower straight-eight engine of 223 cubic inches that would push it up to 78 miles an hour. *All* 1933 Pontiacs were straight-eights, the sixes and V-8s having both been discontinued at the end of the 1932 run. The 1933 car was completely new, from its broad, V-shaped grille (with outswept lower section) to the new, more rounded body and its beaver-tail rear quarters. The new, long hood had four, large, slanting louvres on each side, not far from the cowl. Fenders were semi-skirted and stylishly ribbed with decorative mouldings. Fisher "No Draft Ventilation" was incorporated in all bodies.

Rather than having a tie-bar, headlamps were connected vertically to the fenders and horizontally to the radiator shell, by chromed supports. Only one trumpet horn appeared on the '33 model, set below the left headlamp.

Safety glass was used in all windshields. The starter button was on the dash. And an 18-gallon fuel tank was hidden by streamlined paneling at the rear.

Despite the many changes in the '33 Pontiac "Eight," prices (f.o.b.) started at only $565. Not long before, few could have dreamed that a straight-eight car would ever sell for such prices. Even in 1930 there had been much ballyhoo about the first eights to reach the $995 mark!

The 1934 Pontiac again offered no choice but a straight-eight engine, but horsepower was boosted to 84. Top speed now ranged between 77 and 82 miles per hour, depending on the body model. Wheelbase was lengthened to 117¼ inches, and a new "KY" box girder frame was employed for added strength. The four-door sedan now weighed 3480 pounds, 215 heavier than during the preceding year.

The hood was lengthened seven inches so that it nearly overlapped the cowl, and a horizontal panel of streamlined vent louvres added new éclat to the '34 Pontiac, as well as an illusion of greater length. Even the bullet-shaped headlamps were longer, and fender lights were more streamlined. It was evident that a look of speed was desired.

Independent, knee-action front wheels lent new riding ease, and the pleasing walnut-grained instrument panel carried three large dial-gauges at left and a symmetrical panel with glove compartment at right, with control switches in between.

The starter was actuated by pressing hard on the accelerator pedal, as on the previous year's Chevrolets. The duo-servo, cable-operated Bendix mechanical brakes had 12-inch drums.

Pontiac models for 1934 included: Five-Passenger Touring Car, Two-Door Sedan, Two-Door Trunk Sedan, Four-Door Sedan, Four-Door Trunk Sedan, Two-Passenger Business Coupe, Sport Coupe (with rumble seat), Cabriolet (convertible coupe). The prices were noticeably higher than in 1933, and now began at $695. The new car was still a good buy at the price, however, when compared to older models.

The 1935 Pontiac was completely restyled, with new steel top and V-windshield, and again offered the choice of a six or straight-eight.

REO

Reo first built automobiles in 1904, followed with trucks in 1908. The company was founded by Ransom E. Olds, the "father" of the popular Oldsmobile, after he left his first organization. The name "Reo" was taken from the founder's initials. Reo, unlike Oldsmobile, did not become a part of General Motors.

By 1930, Reo had established a laudable reputation for durability and quality. The 1930 Reo was good, but unspectacular, and more important developments were planned for the following year.

Priced from $1195 to $1945, the best-known Reos were the "Flying Cloud" models. Reo, even in 1930, had interesting features, such as a silent-second transmission that could be downshifted without clashing from high back to second gear at 40 miles per hour. All 1930 models had Lockheed hydraulic brakes.

The lowest-priced Reo used a 60-horsepower, 6-cylinder *Continental* 16-E engine. In fact, Continental engines had been used in the lower-priced Reo series starting with the "Wolverine" models of 1928 and continuing until the end of the 1931 model year. The models "20" and "25" of 1931 used 80-horsepower sixes that were Reo-built.

For 1931, the low-priced "15" series was continued ($1005 and up) with its 60-horsepower Continental engine. Horsepower on the all-Reo "20" and

REO
FLYING CLOUDS

An Eight and a Six

The Flying Cloud Eight—
Five-Passenger Sedan

THEIR distinguished appearance is
a major factor in their great success.
Public faith in Reo is another . . .

REO MOTOR CAR COMPANY, LANSING, MICHIGAN

"25" Flying Cloud models was raised to 85. And the first of the new 125-horsepower straight-8 Reos made their appearance.

Best of all 1931 Reos, by far, were the luxurious "8-35" Reo-Royale models, with streamlined bodies that could easily pass for 1933 models a few years later. The "Royale" had a graceful, sloping windshield, a deep, V-shaped grille, long hood with ventilating doors, and wire wheels. Front doors swung open at the front, and the only characteristics which dated this new car as a 1931 model were the 2-leaf bumpers and the headlamp tie-bar.

"Royale" prices started at $2745, f.o.b. Lansing. A special feature of this 135-inch-wheelbase model was one-shot chassis lubrication.

The "Royale" convertible coupe, announced during spring, had a low-slung folding top with landau irons which lowered gracefully into a special well so that it was nearly level with the rear deck, when folded.

The "Flying Cloud" was available with either 6- or 8-cylinder engine. It had the new body, but the radiator was flat and minus a grille, and the hood had six vertical groups of four louvres on each side, instead of the vent doors. This model looked inconsistent, for the old-style front end clashed with the new-style body.

Placing an ad for the new models in the December, 1930, issue of *The American Boy-Youth's Companion* magazine, the Reo Motor Car Company made this known: "Boys are always welcome in Reo showrooms. Reo dealers everywhere invite you to come in and examine the new Reo-Royale." Obviously, this invitation did *not* include a test-drive, but young visitors would be inclined to leave the showrooms with catalogs that their parents might find of interest.

For 1932, all Reos had "Royale" styling, including the modern V-grille which now flared out near the bottom, twin trumpet-type horns on sport models, and wire wheels. One-piece bumpers were used, and there was no longer a tie-bar between headlamps.

New mechanical features were up to the mark; synchronized-shift transmission with vacuum clutch control, new safety-type centrifuse brake drums (Lockheed hydraulics, as before) double-drop X-type frame, soundproofed bodies, and, as optional equipment, Startix, freewheeling, and safety glass.

The lowest-priced model was the 80-horsepower, 6-cylinder Flying Cloud "6-21," priced from $995.

Other models, all straight-eights, were the 90-horsepower "8-21" and "8-25" models, also, the Royale "8-31" and "8-35," with the 125-horsepower, 356-cubic-inch engine. Royale prices started at $1785.

Reo model-numbers during these years referred to number of cylinders and wheelbase length. And, in 1932, Reo was billing its cars as, "Pioneers of the Air-Stream Design."

Again, in 1933, Reo prices started at just $995. Quoting from *Motor* magazine: "Both the Flying Cloud Six (Model 'S,' 85 h.p.) and Royale Eight (125 h.p.) have more sharply sloping Vee-type radiator grilles. Radiator shells and front splash aprons have been remoulded, and the curve of the front bumper has been altered (dipped in the center) to harmonize more perfectly with them. The front fenders are skirted (partially) and the running boards have curved outer edges, paralleling the body sills."

All 1933 Reos had a redesigned transmission with helical silent-second, built-in freewheeling, and "synchronous meshing of high and second gears."

New features of the Reo "Six" were a downdraft carburetor, automatic choke and automatic heat control.

To increase the smoothness of engine performance, air-cushioned rubber mountings were used, with a torque arm running from the flywheel housing to the frame where it was supported in blocks of rubber.

For economy, Reo had cut down on model varieties for 1933. There was a choice of either the 117-inch-wheelbase "Flying Cloud" Six or 131-inch-wheelbase "Royale" Eight. The largest Royale had become a victim of the Depression. Reo car sales had declined to 3082 in the first ten months of 1933. For the same period in 1932, the figure had been 3540. It had been 6026 in 1931, and 9895 in 1930.

Reos for 1934 offered new styling and a sensational new mechanical development, an *automatic transmission!* Gone was the customary gear-shift lever on the floor, as, after considerable testing, the Reo "Self-Shifter" was offered to an interested public. With the price of the standard business coupe at only $795, the new, automatic transmission was, understandably, an option. Strangely, though, Reo continued to charge extra for bumpers and a spare tire which, by 1934, were taken for granted.

News of the "Reo Self-Shifter" was made public in May, 1933, after two years of road tests, and the device was said to be foolproof. This automatic transmission was more than a mere flash in the pan, for it was offered again in 1935. But Reo was about to abandon automobile operation and concentrate on the truck field, which, of late, had been a more profitable one. So the rare 1936 model, with new styling, was Reo's very last passenger car.

Of the old Reos, the 1927 to 1929 models show up occasionally. Some very nice "Royales" of the early '30s have also survived. But the later models, especially the 1936, are almost never seen, even though there are quite a few Reo *trucks* around.

See the brilliant Ne~

NO GEARS

1934 Reo...with

NO SHIFT LEVER

NO GEARSHIFT LEVER

A Triumph in Aerodynamic design and Long Life Construction

The car without a gearshift lever is presented today by Reo in an entirely new design—a design in which we confidently believe you'll recognize the smartest combination of advanced style and good taste yet offered to the motoring public.

The new Reo Flying Cloud for 1934!

A car of flashing performance and superb construction! A car evolved legitimately and logically from the distinguished Royale, which was America's FIRST car in the ultra modern dynamic vogue.

Originator of this vogue, Reo can be depended upon for its development. You will sense this when you see the car. You'll know instinctively that Reo has the answer to the questions of STYLE.

An Exclusive Advantage

And Reo supplied the answer to the industry's long quest for a practical, workable *automatic transmission.* All over the world, the SELF-SHIFTER is now acclaimed as the greatest advance since the self-starter—and yet it is still to be had ONLY in the new Reo!

The engineering development of 1933 remains the BIG development of 1934. Nothing comparable has been introduced.

Of particular importance to new car buyers is the fact that the SELF-SHIFTER has so emphatically *proved its case.* It is NOT an expedient or an experiment.

In the hands of thousands of owners, over millions of miles, under every condition of road and climate, it has proved that gearshifting by hand is PASSING—that automatic shifting is a *fundamental* principle which will come into general use through sheer public demand for its manifest advantages!

Driving Becomes Piloting

Driving is so much simpler—so much SAFER and more enjoyable —that people simply refuse to consider hand-shifting after a few experiences with the SELF-SHIFTING REO.

Literally, it changes driving into piloting. There is virtually nothing to do but steer. The "take-off" is like that of an airplane—a swift, smooth, uninterrupted surge of power!

Try it yourself—and see!

Start from a dead stop and sweep through to high without reaching for a gearshift lever—without movement of hand or foot. Slow down and change automatically back to second! Drive for hours without touching the clutch! Think of the greater SAFETY in such a car—of the fatigue and tension saved by being able to keep both hands on the wheel and concentrating all attention on *safe control!*

Reo's Greatest Value

It is traditional in the industry that Reo offers a SUPERIOR type of construction—better than average performance—longer than average life. Never was this tradition more truly exemplified than in the new Flying Cloud for 1934. It is an even sturdier and roomier car than previous models which sold for as much as $1795. Its amazingly low price makes it by all odds the finest value Reo has ever offered.

QUALITY in a Reo may be taken for granted. But the SELF-SHIFTER is such a revolutionary advance, so startling in its effect on car operation, that it can be understood and appreciated only after a drive. We urge that you do this—call your Reo dealer today and experience the thrill of a trip in the most advanced car of all—the car without a gearshift lever.

It will make you wonder how long any car of the hand-shift type can continue in public favor—make you realize that it is a GOOD INVESTMENT—for more reasons than one—to buy a Reo!

Outstanding Features You Get in the New Reo

Reo Self-Shifter—no gears to shift . . . 6 cyl. 85 h. p. Reo-built engine . . . counter-weighted 7-bearing crankshaft . . . 118 in. wheelbase—a LARGE CAR of exceptional riding qualities . . . Air cushion engine mountings . . . Airplane type shock absorbers . . . Positive action hydraulic brakes . . . Draft free ventilation.

No gears to shift—and therefore no danger of stalling your motor behind slow traffic on steep hills. The self-shifter automatically finds the proper ratio.

Ample room for three—unusually large front seats —no gearshift lever to take up valuable space. The sedan is a real 6 passenger car.

The new Reo draft-free ventilating system affords unobstructed vision for driver and passenger alike. Easily adjusted—quiet—amazingly effective.

Unusually large and convenient space for luggage. A weather-tight trunk built into the car in a harmonious blend with the aerodynamic design.

$795
Business Coupe

$895
Standard Sedan

Prices f. o. b. Lansing, plus tax.

Self-Shifter—bumpers, spare tire and lock, spring covers, included at slight extra cost.

REO MOTOR CAR CO.,
LANSING · MICHIGAN

Read these before you buy any car— Write for interesting booklets today See your Reo dealer for demonstration

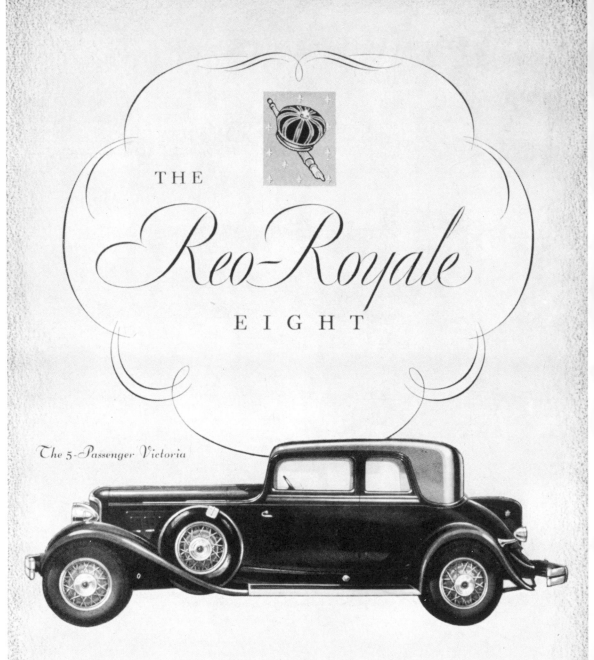

THE

Reo-Royale

E I G H T

The 5-Passenger Victoria

Introducing a stunning new fashion
in fine car design; with interiors that
mark a new era in luxury and good taste.

REO MOTOR CAR COMPANY, LANSING, MICHIGAN

ROCKNE

From 1927 to 1930, Studebaker had offered its lower-priced Erskine "Six," with little success; in 1931, replacing it with an equally inexpensive Studebaker. But for the 1932 season, Studebaker decided to take a chance once again and launch another low-priced car, with a new name. The chosen name was *Rockne,* in honor of the late, great football coach of Notre Dame University, Knute Rockne, who had died in a plane crash in 1931. Rockne had made plans to retire from football after the 1931 season and become Vice-President of Studebaker's new subsidiary company. He had been associated with Studebaker's sales staff for many years. In Rockne's stead, George M. Graham was named Vice-President in Charge of Sales.

The "Rockne Six" for 1932 came in two sizes, the "65," with 66-horsepower and 110-inch wheelbase, and the 72-horsepower "75" with 114-inch wheelbase. Piston displacement of the engine in the "65" was listed at 190 cubic inches, and in the "75," 205 cubic inches.

With prices starting at only $585, Rockne had these five body models in both series: Business Coupe; Rumble Seat Coupe; 4-Door Sedan; Convertible Roadster (Cabriolet); Convertible Sedan. In addition, there was a 2-Door Sedan (Coach) in the "65" series only.

The new Rockne had plenty of style, with a V-shaped grille, slanting hood louvres, graceful front fenders that flowed into the running boards and lines that were even more modern than its big brother, Studebaker.

The 1932 Rockne featured switch key starting, freewheeling, fully synchronized transmission, hydraulic shock absorbers, quadruple counterweighted crankshaft and other advancements, all as standard equipment. The engine was cushioned on live rubber at four points. It was an excellent buy, and Rockne sold fairly well for a car born in hard times; 22,000 units in 1932. In fact, Rockne, in its first nine months, rose to fifth, fourth and even third place in sales in many important market areas in the United States. And in August and September, 1932, Rockne held eighth place in overall nationwide sales. But it was unwise to offer two different basic models, when competing in a low price field.

For 1933, only one series was continued, the former "65" model, now known only as the "Rockne Six." Horsepower was kicked up to 70, and the gear ratio was changed to 4.55 to 1. Wheelbase was left at 110 inches, and prices still began at $585.

Front fenders, though unskirted, were redesigned to hide a greater portion of the steering and axle assembly, and minor changes were made in hood and grille design. The instrument panel was somewhat diamond-shaped, with speedometer in upper center, flanked by a smaller gauge at either side and one below, all gauges being black-faced and circular. Freewheeling was still offered. The new tire size was 5.25 x 17″, and de luxe models had twin side-mounts as well as twin trumpet horns.

Body models were the same as on the '32 "65s," and a Rockne panel delivery truck was added, at $615, f.o.b. But sales declined to 14,366 in 1933, and as Studebaker was in terrible financial shape that year, no new Rockne was offered for 1934.

RUXTON

The 1930 "Ruxton" was an unusual car, introduced in 1929 by New Era Motors, Inc., New York City. New Era was a sales organization and not a manufacturer, so they originally contracted with the Gardner Motor Car Company of St. Louis for the assembled cars. However, by December, 1929, the Gardner deal was off and Gardner came up with its own unique, front-drive car. The New Era Motors contract was awarded to another St. Louis manufacturer, the failing Moon Motor Car Company which was delighted to have the opportunity to produce the new Ruxton.

Through an exchange of stock, the Moon Motor Car Company purchased from New Era Motors, Inc., "all patent rights, granted and pending, to the front-drive Ruxton car . . . as well as plant equipment, engineering data, finished and unfinished cars." The few, remaining Moon dealers who had managed to hang on through previous storms were to be the (luckless) distributors of the Ruxton.

In the October 5th, 1929, issue of *Saturday Evening Post,* readers saw a bold advertisement which began: "Now at your service . . . America's first Front-Wheel-Drive motor car." The new Ruxton was illustrated, but because of limited finances, New Era Motors advertised in black-and-white instead of in color. This was most unfortunate, because one of the Ruxton's unique features was its colorful paint "job" as conceived by automotive artist Joseph Urban.

Because of the front-drive mechanism, the Ruxton sedan could be built low. In fact, it was less than five feet in height! The Ruxton had a small radiator, set above the shrouding that covered the front-drive transaxle, and was flanked on either side by the distinctive, exceedingly narrow Wood-lite headlamps and matching fender lamps. The car had no running boards, and the sides of the body covered the customary chassis aprons. The 100-horsepower straight-eight engine was more than adequate.

The excitement of Ruxton's entry into the market was considerably dampened by the almost simultaneous appearance of both the "Cord" and "Gardner" front-drive models. Only 375 of the classic Ruxtons were built between 1929 and 1931. The majority were sedans, but a couple of collectors have run across phaetons.

Pretty as it was, the Ruxton was a commercial failure. Moon and its related cars were soon "orphans," and, by 1933, owners of these discontinued makes had to seek parts at such agencies as the Moon Motor Car Service Company of Kokomo, Indiana, or Moon-Diana Service, Inc., in New York City. Supply companies for various discontinued cars thrived for a time during the early 1930s. There was a Locomobile Service Company in Philadelphia, an Elgin Motor Car Service Company in Flint, and many more—even a Saxon Motor Car Company which gave its address as, "Box 132, Roseville, Michigan." But, by the late '30s, many of the "orphan" cars of the teens and twenties were long gone, and most of the suppliers of parts for discontinued autos were going out of business as the demand for their wares dwindled to almost nothing.

Rare as the Ruxton may be, a few interesting specimens (usually '30 sedans) show up for sale, from time to time. Few, however, are painted in the original rainbow color-band motif which was so unusual.

STUDEBAKER

Studebaker has become an "orphan" car in recent years, since production was halted in 1966 after a last-ditch stand in Studebaker's Canadian branch.

Studebaker history goes back to 1852 and, during the latter half of the nineteenth century, this was the name known as a leading producer of horse-drawn vehicles. Electric- and gasoline-powered Studebakers followed in the early 1900s and, by 1930, Studebaker (with assembly plant in South Bend), was one of the better-known "independents," having moved from eleventh to ninth place in sales that year.

"Builder of Champions" was a Studebaker slogan in 1930, and though, at that time, there was no "Champion" model as such, there were seven series.

First, there was the new Studebaker "Six," on a 114-inch wheelbase, with a 70-horsepower engine. It was priced at only $895 to $1125 (f.o.b.) and sold for less than any previous Studebaker. Its specifications were the same as the 1930 "Erskine" (Studebaker's price leader) and it actually became a midseason replacement of that car.

The "Dictator Six" was the lowest-priced Studebaker available from the very beginning of the 1930 season; the 4-door sedan sold for $1165. The "Dictator" was rated at 68 horsepower, had a 115-inch wheelbase and 4.78 gear ratio.

One of Studebaker's lowest-geared of all cars was the "Dictator *Eight*" for 1930, which had a miserable 5.11 to 1 gear ratio that worked the 70-horsepower straight eight to death at high speeds and half-to-death at cruising speeds. The "Dictator Eight" also had a 115-inch wheelbase, and the 4-door sedan sold for $1285.

The "Commander Six" and "Commander Eight" shared a 120-inch wheelbase, and their respective horsepower ratings were 75 at 3000 RPM, and 80 at 3600. The sedan prices were $1425 and $1515. The Commander Six was the most efficient of all Studebaker's 1930 models because it developed its peak of power at a lower engine speed and had a favorably high gear ratio of 3.91 to 1. In fact, the "Commander Sixes" of 1928 through 1930 were the only high-geared models built by Studebaker in the late '20s or early '30s (with the possible exception of optional differential ratios on certain other models.) One might surmise that, during that time, high cruising speed was sacrificed in favor of faster pick-up and more pulling-power on hills. There were good reasons for this at the time; most highways were narrow and sometimes roughly-paved, two-lane thoroughfares, and legal speed limits in most states were quite low, sometimes only 35 on the open road! The 8-cylinder "Commander" had a more typical gear ratio: 4.70.

Studebaker's finest 1930 models were the two sizes of "President Eights:" the "FH" series on a 125-inch wheelbase, and the "FE" on 135. Both had a 4.31 gear ratio and 115-horsepower straight-eight engines; the comparative prices of the sedans were $1765 and $1995.

Studebaker's first straight-eight car had been the 1928 "President." In 1929, the "Commander" was also available as an eight, and by 1930 even the "Dictator" series offered an eight for those who preferred this engine.

Larger 1930 Studebakers had thermostatic radiator shutters, and visorless windshield pillars which swept forward near the top in snappy "military" fashion.

One fine-looking automobile was the "President" roadster. Studebakers are not considered "classic" cars, but exceptions must be made for certain "President" models. Another luxurious "President" for 1930 was the $2295 "State Victoria," which had 6 wire wheels, a luggage grid, and Duplate shatterproof glass. Interesting mechanical features were the double-drop frame, coincidental steering-and-ignition lock pioneered by Studebaker and a new, "full power" muffler.

Studebaker defended the construction of its composite steel-over-hardwood bodies by declaring that it was the accepted fine car coachcraft. This was true at the time, for most of the cars that had switched to all-steel bodies were the less expensive makes.

he last word in driving control!

The Triumphant New Studebakers offer you 32 startling betterments for 1932 . . . chief of which is incomparably finer Free Wheeling in all forward speeds *plus* Synchronized Shifting and Automatic Starting. Studebaker virtually eliminated the clutch as a factor in driving when it pioneered Free Wheeling in 1930—and now Studebaker has simplified and improved the entire transmission mechanism *without adding anything new for the driver to do!* The Triumphant New Studebakers . . . with longer, wider bodies . . . Full-Cushioned Power . . . and other epochal improvements . . . are the only line of cars in their price class to provide Safety Plate Glass without extra charge in all windshields and all windows of all models. Drastically lower in price, they reflect all the experience and vitality of Studebaker's 80 enterprising years.

NEW LOW PRICES

PRESIDENT EIGHT, 122 H.P., 135" wheelbase
$1690 *to* $1890 *Reductions up to $560*
COMMANDER EIGHT, 101 H.P., 125" wheelbase
$1350 *to* $1465 *Reductions up to $235*
DICTATOR EIGHT, 85 H.P., 117" wheelbase
$980 *to* $1095 *Reductions up to $120*
STUDEBAKER SIX, 80 H.P., 117" wheelbase
$840 *to* $955 *Prices at the factory*

To start the Triumphant New Studebakers you simply switch on the ignition with a key. The engine instantly responds — and even should it stall at any time, it automatically starts again.

The Studebaker Synchronized Shift assures instantaneous, silent shifting in all gears and at any car speed. There's no clashing. You shift as fast or as slowly as you wish.

With their steel core safety steering wheels of super-strength, and steering gear that automatically rights itself after a turn, the Triumphant New Studebakers hold their course true under all conditions.

The improved Studebaker brakes, at a woman's normal foot pressure, are adequate to any emergency of road or traffic. Brake drums are larger. Lining that's molded and thicker doubles the life and halves the wear.

Studebaker Free Wheeling is controlled by a touch of a lever on the dash. There is no necessity for keeping your foot constantly on a button.

Triumphant New
STUDEBAKERS

Though Studebaker had experimented with hydraulic brakes, and had offered them on certain models during the mid-'20s, their 1930 cars had 4-wheel mechanicals.

For 1931, Studebaker's "Dictator" and "Commander" models, like the "Presidents," were available only as straight-eights. The "Dictator" had 81 horsepower and was priced at $1095 and up, on a 114-inch wheelbase. For $1585, the "Commander Eight" developed 101 horsepower and had a new 124-inch wheelbase. The "President Eights" ($1850) had 122 horsepower and two wheelbases, again 130 or 136 inches. "President" gear ratio was 4.31 as in 1930, and all other 1931 Studebakers had a standard gear ratio of 4.73.

The 1931 models had new V-shaped grilles, new one-piece bumpers that dipped in the center, and big, new, ovaloid headlights minus a tie-bar. Streamlined fender lamps were also included.

Interestingly, though some 1930 Studebakers did not have an outside sun visor, this feature was *reintroduced* on the 1931 versions in a surprising reversal of the trend.

Biggest news of all for 1931, however, was the adoption of freewheeling on all Studebaker models. Studebaker hailed freewheeling as "the greatest automotive advancement since the electric starter." Studebaker pioneered this device on July 10, 1930, when it was first available on the "President" and "Commander" models. In September, 1930, freewheeling was available on the "Dictator Eight," and by January, 1931, even the Studebaker "Six" had it, following many other automakers. It was later outlawed in many states where it was illegal to coast a car down a hill and, by 1935, Studebaker was one of the last manufacturers to abandon freewheeling.

Studebaker advertised in 1931 that there were already 100,000 Studebaker Eights on the road, and that, "the general stampede of the automotive industry to design and rush into the market new eight cylinder cars to meet the demands of an eight-minded public, found Studebaker already impregnably entrenched with three years of eight cylinder leadership." Of course, there had been other straight-eights on the market before Studebaker's; Duesenberg had offered the first American straight-eight in its 1921 model, and there had been a Packard straight-eight as early as 1923. By 1927, straight-eights were also offered by Auburn, Davis, Elcar, Gardner, Hupmobile, Jordan, Kissel, Locomobile, McFarland, Marmon, Paige, Rickenbacker, Roamer and Stearns-Knight.

One favorite among 1931 Studebakers was the "Commander Eight" four-door brougham, with wire wheels, side-mounts, and a trunk at the rear, in addition to metal-covered rear side quarters which gave the car an expensive "close-coupled" appearance. However, the sportiest 1931 Studebaker was the "President Eight" convertible roadster with roll up windows of safety glass, six wire wheels, and a finish of pale green with darker green fenders and trim. This model was a beauty, and is understandably scarce; there is one which used to be frequently seen at antique and classic car shows on the West Coast. It would be most interesting to know how many of these exist now; there may be a couple that collectors have not yet discovered!

Features found on some (if not all) 1931 Studebakers were a self-righting steering gear and adjustable steering column, metal spring covers and ball-bearing spring suspension, adjustable front seats, starter button on dash, dual carburetion, duo-servo mechanical brakes, filters for air, oil and gasoline and positive-feed fuel pumps. Also, automatic circuit-breaker for electrical system, Lanchester vibration dampener with centrifugal governor, no-glare windshield, floodlight in front compartment (for reading maps at night) and a treadle-type accelerator pedal. A semi-automatic choke was also included.

For 1932, Studebaker featured new, larger bodies with "air-curve coachcraft." The windshield visor was gone for good, but the design of hood and grille was similar to the '31s, in most respects. The ovaloid headlights were continued, as well as the modern bumpers. Twin trumpet horns appeared on some models. The '32 Studebakers were not as attractive as their predecessors. They seemed a bit too low and squat, and the windows were noticeably smaller, with a consequential loss of visibility.

The new Studebakers for 1932 were available at reduced prices, yet were the first moderately-priced cars to include shatter-proof glass throughout all models at no extra cost. But Studebaker safety glass of 1932 vintage had a marked tendency to yellow and craze with age, as the plastic lamination discolored between the two outer sheets of glass. Thus, after a few years, it was frequently necessary to replace this kind of glass. (Some readers may remember that the safety glass of 1936 vintage, used on Ford and Chrysler products, tended to whiten with age.)

A carburetor silencer, automatic vacuum spark control and automatic starting (Startix) were also featured on 1932 Studebakers. The Bendix mechanical brakes had linings which were 25 per cent heavier than before. New "Reflex" taillights had reflecting lenses which showed up well even with the light out.

Dash panels featured round gauges, rather than the usual row of square gauges (white-faced, behind glass) which had been a Studebaker characteristic, of late. The new speedometer was the pointer-type, and the hydrostatic thermometer-type fuel gauge was replaced by a more reliable electric-type with needle pointer. "President" models had a clock and a "pass-around" cigar lighter as standard equipment.

Freewheeling on 1932 Studebakers was controlled by a lever under the center of the dash, and a gauge at the extreme left indicated whether or not the device was engaged.

The Studebaker "Six," on a 117-inch wheelbase, had 80 horsepower and was priced at $840, and up.

The "Dictator Eight," reduced in price ($980, and up) shared the 117-inch wheelbase and had 85 horsepower.

The "Commander Eight," on a 125-inch wheelbase, still had 101 horsepower; its new price range began at just $1350.

Also reduced in price was the "President," with a range of $1690 to $1990. This car was a lot for the money, on a 135-inch wheelbase, boasting the 122 "horses" of its 337-cubic-inch straight eight.

All closed models were wired for radio installation. The "non-resonant" bodies were well insulated.

All 1932 Studebakers had 18-inch wheels, and 6-ply tires were offered on "Presidents" and "Commanders." Tire prices were at a new low during the Depression, and a four-dollar tire in the cheaper lines was now possible.

One of the most glamorous and unusual of all the new Studebakers that year was the "St. Regis Brougham." It was, also, one of the most distinguished new types for 1932 in any line, for its long hood was further accentuated by its very short body and rear quarters. An interesting forerunner of the late-1960s style of "pony" or "personal" cars, the "St. Regis Brougham" had two extra-wide doors which gave access to both front and rear seats. The body was that of a close-coupled coach, and the cab was nearly as short as that of a coupe. There was only a very small side-window behind each door, and the trunk was attached as a separate unit. It looked very European, and there was nothing else like it on the road.

The 1933 Studebakers were extremely ugly, because the broad, outswept grille did not harmonize with the rest of the car. But they are extremely rare, and, consequently, quite interesting.

One commendable feature of '33 Studebaker styling, however, was the new beavertail panel which covered the gasoline tank and decreased wind drag. Front fenders were semi-skirted. All 1933 Studebakers were equipped with Bendix "B-K" vacuum-type power brakes, leaving most of the braking effort to engine suction rather than to foot pressure; a feature which, undoubtedly, appealed to women.

Improved power and added speed were made possible by new 1¼″ downdraft Stromberg carburetors (dual on eights) and compression was raised to 5.5 with 6 to 1 optional.

The "Six" had 85 horsepower; displacement was 230 cubic inches. The "Dictator" model was not offered for 1933, which was probably just as well. The name "Dictator" for a car model never seemed a wise choice, especially in light of what was developing in Europe during the early thirties. Yet, Studebaker revived this odious name for a model the following year.

Because of the absence of the "Dictator," the "Commander" and "President" models were downgraded, with respective prices starting at only $1000 and $1325, and horsepower ratings at 100 and 110. The old, *big* "President" model was replaced by the new top-of-the-line Studebaker, the "Speedway President" series, which had 132 horsepower and the mighty 337-cubic-inch power plant formerly found in "President" models. The "Speedway President" had a 135-inch wheelbase, and its price range was $1625 to $2040.

An improved intake silencer and a Burgess straight-through muffler were used. All models now had ball bearing spring shackles, and lubrication points were reduced so that only four places on the chassis required attention at 2500-mile intervals. The rest of the fittings could remain without servicing for 5000 miles. A backfire circuit breaker was added to the Startix unit. As on some other 1933 cars, an automatic choke was added.

Studebaker sales were lagging in 1933; these cars were certainly not getting by "on their looks," and only 14,824 Studebakers were sold in the first ten months of 1933, in comparison with 23,220 in the first ten months of 1932. Sales of the low-priced "Rockne" were no better, with 15,252 "Rocknes" sold during the first ten months of 1932 and 14,366 in 1933.

To stimulate business, Studebaker sponsored a contest. To participate, a contestant had to take a demonstration ride in a new Studebaker "Commander," and then answer, in fifty words or less, the question, "What is the most important feature of the new Commander and why?" Application blanks were available at Studebaker dealerships. First prize was a new Studebaker "Commander." Fifty other prizes included ten automobile radios, ten motor robes, ten spot lights, ten camera sets, and ten clock-and-mirror sets.

Studebaker did a complete restyling job for 1934, with new, curvier all-steel bodies, rear pontoon fenders with streamlined taillights, and modernized broader hoods and body sides which, however, were somewhat reminiscent of the 1929 "pregnant" Buick. Ventilating vanes on front windows (like those on the new Chrysler products that year) could be lowered together with the windows, if desired.

Prices were lower than ever, with a "Dictator Six" selling for as little as

$645, "Commander Eight" prices starting at $890, and even a "President" for as little as $1170! Many other manufacturers hiked prices a bit in 1934, but Studebaker was fighting to stay alive at that time.

As in 1933, 17-inch wheels were standard; they were the steel artillery-type, but wire wheels were optional. Bendix power brakes were still featured.

A 6.3 compression ratio was provided by an aluminum cylinder head, and aluminum pistons were used. The three basic models (with wheelbases of 114, 119 and 123 inches,) had horsepower ratings of 88, 103 and 110. The "Dictator Six" was the lowest-priced, the "Rockne" having been dropped.

The "Commander Eight" was the hardest-working of the three models, as it was very low-geared (4.82 to 1) and developed its peak horsepower at what was, then, a screaming 4000 RPM! The only 1934 cars that equalled the "Commander Eight" for engine speed were the supercharged Graham "Custom Eight" (135 h.p. @ 4000) and the incomparable Duesenberg (265 h.p. @ 4200 *without* the supercharger.)

Freewheeling was still offered, though most automakers had dropped the feature. Owners of freewheeling cars were squawking that they had been wearing out their brakes with all the coasting they'd been doing. And, as mentioned earlier, coasting downhill was illegal in many states. Some owners wired the freewheeling control lever to the inactive position to avoid using the device, or being accused of doing so.

Six-beam headlamps were a safety "plus."

The 1934 Studebaker had a new front-end design, with narrower grille (more attractive than before) and new V-type bumpers. The sales slogan for the year was: "FROM THE SPEEDWAY COMES THEIR STAMINA, FROM THE SKYWAY COMES THEIR STYLE." And the 1934s were referred to as the "startling new Studebakers." Most startling of all was the bulbous "Land Cruiser," available on any of the three chassis. The "Land Cruiser" was an imitation of the famous Pierce "Silver Arrow," with a fastback and wide-view 4-piece rear window. But, somehow, the Studebaker version lacked the beauty of the car that inspired it. The "Land Cruiser" resembled an overturned bathtub, or a bulging blimp. At Studebaker showrooms, startled customer reactions such as "Good Lord!" and "Oh, what an *ugly* car!" did nothing to cheer the hapless salesmen trying to unload the big beasts.

Despite the freakish ugliness of the 1934 "Land Cruiser," it is worthy of preservation because it's an early example of streamlining, and was one of the earliest sedans ever to have a built-in trunk flush with its sloping rear deck.

Also, it was one of the early models offering snap-on rear fender skirts that covered half the wheels.

At the Century of Progress Fair in Chicago, a giant replica of a 1934 "Land Cruiser" was set up, not as an eyesore but as a, so-called, "attention-getting display." The car colossus was 80 feet long, 28 feet high, and 30 feet wide! Its headlight lenses alone were five feet in diameter, and the side doors were fourteen feet wide. Below this giant display was a theater which seated eighty persons, and free movies were shown on the subject of the new Studebakers. One of the films depicted the testing of Studebaker's new, steel bodies. A sample '34 "Dictator" sedan was taken at random from the assembly line, then rolled over and over down a 104-foot embankment in the presence of the cameras. Twice this test car was shoved into a rock quarry, yet it could still be driven away under its own power!

The giant car was a good publicity stunt, but no doubt it scared a lot of little children at the Fair when they saw it for the first time. Another giant Studebaker, a 1930 roadster, was constructed earlier for a 1930 "talkie" film entitled, "Just Imagine." It was one of those interesting trick films which demanded giant props for the "little people" to crawl around on.

Studebaker discarded their exciting publicity stunts, after 1934.

Studebaker's 1935 models resembled the 1934s in body styling, but had an altered hood and grille treatment, new bumpers, and hydraulic brakes. The 1936 Studebaker was completely restyled, however, with a steel top and a much improved design. The low-priced Studebaker "Champion" model was introduced in 1939 and met with considerable success.

STUTZ

In 1929, Stutz added a lower-priced companion car to its famous "Bearcat" and "Safety Stutz." The new model, the "Blackhawk," was priced at $2695 and came with either a 6 or 8-cylinder engine. The "Blackhawk" was continued into 1930, with the 6-cylinder overhead-camshaft engine developing 85 horsepower and the straight-eight developing 90. Both 1930 "Blackhawks" were priced at $2395 (sedan) and had 127½-inch wheelbases and gear ratios of 4.75.

Stutz cars were also reduced in price for the 1930 season. While in 1929, the Stutz "M" sedan had sold for $3695, now the same model ("MA" or "MB") was priced at $2995, with a straight-eight o.h.c. engine that put out 113 horsepower at 3300 RPM.

Most interesting of the 1930 Stutz models was the beautiful "Versailles," a four-door sedan with custom body by Weymann. Unlike most American cars, this model had no belt moulding below the side windows. The doors (hinged on center posts) extended all the way to the running boards, concealing the chassis apron. The windshield was decidedly slanted, and the visor was merely a slight extension of the roofline. Rear quarters were closed, and much of the body was made of wood with handcrafted fabric covering. Fabric-covered bodies were much more popular in England and abroad, and the "Versailles" had a distinctively British appearance, despite its name.

During both 1929 and 1930, Stutz cars could be had with radios installed.

In 1930, a Stutz "Torpedo Speedster," with boat-tailed body, ran stock at the Indianapolis Race and came in tenth. It survived the gruelling 500-mile run on the famous track at better than 85 miles per hour average speed.

Motor magazine for January, 1931 related the following news: "Minor improvements have been made in the Stutz for the coming year. There is a six-cylinder model LA (85 h.p.) with a wheelbase of 127½ inches, and two eight-cylinder models (113 h.p.,) the MA with a wheelbase of 134½ inches and the MB with a wheelbase of 145 inches. All are equipped with over-head camshaft engines of the same size as used last year. (The Stutz Six was the continuation of the 1930 Blackhawk L-6.)

"Bodies have been stiffened considerably at the front pillars, and the MA and MB have new instrument board designs. All cars are now equipped with a D-K vacuum booster.

"An interesting detail is the use of three ventilating doors in the hood. Contrary to conventional practice, the front door is hinged at the rear so that it acts as an air scoop, directing air into the hood. This feature has reduced the temperature under the toe-board 40 degrees and in very hot weather it provides a marked increase in hill-climbing ability, as well as about 3 miles more speed. It is also for this reason that the first four louvres on the model LA are reversed."

Prices of sedans were $2245 for the "LA Six," and $3695 for the "MA Eight." The "DV-32" model was also introduced during 1931. It had dual overhead camshafts and dual intake and exhaust valves so that there were *four* valves per cylinder instead of the customary two. With this system, 156 horsepower was achieved at 3900 RPM!

The "Bearcat" was revived in 1931, on a 134½-inch wheelbase with DV-32 engine. This car was guaranteed, in writing, to go 100 miles per hour. (The original Bearcats of 1914 could get 75 m.p.h. from their mammoth 4-cylinder Wisconsin engines.) Also in 1931, a "Super Bearcat" was born, with a very short body on a 116-inch wheelbase. Because of its unusual stubbiness, the "Super Bearcat" somehow resembled a big toy.

For 1932, Stutz continued the 85-horsepower "LAA Six," the "DV-32," and the 113-horsepower "Eight" which had become the "SV-16" model. Prices of sedans were $1620 for the "Six," and $2995 for the "SV-16." The "DV-32" sedan was priced at $3995 (all prices f.o.b.). Bendix vacuum brakes were used on 8-cylinder Stutzes.

Sales for 1932 were reported less than 200. But, disregarding the lack of sales and working capital, Stutz continued to stress quality rather than quantity with fancy, custom bodies supplied by such coachbuilders as Waterhouse and Weymann, the latter continuing to offer a wood-framed fabric-covered body designed for extreme lightness.

Stutz, for 1933, featured the same, general specifications for its three models, though there were many refinements. On the eights, a Bendix vacuum-operated clutch control was adopted, as well as an automatic choke, thermostatically-controlled hood doors and shock absorbers, tandem mufflers, three-speed silent-second synchro-mesh transmission with freewheeling, and push-button starter control. Whitewall tires and drop-center rims were standard.

Twin trumpet horns added a dashing touch. Some closed models had semi-streamlined bodies with a curving top and built-in trunk, but the front end of the Stutz remained dated, as it had an absolutely flat radiator with vertical shutters more typical of 1930 than 1933.

Prices of the "Six" began at $1895, with "SV-16s" at $2595 and up, and the "DV-32s" starting at $3295.

Brand-new in ideas for 1933 was the Stutz "Pak-Age-Car," a light delivery truck which was powered by a 4-cylinder Hercules engine. The entire power unit was at the rear and could be replaced by factory-trained experts in only fifteen minutes! The "Pak-Age-Car" had a lightweight walk-in cab, similar to those on walk-in vans of later years. Though the "Pak-Age-Car" looked like a box on wheels, it was the forerunner of a very popular type of commercial vehicle.

Standard Stutz cars were known as the "Challenger" series in 1933. De luxe models were named the "Custom" series. Le Baron and Weymann built bodies for many of the "Custom" Stutzes produced. Considering that Stutz was on the verge of bankruptcy, an amazing variety of models was available. Automatic chassis lubrication was a special feature usually found on only the costly cars of the late twenties, but Stutz still offered it in 1933.

The Stutz 6-cylinder series was dropped for 1934. Only the 322-cubic-inch "Eights" remained, virtually unchanged. The lowest-cost "SV-16" sedan sold for $2995 at the Indianapolis factory, where things had almost come to a standstill. F.O.B. price of the "DV-32" was $20 higher than before, at $3695 for the sedan. While only 115 new Stutzes were reported sold in 1933, it has been stated that only *six* of the following 1934 models were actually sold during 1934. Consequently, no new Stutz automobiles were built for 1935. During the late 1930s, Stutz remained in business, continuing to build the practical little "Pak-Age-Car" in limited numbers. Their production was eventually taken over by Diamond T.

VIKING

General Motors Corporation introduced two new cars during 1929. One was the Buick-built "Marquette," discussed earlier. The other was the rare "Viking" car, produced and sold during 1929 and early 1930 by the Oldsmobile Division at Lansing. Like the Marquette, the Viking was on the market for less than two years; it is the scarcer of the two cars.

The Viking had a 90° V-8 engine which developed 81 horsepower and had the unusual horizontal-valve arrangement later found in the Oakland V-8s, though the two engines differed.

Gear ratio was 4.63 to 1, the wheelbase was 125 inches, and wood wheels were standard equipment, with wire wheels optional. Hood louvres were vertical, with the group set somewhat toward the rear. A raised panel at the top center of the hood widened as it ran back from the radiator and flared out over the cowl. There was a door-type ventilator on each side of the body, between front door and cowl band. The radiator had black vertical shutters, and the simple Viking emblem consisted of a stylized "V" set in a circular field of orange, black and silver.

When it was introduced during the spring of 1929, the Viking was priced at $1595., f.o.b., for a choice of three models: the Four-Door Sedan, Convertible Coupe, or Close-Coupled Sedan. For 1930, a fourth model was added, the Super De Luxe Sedan, upholstered in broadcloth and equipped with "torchere" side lights. The base price was also raised to $1695 for the 1930 season.

De Luxe equipment (at $160 extra) consisted of six wire wheels with locking fender wells, a trunk rack, and a pair of two-piece bumpers.

Viking's Fisher body was of composite steel-over-wood construction. Styling was similar to that of other middle-priced General Motor cars, and, in some respects, the Viking resembled a "big Chevy." But, unlike most General Motors products of 1929–30, the Viking did not have the usual all-black instrument panel. On the Viking, the instrument board contained a large silvery, etched panel in the center, framed by a heavy black rim. Five black, circular gauges were set in the panel, the speedometer being slightly larger and mounted in the center. The only noticeable difference between 1929 and 1930 Vikings, inside, was that the '30 model had a new, etched instrument panel that was set in a walnut-finished hooded cowl.

Like other General Motor cars that year, the Viking had mechanical brakes in 1930.

According to Olds Motor Works officials, the Viking was designed not only as a companion car to the 6-cylinder Oldsmobile, but also to fill "a genuine need for an 8-cylinder car in the medium-price field which would provide the advantages and characteristics of costlier motor cars." However, the Viking proved to be a disappointment to its makers. Between its spring introduction and early August, only 2277 Vikings were sold. The total reached 3713 by November. During 1930, an additional 2545 Vikings were sold. This was not enough volume to suit General Motors, and the car was withdrawn during 1930. Years later, Ford Motor Company experienced a disappointment, similar to General Motors' when they introduced and tried to popularize a medium-priced car, the Edsel. Since its withdrawal in 1960, the Edsel has become of considerable interest to collectors. There are quite a few Edsels around, but Viking cars are *extremely* scarce.

WILLYS

The history of Willys-Overland (of Toledo) goes back to 1907. Early Overland cars were inexpensive but reliable vehicles, and the first Willys-Knight automobile appeared in 1915.

The Knight engine (used in all cars which bore the name "Knight") differed from others in that it had sliding sleeves between pistons and cylinder walls. These sleeves were notched, in order to line up with corresponding openings in the stationary cylinder walls; the sleeves served as valves, eliminating the need for the usual mushroom-type "poppet" valves found in other internal-cumbustion engines. Knight "sleeve-valve" engines were used in many American and European makes during the teens and twenties, and were said to be quieter in operation, as well as more practical. The sleeve-valve engine was said to improve with use, as the gradual buildup of carbon in cylinders improved valve efficiency instead of impairing it. Willys was the most popular Knight-engined car in the United States, far outselling other sleeve-valve cars such as the Stearns-Knight, Handley-Knight, R & V Knight, Falcon-Knight, etc.

There used to be an old joke about the lady who drove her Willys-Knight to a repair garage. After taking the engine apart, the mechanic confronted the lady. "I know the trouble, ma'am," he said. "Your valves are 'gone.'" The mechanic scratched his head and continued, "I don't know where they went . . . but they're sure *gone!*"

The sleeve-valved 1930 Willys-Knight "Great Six" (66-B) sold for $1795 and up, with a choice of coupe, 5-passenger (Victoria) coupe, roadster or sedan. The seven-main-bearing six in this car developed 87 horsepower and had a displacement of 255 cubic inches.

There were four vent doors, in one long panel, on each side of the hood. The massive radiator had vertical thermostatic shutters. Wire wheels were standard equipment, but wood wheels were available for those who preferred them.

The closed models were not particularly attractive, but the interiors reflected a novel, "arty" decor in hardware and upholstery design. The dashboard was fairly elaborate, done in pleasing walnut-finish inlays, with a square, silvery panel of various white-faced instruments in the middle, a shield-shaped speedometer at the very center. A further touch of modernism inside the Willys-Knight sedans was given by the corner lamps, shaped like futuristic torches with colored ground-glass lenses that gave a "warmly diffused amber glow."

Most striking, by far, of the 1930 "Great Sixes" was the roadster, which had an unusual checkerboard decoration on the doors and sides of the cab. Frequently the fenders and running gear on this roadster were painted a lighter color than the body.

Early 1930 models featured tubular bumpers. These were later replaced by a larger, three-leaf type. Though there was a chromium cowl band, parking lamps were mounted atop the front fenders. Other features of the "Great Six" were "finger-tip control" (a revolving horn button, notched around the edges, which also served to control the starter and headlight beams), "one-shot" chassis lubrication, a back-up light, an amber-backed rear vision mirror to reduce glare and an emergency brake lever at the left of the steering column.

The headlights and triangular tie-bar were designed to harmonize with the radiator which was highly peaked with a raised, domed section in upper center. Another distinguishing feature of the "Great Six" was the moulding which swept gently upward from the rear, along the lower portion of the body, until it joined the "saddle" moulding which ran down the side of the cowl.

In addition to the "Great Six," there was the 53-horsepower Willys-Knight "70-B" model. This had a 112-inch wheelbase and a 177.9-cubic-inch 6-cylinder engine with a bore and stroke of only $2^{15}/_{16}''$ by $4\%''$. It sold for as little as $975, and was discontinued in 1931 but revived in 1932 as the Model 95.

The 1930 Willys "Six," on a 110-inch wheelbase, had a conventional L-

Presenting

THE NEW

WILLYS-KNIGHT GREAT SIX

*The most distinctive and most
luxurious Willys-Knight
ever designed*

The new Willys-Knight Great Six is
the most beautiful and most luxurious
automobile that Willys-Overland's
designers have ever created.

Such graceful sweep of line, such perfection of symmetry, such rich harmony
of color, such tasteful elegance of
finish—all combine in a distinguished
ensemble that testifies to the achievement of new ideals in motor car design.

In engineering as in artistry, the new
Willys-Knight Great Six is advanced
to a degree which few of the most
costly automobiles ever attain. The
patented Willys-Knight double sleeve-
valve engine reaches its highest
development—faster, more powerful
and more efficient than ever before.

WILLYS-OVERLAND, INC.
TOLEDO, OHIO
WILLYS-OVERLAND SALES CO. LTD.
TORONTO, CANADA

WILLYS-KNIGHT GREAT SIX SEDAN
ROADSTER ・ COUPE ・ 5-PASSENGER COUPE
—*each model*

$1895

*Six wire wheels and trunk rack standard equipment
Willys-Knight "70-B" models $1045 to $1265. Wire
wheels included. All prices f. o. b. Toledo, Ohio, and
specifications subject to change without notice.*

THE ROADSTER

THE SEDAN

head, poppet-valve, 6-cylinder engine of 193 cubic inches developing 65 horsepower at 3400 RPM. It took the place of the low-price, 6-cylinder Whippet car of 1929. With a 4.09 gear ratio, the 1930 Willys "Six" was the highest-geared of all Willys products built during the late twenties or early thirties. It was a snappy performer for its size; 72 miles per hour was the top speed, and the Willys "Six" could do 48 in second gear. Prices started at only $645.

Later in 1930, a new Willys straight-eight was added to the line. The engine was of the common poppet-valve variety, and prices of the Willys "Eight" were in the $1245 to $1395 range. By November, 1930, some 30,249 Willys "Sixes" and "Eights" had been sold, plus an additional 12,993 Knight-engined models.

The final year for Willys-Overland's low-cost Whippet car was 1930. Only 17,961 Whippets were built, though some 155,632 of them had been produced between January and November of the preceding year. The decline of the Whippet was hastened by the conception of the 1930 Willys "Six," similar to the Whippet "Six" except for a slightly larger engine. The last Whippet of 1930 was the 4-cylinder model "96-A," with 40 horsepower and a 103½-inch wheelbase (specifications similar to the 1930 Model "A" Ford.)

The first Whippet had been the 1927 model, which had replaced the old Overland car in the latter months of 1926. The Whippet, once known affectionately as the "Toledo Vibrator," was one of very few cars ever named for a dog. Though the Whippet was a cheap car, built only for basic transportation, it is now considered by many to be a true collector's car.

In January, 1931, Willys-Overland took pleasure in announcing that it had built, over the past years, a grand total of 2,425,000 cars.

All Willys models were reduced in weight for 1931, and were considerably restyled. Though the Willys-Knight (with sleeve-valve engine) was still available, advertising emphasis was now upon the Willys "Sixes" and "Eights," with their conventional poppet-valve engines.

The radiator design for 1931 was pleasing; the shell high, arched and narrow, and bisected down the middle by a thin strip of chrome. Hood louvres on the Willys "Six" were horizontal, while the "Eights" and Willys-Knights had vent doors as before. One-piece bumpers were found on all models, and fender parking lamps were low and streamlined.

Bendix duo-servo, cable-operated, mechanical brakes were adopted, eliminating the looseness and rattling of rod-controlled brakes. As an added feature, various models could be had with lower "mountain" gear ratios (4.9 on poppet-valve models and 4.6 on the Knights.)

THE MOST POWERFUL SIX-CYLINDER ENGINE OF ITS SIZE IS IN THE

WILLYS · KNIGHT

GREAT SIX

THE patented double sleeve-valve engine of the Willys-Knight Great Six develops more power and torque than any other six-cylinder engine of its size in American records. This Great Six is the fastest, liveliest and most powerful Willys-Knight ever built . . . Sleeve-valve smoothness and economy also feature the Willys-Knight "70-B", the largest, smartest and most powerful low-priced Knight-engined car in history.

WILLYS-OVERLAND, INC., TOLEDO, OHIO
WILLYS-OVERLAND SALES CO., LTD., TORONTO, CANADA

GREAT SIX SEDAN **$1795**
Other models at same price. "70-B" prices, $975 to $1195. Equipment, other than standard, extra. Prices f. o. b. Toledo, Ohio, and specifications subject to change without notice.

Models "97" and "98-D" had the 65-horsepower, 6-cylinder engine. Their respective wheelbases were 110 and 113 inches, and standard gear ratio was 4.6. Sedan prices were now only $675 and $795, and the f.o.b. price of the 97 roadster was just $495! Until recent years, the 1931 Willys "Sixes" were much easier to find than the Willys-Knights; now they have all virtually disappeared into private collections.

The "8-80" Willys Eight of 1931 had 80 horsepower and a standard gear ratio of 4.40. The sedan sold for $995.

The Willys-Knight "66-D" sedan was priced at $1095. Like the Willys "Eight," it had a 121-inch wheelbase. Standard gear ratio was 4.18 to 1, and the horsepower was 87, as before.

Safety glass and freewheeling were available at extra cost. A line of Willys trucks was on the market, too, with prices as low as $395 for the ½-ton chassis or $595 for 1½-ton chassis.

In ten months, 38,511 Willys poppet-valve and 7,561 sleeve-valve 1931 models were sold. Serious plans were made for the near-future discontinuance of sleeve-valve models.

For 1932, Willys and Willys-Knight made few noticeable changes. The radiator grille, though generally similar to the 1931 version, was slightly "veed," and the water filler cap was now under the hood, having been replaced above by an ornament. The horn was now a trumpet-type, hung below the left headlamp, replacing the disc-type vibrator horn formerly seen on the left end of the tie-bar.

There were four basic 1932 models. The "6-90" replaced the old "98-D." The "8-88" replaced the "8-80-D." Both of the 6- and 8-cylinder poppet-valve "Silver Streak" models were registered as Willys-Overlands instead of just Willys, as in 1931.

The two Willys-Knight models for 1932 were the "95" and "66-D." The "66-D" had the door-type hood vents and a grille with alternating chromed and lacquered bars. All other models had horizontal hood louvres and dark grilles. Hoods were extended an additional two inches over the cowl for 1932. The very simple dashboard of the Willys-Overland "Six" was virtually unchanged from 1931, having four gauges above four knobs, set in a row within a recessed center portion. However, walnut-grain replaced the black finish of the earlier Willys dash.

The high 4.09 differential gears found on the 1930 Willys Six were now available once more, though only on special order.

New, smaller wire wheels on the "6-90" took 5.25 x 18-inch tires, and brake drums were enlarged an inch to 12″ diameter. Models "66-D" and "8-88" had freewheeling at no extra cost.

Mohair upholstery was included in "6-90" models; previous versions had also offered broadcloth. All bodies were well soundproofed.

The "8-88" had larger, 13-inch brake drums, with 5.50 x 18 tires on standard and 6.00 x 18s on custom models.

The 1932 Willys-Knight model "95" was unchanged mechanically, except that its brake drums had been enlarged to 12 inches, while the new tire size was 5.50 x 18.

The larger Willys-Knight, the "66-D," was available with either sedan or Victoria body, had wire wheels and side-mounts, as well as twin-trumpet horns. Willys-Knight, as an individual make, fell from twentieth to twenty-third place in total national sales for 1932; only 3265 Willys-Knights were sold in ten months. On the other hand, Willys-Overland "Silver Streaks" (in twelfth place) were doing somewhat better, with 20,882 sales in the same period, though volume was down 45.7% from 1931. Most of the buyers who chose the final Willys-Knight cars were previous owners of Knight-engined cars, preferring to remain loyal unto the bitter end. For Willys-Knight, that came with the termination of the 1932 season.

Some readers may ask, "Wasn't a straight-eight Willys-Knight with sleeve valves ever offered?" The answer is no, though, as late as 1930, a Stearns-Knight automobile was available with a straight-eight sleeve-valve engine. The last of these had 128 horsepower. As for the Willys-Knights, both fours and sixes were offered in the early years and, in 1918, a sleeve-valve V-8 Willys-Knight also was available.

Willys truck sales declined in 1932, too; only 1002 units were sold in the first ten months, as opposed to 2881 during the corresponding 1931 season.

For 1933, Willys-Overland effected a drastic and revolutionary change in their entire line of cars. In fact, nothing seemed the same except for the 113-inch wheelbase of the "Six," which had a new engine as well as a new look.

The biggest news was the 4-cylinder Willys "77" series. The "77" was designed strictly as an economy car. Having a skimpy 100-inch wheelbase, it weighed only 2100 pounds and cost $445. The headlamps were sunken into the semi-skirted fenders. The hood sloped downward from the windshield to meet a small, tapered grille, four vent doors of graduating sizes were located near the rear of each side of the hood and wheels were the utmost in utility; steel discs with radial ribs that simulated spokes. Wire wheels were available, if preferred. The tire size was 5.00 x 17. The body was not only short, but also quite narrow, as the tread was only 51 inches across. This meant, obviously, that the diminutive "77" sedan would carry only four adults. The rear quarters sloped considerably, and the spare wheel was set into a niche in the rear deck for aerodynamic efficiency. This homely little car looked like a surrealistic cross between a Chihuahua and a baby pig, but it was at least out of the ordinary in looks. One either loved it or hated it, and the "77" attracted much attention at the 1933 Motor Shows.

The little engine of the Willys "77" gave 48 horsepower at 3200 RPM; piston displacement was 134.2 cubic inches. With a bore and stroke of 3⅛ x 4⅜ ", it was of similar dimensions to the engine used in the 1928 Whippet which had delivered 32 horsepower at 2800. The 1933 power plant offered many refinements, the most notable being Floating Power, the patented, improved engine mounting first introduced on the 1931 "PA" Plymouth. Willys had made a deal with the Chrysler Corporation to share the rights to this unique feature, and it added considerably to the smoothness of the "77." Top speed of the little car was seventy, and people began to forget the old nickname of "Toledo Vibrator."

Though Willys-Overland had permanently discontinued the Knight-engined models during 1932, a 6-cylinder Willys was still available for 1933. It was known as the "99," and had a poppet-valve, 80-horsepower engine of 213.3 cubic inches, which peaked out at 3400 RPM. The seldom-seen "99" model had styling similar to the "77," but it was somewhat larger. Priced at $675 for sedan, the "99" was a bargain, but never sold as well as the 4-cylinder Willys.

Quite a few of the economical "77s" were still in use during the days of World War II. They were in demand throughout the gas-rationing era because a "77" could produce 30 miles or more out of one gallon of fuel. In more recent years, several "77" coupes have been modified for racing, and are frequently described and illustrated in various hot rod and custom car magazines.

Convertible "77s" were built, but they are exceedingly scarce.

How long was the "77" on the market? It was continued, with similar body lines but with various changes in details, through the 1936 season. From 1933 to 1936, the grille was modified and circular hood vents replaced the original doors. The price by 1936 had fallen to only $395, f.o.b. for the coupe. The de luxe coupe with rumble seat and the convertible coupe were both discontinued during the four-year run of the "77." The 1936 models still had 48 horsepower, 5.00 x 17″ tires, mechanical brakes and a 100-inch wheelbase.

A major change in design came in 1937 with the "shark-nosed" hood-and-grille combination and, in the ensuing years before World War II, the Willys "American" evolved. During the war, Willys produced most of the military Jeeps ordered by the Army.

WILLYS 8 SEDAN DE LUXE, $1395

BRILLIANCE IN ABILITY WITH WILLYS SIXES AND EIGHTS

WILLYS SIX PRICES START AT

$695

Complete line of body types, $695 to $850. Willys Eight prices, $1245 to $1395. Prices f. o. b. Toledo, Ohio, and specifications subject to change without notice.

YOU will find it extremely interesting to drive one of these excellent new cars. Their action on the road, on crowded street or steep hill, shows what great engineering progress has been made with lower-priced Sixes and Eights. Willys cars reach a speed of well over 70 miles an hour—a speed which is easily and comfortably sustained. In second gear, speed as high as 48 miles an hour assures sparkling pick-up, so necessary in modern traffic conditions. The engines are rubber insulated against vibration. Superb riding qualities result from extra long springs and four double-acting hydraulic shock eliminators. The internal four-wheel brakes are fully enclosed, protected from dust and moisture. And only in cars of much higher price would you expect to find such beauty of design and interior luxury. Inspect the new Willys line at the showroom of your nearest Willys-Overland dealer.

SIXES AND EIGHTS

WILLYS-OVERLAND, INC., TOLEDO, OHIO . . WILLYS-OVERLAND SALES CO., LTD., TORONTO, CANADA

MISCELLANY

BUICK CENSUS

In August, 1930, as a promotional idea, the Buick division of General Motors engaged census specialists R. L. Polk and Company to compile a complete list of all the older Buicks still in service. The results were amazing and a tribute to Buick's durability. As of registrations checked (to Aug. 1, 1930) these Buicks were still in service:

Year Built	Number In Use in 1930	Year Built	Number In Use in 1930
1904	1	1917	9984
1905	1	1918	16,543
1906	10	1919	15,388
1907	3	1920	33,829
1908	17	1921	21,353
1909	12	1922	64,185
1910	39	1923	133,879
1911	29	1924	136,176
1912	99	1925	147,111
1913	160	1926	218,563
1914	609	1927	228,913
1915	1643	1928	199,373
1916	5011	1929	165,462

Total Buick registrations in the United States, as of August 1, 1930, amounted to 1,532,691. This did not include the many thousands of cars that had been shipped or sold overseas. And, of course, these figures did not include any old Buicks that were unlicensed, of which there were many.

LIGHTERS

According to a 1930 advertisement, *Casco* cigar lighters were chosen by 98% of the manufacturers who factory-equipped their cars with such devices. The Casco was a simple item, comparable to modern-day lighters except that it had a knob of bakelite. The new "Vis-o-lite" Casco came in two models: the $3-type had a spool-shaped knob of opaque bakelite, with a lens in the center which lit up when the filament was hot. The $4 lighter had a plain knob (notched around the edge) of translucent marbleized bakelite so that the entire knob was illuminated when the heat was on.

For a dollar extra, a small, swing-out ash cup was included with either lighter. The entire lighter-and-ash cup assembly could easily be clamped to the lower edge of most dashboards, and required only one "hot" wire to be fastened to the ammeter lead. Any metal dashboard became the "ground" when the accessory was installed.

An earlier type of lighter, still in use, was the "pass-around," which could be pulled out and away from the dash by its cord. This saved backseat passengers a considerable amount of awkward reaching.

TURN SIGNALS

Though directional signals, as we know them, were not included on most American cars until the 1940s and 1950s, a device called the "Turn Signal" was available as early as 1933. It was shaped like a small, double-ended stake, and featured an arrow-shaped window of light at either end. Since this clever gadget was designed for installation at both the front and rear end of any car, attached to the body, fender, or just above the bumper, it was usually sold in pairs.

The side lighted (right or left) indicated the direction of the turn. Like later directional signals, it could be hand-controlled by the driver.

The enterprising manufacturer was the Turn Signal Corporation, Philadelphia, and one of the producers of this interesting and useful accessory was Howard E. Coffin, better known for his earlier association with the Hudson Motor Car Company.

The sales motto for the Turn Signal was: "THE MAN BEHIND CAN'T

READ YOUR MIND." The idea was years ahead of its time, and most drivers continued to rely on arm signals.

AUTOMOBILE RADIOS

In less than five years, the manufacture of radios for automobiles became a twenty-million-dollar industry. The booming market for this popular item was nonexistent on March 7, 1929, when C. Russell Feldman formed his Automobile Radio Corporation, having bought the patent rights from a man named M. Heina who had previously made a few experimental installations of automobile radios.

Earliest custom installations had cost more than $250 per car, but eventual mass production and widespread advertising had increased sales during the early thirties and, as volume increased, prices had gone down. During 1933 alone, half a million radio sets were installed in new or used cars!

By the end of 1929, three manufacturers had announced that they would offer automobile radios for the coming year—*Transitone, Delco-Remy,* and *American Bosch.*

The Transitone had a single dial control. Early units, when installed, resembled nothing more than the type of handle which controls the shower over the bathtub. There was no illuminated dial, so tuning (in the dark) was done simply by "feel," as one swung the handle from station to station. Most of the vital radio parts (and there were many) were installed under the dash. The Transitone had six tubes providing three-stage radio amplification, a detector and two-stage audio amplification. There was also a speaker, an aerial to be mounted in the car roof, and two additional batteries. The "A" power was derived from the car's own storage battery, "B" and "C" batteries provided 135 and 9 volts, respectively. Manufacturer of the Transitone was C. Russell Feldman's pioneer Automobile Radio Corporation of Detroit.

For 1930, the Chrysler "77" and "70" closed models and the Dodge "Senior" brougham, coupe, and landau sedan were factory-equipped for the Transitone; they were completely wired for immediate installation, if ordered by the owner. In addition, 1930 De Sotos were also wired for Transitone, on special order.

General Motors Radio Corporation produced the Delco-Remy automobile set with single dial control, automatic volume control, five tubes and magnetic cone speaker. A lock switch was provided to protect the set against unauthorized use. The aerial consisted of five parallel wires in the roof, and "B" and "C" battery power was a necessity, also. Delco-Remy sets were recommended for the 1930 Cadillac and La Salle closed models which were factory-wired for future radio installation. Incidentally, General Motors was also producing radios and phonographs for home use at this time.

The Bosch Motor Car Radio by the American Bosch Magneto Corporation was a screen grid set with cone speaker, designed so that it would not be necessary to drill through the dashboard or disturb any of the upper upholstery panels for aerial installation.

At the indication of the future popularity of radios in cars, other automakers began to offer car models that were especially wired. Marmon-Roosevelt cars were factory-equipped for future radio installation, though no particular brand was suggested; selection was to be made by the dealer, at the buyer's request. Stutz was another early user of radios.

Pioneer,auto radios of 1929 and 1930 were complicated by the need for extra batteries and other cumbersome paraphernalia. Some small and medium-sized cars simply did not have room for the equipment required. Simplification of radio sets for cars was gradually accomplished during the early thirties.

In 1930, installation of one-way and two-way radios in police patrol cars began in the United States.

TWO FAMOUS NAMES ARE JOINED!

"Philco, largest manufacturer of radio in the world, has incorporated Transitone Automobile Radio Corporation. Transitone, the pioneer success in automobile radio, becomes the PHILCO-TRANSITONE." Thus read a portion of an interesting advertisement which appeared in January, 1931. Most exciting news of this merger was that the new Philco-Transitone auto radio had been simplified, and reduced in price to only $65, including 7 tubes, dashboard tuner, amplifier, speaker, "B" battery box and cables. The new unit included an oval-shaped panel with tuning dial, and two control knobs and a lock which could be fitted into the dashboard of most cars. It was especially recommended for the following 1931 cars, already wired for easy installation: *Chrysler, De Soto, Dodge, Franklin, Hupmobile, Jordan, Packard, Peerless, Pierce-Arrow, Plymouth, Studebaker* and *Stutz.*

The new Philco-Transitone had an automatic volume control to counteract fading under changing conditions as the car travelled along. Naturally, there was also a hand-operated volume control. Sixty-five dollars was a great deal of money in depression days, but it was a bargain for the pleasure it added to driving. The Philco-Transitone settled the question, once and for all, posed by many car owners: "Shall we go for a ride, or shall we stay home and listen to the radio?"

By January, 1933, the price range of the Philco-Transitone was $59.50 to

There's Only One

TRADE MARK REG. U S PAT OFFICE

Kari-Keen
KARRIER

The Baggage Car of the Auto

SALES of Kari-Keen Luggage Karriers continue to reach new high levels. Only this matchless combination of beauty and large carrying capacity could appeal to so many thousands of car owners.

When you swing it open, Kari-Keen provides a safe roomy space for luggage that would otherwise have to be crowded in with the passengers . . . bulky traveling bags, big crates and boxes, cans of cream, salesmen's sample cases, etc. It is also used closed for small loads.

Beautiful Lacquer Colors
Brilliant Chromium Trimmings

Made of pickled steel with new, brilliant chromium trimmings. Available in black or handsome lacquer colors to match any model.

Write for full information. The rapid growth in Kari-Keen sales has no equal in trunk or luggage carrier history. Get the facts.

Kari-Keen Mfg. Co., Inc.

2117 East 7th Street, **Sioux City, Iowa.**

SALES AGENCIES

Philadelphia, 2506 N. Broad St.
Chicago, Ill., 2017 Michigan Blvd.

Los Angeles, 440 Seaton St.
Oakland, 1620—18th St.
Portland, Ore., 32 Grand Ave. So.

San Antonio, Texas, 403 Brooklyn Ave.
Boston, Mass., 1258 Boylston St.

Toronto, Canada, Canadian Sliding Seat Co., 680 Bay St.

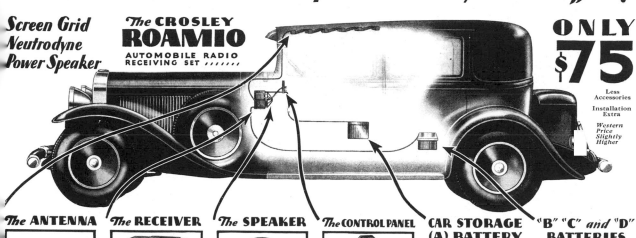

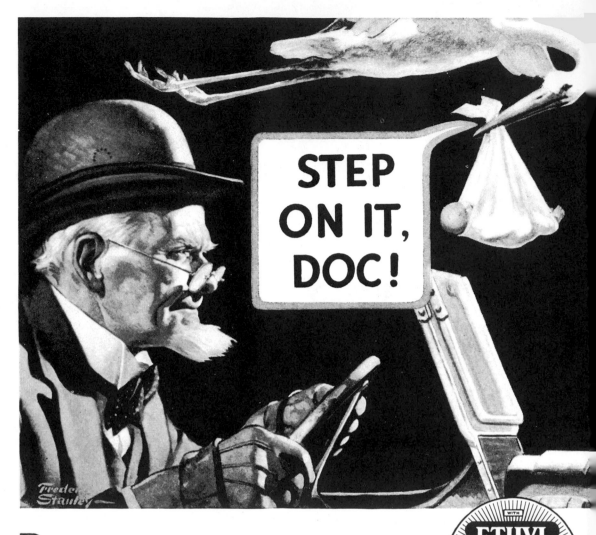

℞ *For cars that are showing age: Drive up to a pump that is marked with the Ethyl emblem and say, "Fill 'er up with Ethyl." Repeat treatment regularly. Ailing motor will recover its contented purr. Harmful knock will disappear, and added power will displace sluggishness.*

ETHYL
(TRADE MARK)
REG U S PATENT OFF
BRAND OF
ANTI-KNOCK
COMPOUND
ETHYL GASOLINE
CORPORATION
NEW YORK, U.S.A.
THE WORLD'S HIGHEST QUALITY MOTOR FUEL

HERE is a prescription for the doctor pictured above —and for everyone else who has to make his car do a while longer. Just remember: The next best thing to a brand-new car is Ethyl in the tank of your present car.

And with pennies counting as they do today, remember this too:

The savings that regular use of Ethyl Gasoline makes in repairs and upkeep *more* than offset its slight additional cost. Ethyl Gasoline Corporation, New York City.

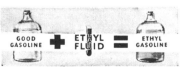

GOOD GASOLINE + ETHYL FLUID = ETHYL GASOLINE

Ethyl fluid contains lead. © E. G. C. 1933

BEWARE OF IMITATIONS

All Ethyl Gasoline is red, but not all red gasolines contain Ethyl fluid. The color is for identification only and adds nothing to performance. Look for this Ethyl emblem on the pump (or its globe).

* * *

The all-round quality of Ethyl is doubly tested: first, at the time of its mixing, and second, through inspection of samples taken from pumps. The Ethyl Gasoline standard of anti-knock quality is higher today than ever before.

NEXT TIME STOP AT THE ETHYL PUMP

In that the Double Eagle is safer and stronger than normal use requires, it is rightly called a luxury tire

MONEY CAN BUY NO MORE!

Goodyear readily admits that in the commercial sense the Double Eagle tire has definite limitations.

It does not seek to compete with standard tires — either in price, production, function or character.

What it does do, is to provide *safety, strength, freedom from annoyance and trouble* in superlative, even extravagant measure.

That is why so many careful men willingly pay premium to get this Tire of Tires—knowing that in terms of security and dependability, money can buy no more!

$89.50, *including cost of installation.* A new model had been introduced, with a dial and control box in the shape of an inverted shield. The control box could be clamped to the steering column, making it unnecessary to drill or mar the dashboards of cars not designed for radio installation. And the 1933 radio operated entirely off the main storage battery, requiring no "B" or "C" power units.

Further price reductions were made as sales volume picked up, and by July, 1933, the new Philco auto radios were available for as little as $39.95, installed; this price remained the minimum cost of a number of brands of auto radios for many years! And with payments as low as $1.50 per week, many radio fans ordered "one for the road."

Certainly, Philco and Transitone were not the only names in early auto radios. As mentioned before, there were Delco and American Bosch. RCA Victor got into the act with a good, competitively-priced model, as did Motorola, Auto-Lite, Atwater Kent and others. And by the end of 1933, the Crosley Radio Corporation in Cincinnati was offering the Crosley Roamio "103," for $44.50, with a steering-column-attached control box. Often these control boxes resembled miniature table radios especially the "cathedral" type, arched at the top, which was the most popular shape for small radios in the early '30s. All vital parts of the Roamio, including tubes, amplifier, etc., were enclosed in a separate box under the dash. The six-inch speaker, included in the compact package, played "music loud enough for *dancing.*" How anybody could dance while driving a car was not explained.

TIRE COVERS

Covers for spare tires were popular accessories during the thirties. They enhanced the beauty of the car and protected the spare tire, or tires, from the drying and cracking effects of sun and weather.

The Federal Pressed Steel Company manufactured Federal All-Steel Tire Covers. They were available in black finish with striping, or could be ordered unpainted so that they could be finished to match the particular automobile on which they were to be installed. Federal covers were available on 1930 models of Cadillac, La Salle, Hupmobile, Studebaker, Willys-Knight and Hudson, and could be fitted to practically any other automobile.

During the 1920s, many manufacturers or dealers supplied fabric or leatherette covers for spare tires, with the brand of the car or dealer's name painted on. It was good advertising, as well as protection for the spare. However, many of these rather perishable covers became frayed or weatherbeaten after a few years, and new steel covers were most practical as replacements.

TRUNKS

During the twenties and early thirties, there was a great demand for auto trunks that could be mounted at the rear. After 1933, when many manufacturers began to include built-in trunks in their sedans, the demand for detachable trunks diminished.

But in 1930, one of the popular brands of accessory trunks was the "Kari-Keen Luggage Karrier," manufactured at Sioux City, Iowa. This trunk could be had in colors that harmonized with the body of the car to which it was to be attached, unlike the usual black metal, wood or leatherette. The "Kari-Keen" was different, also, in that it could be swung open for heavy loads, so that it resembled a miniature pick-up bed.

HORSEPOWER

Though the horsepower ratings have been mentioned for many of the models discussed in this book, it should be of interest to compare the horsepower figures for the various American cars built between 1930 and 1934. The number preceding each horsepower rating represents the number of cylinders.

	1930	*1931*	*1932*	*1933*	*1934*
Auburn	6−70	8−98	8−98	8−100	6−85
	8−100		12−160	12−160	8−100
	8−125				8−115
					12−160
Austin	4−13	4−13	4−13	4−13	4−13
Blackhawk	6−85				
	8−90				
Buick	6−80½	8−77	8−78	8−86	8−88
	6−98	8−90	8−90	8−97	8−100
		8−104	8−104	8−113	8−116
Cadillac	8−95	8−95	8−115	·8−115	8−130
	16−185	12−135	12−135	12−135	12−150
		16−165	16−165	16−165	16−185
Chevrolet	6−50	6−50	6−60	6−65	6−60
					6−80
Chrysler	6−62	6−68	6−82	6−83	6−93
	6−66	6−70	8−100	8−90	8−112
	68				
	6−75	6−93	8−125	8−108	8−130
	6−93	8−88		8−135	8−145
	6−100	8−125			
Cord	8−125	8−125	8−115	8−115	
Cunningham	8−110	8−110	8−140	8−140	8−140
De Soto	6−55	6−72	6−75	6−79	6−100
	8−72	8−75			

	1930	1931	1932	1933	1934
De Vaux		6–70	6–70		
Dodge	6–61	6–68	6–79	6–75	6–82
	63				
	6–78	8–84	8–90	8–100	
	8–78				
Duesenberg	8–265	8–265	8–265	8–265	8–265
	8–320 *	8–320 *	8–320 *	8–320 *	8–320 *
Durant	4–40	4–50	6–71		
	6–58	6–58			
	6–70				
Elcar	6–61	6–61			
	8–90	8–140			
	8–140				
Erskine	6–70				
Essex	6–60	6–60	6–70	6–70	(changed to
				8–94	Terraplane)
Ford	4–40	4–40	4–40	8–65	8–92
				78	85
			8–65	4–50	
Franklin	6–95	6–100	6–100 *	6–100 *	6–100 *
			12–150 *	12–150 *	12–150 *
Gardner	6–70	6–70			
	8–90	8–100			
	8–126	8–126			
Graham	6–66	6–76	6–70	6–85	6–85
	6–76	8–85	8–90	8–95	8–95
	8–100	8–100			8–135 *
	8–120				
Hudson	8–80	8–87	8–101	6–73	8–108
				8–101	
Hupmobile	6–70	6–70	6–70	6–90	6–80
	8–100	8–90	6–75	8–93	6–90
	8–133	8–100	8–90	8–109	6–93
		8–133	8–93		8–96
			8–100		8–109
			8–133		8–115
Jordan	8–80	8–80			
	8–85	8–85			
Kissel	6–70	6–70			
	8–95	8–95			
	8–126	8–126			
Lafayette					6–75
La Salle	8–90	8–95	8–115	8–115	8–90
Lincoln	8–90	8–120	8–120	8–125	12–150
			12–150	12–150	

* Supercharger equipped

	1930	1931	1932	1933	1934
Marmon	8–84	8–84	8–125	16–200	16–200
	8–110	8–125	16–200		
	8–125	16–200			
Marquette	6–67				
Nash	6–60	6–65	6–65	6–75	6–88
	6–74½	8–78	8–78	8–80	8–100
	8–100	8–87	8–94	8–85	8–125
		8–115	8–115	8–100	
				8–125	
Oakland	8–85	8–85			
Oldsmobile	6–62	6–65	6–71	6–80	6–84
			8–82	8–90	8–90
Packard	8–90	8–100	8–110	8–120	8–120
	8–106	8–120	8–135	8–145	8–145
			12–160	12–160	12–160
Paige (com'l.)	6–76				
Peerless	8–85	8–85	8–120		
	8–120	8–120	16 (pilot model)		
Pierce-Arrow	8–115	8–125	8–125	8–135	8–140
	8–125	8–132	12–140	12–160	12–175
	8–132		12–150	12–175	
Plymouth	4–46	4–48	4–65	6–70	6–77
	48	56			
				6–76	6–82
Pontiac	6–60	6–60	6–65	8–75	8–84
			8–85		
Reo	6–60	6–60	6–85	6–85	6–85
	6–80	6–85	8–90	8–125	8–125
		8–125	8–125		
Rockne			6–65	6–70	
			6–72		
Roosevelt	8–77				
Ruxton	8–100	8–100			
Stearns-Knight	8–128				
Studebaker	6–68	6–70	6–80	6–85	6–88
	6–75	8–81	8–85	8–100	8–103
	8–70	8–101	8–101	8–110	8–110
	8–80	8–122	8–122	8–132	
	8–115				
Stutz	8–113	6–85	6–85	6–85	8–113
	8–135	8–113	8–113	8–113	DV8–156
			DV 8–156	DV 8–156	
Terraplane				6–70	6–80
				8–94	
Viking	8–81				
Whippet	4–40				

	1930	1931	1932	1933	1934
Willys	6–65	6–65	6–65	4–48	4–48
		8–80	8–80	6–80	
Willys-Knight	6–53	6–87	6–60		
	6–87		6–87		

In looking at the preceding chart, you'll notice that the Duesenberg was the highest-powered car each year during the early '30s. At the lowest end of the horsepower scale is the tiny, 4-cylinder AMERICAN AUSTIN. But the "Duesie" and the midget car represented extremes, being far from the average so far as size and power were concerned.

In 1930, the usual horsepower was about 10 per cylinder; Ford and Durant fours, for instance, had 40 h.p. The Plymouth 4-cylinder engine gave a little more: 46 in the early months of the year and later, 48.

Among light sixes of 1930, Chevrolet (the lowest priced) had 50 horsepower, De Soto had 55, and Durant's "614" had 58. There were many light sixes with horsepower in the sixties, such as Chrysler, Dodge, Elcar, Essex, Graham, Marquette, Nash, Oldsmobile, Pontiac, Reo, Studebaker and Willys.

Lowest-powered of the 1930 straight-eights was the De Soto, at 72 horsepower. Highest-powered, of course, was the Duesenberg; then the 140-horsepower Elcar. There were four 100-horsepower straight-eights: Auburn, Graham, Hupmobile and Nash.

There were no 12-cylinder cars available for 1930, and only one 16-cylinder model, the Cadillac V-16, with 185 horsepower.

Just four years later saw the near-extinction of the 4-cylinder car. The most noticeable exception was, of course, the Willys "77." The miniature Austin was selling in rather few numbers that year, and there were even fewer of the rare Continental "Red Seals." Most powerful of the remaining fours was the Willys. The 50-horsepower Ford "Model C" had been dropped during 1933.

Light sixes had more power by 1934. Chevrolet offered both 60 and 80 h.p. models, and Plymouth had 77 and 82. Dodge had 82 horsepower, De Soto had 100 and Chrysler had 93. The Oldsmobile "Six" had 84 horsepower and was the only L-head six offered by General Motors in 1934. Ford built no sixes in those days, but Hudson was in the low-price field with the 80-horsepower "Terraplane." Graham and Reo sixes each had 85 horses, and Nash and Studebaker built 88-horse sixes. Nash also introduced its lower-priced "Lafayette Six" (75 h.p.). Hupmobile "Sixes" had 90 and 93 horsepower, while Auburn's new "Six" (their first since 1930) had 85.

INDEX